Just Champion

The Stories Behind Rangers' 2020/21 Title Triumph

Jeff Holmes

Foreword by
CONNOR GOLDSON

First published by Pitch Publishing, 2021

Pitch Publishing
A2 Yeoman Gate
Yeoman Way
Worthing
Sussex
BN13 3QZ
www.pitchpublishing.co.uk
info@pitchpublishing.co.uk

ISBN 978 1 80150 004 3

Typesetting and origination by Pitch Publishing
Printed and bound in the UK by TJ Books, Cornwall

Contents

This book is dedicated to three special guys. Whether we went to the games together, or enjoyed chatting about our team, Ibrox was a special place for all three.

You will never be forgotten.

John Geddes
28 August 1957–30 November 2020

Sean Graham
30 March 1968–16 January 2021

Jim Baillie
28 November 1954–2 February 2021

Acknowledgements

A BOOK such as this is only as good as the sum parts of its contributors, and in that respect I've been blessed with a lengthy list of the best. When it was decided that I should ask others to turn their attention to specific key games, working out a list of who I wanted to contribute took almost as long as coming up with a title (and anyone who knows me knows that it's my Achilles heel).

Each contributor had a unique story to tell. The only qualification necessary was a love of Rangers. So I set about working my way through a preferred list of contributors, and pleased to report that to a person (just about), this is what we have. Twenty-nine folk, all members of the Rangers family and from all walks of life, be they a former player, manager, coach or director. Or a Sir, an MBE or a British Ambassador, or a supporter of our famous club; each one was only too happy to tell *their* story. Everyone is someone in this life and, in my eyes, we are all equal. I'm indebted to each contributor, and I thank you all from the bottom of my heart. On this occasion, I'm the Pritt Stick. My role has been to stick the stories together, but the following list of contributors (in chapter order) showcases the important folk. Quite often you read a testimony saying, 'I couldn't have done it without ...' well, I really couldn't, so thank you.

To the guys who took the battle to the invaders. I'm deeply indebted to Dave King, John Gilligan and Paul Murray for the opportunity to include their thoughts in this book.

To Connor Goldson for a marvellous foreword. I'm honoured that the vice-captain of our club took the time to contribute, in between marshalling that incredible Iron Curtain Mk II defence. Connor has been a great credit to Rangers this season and is surely destined for our Hall of Fame.

Contributors: Mark Walters, Marco Negri, Lisa Swanson, Josh Holmes, John Wallace, Sammy King, HM Ambassador Chris Sainty, Don MacLean, Chris Mayhead, Fraser Aird, Derek Johnstone, Stephen Millar, Andy Cameron MBE, Stephen Purdon, Alan Denniston, Tam Young, Tim Webb, Andy Scott, Murdo Fraser MSP, John Macinnes, Ally Dawson, Satty Singh, Alex Totten, Nancy Honeyball, Alex McLeish and Sir Brian Donohoe.

Thanks also to David Graham, at Rangers, Willie Vass, Lyndsey Maitland, Catherine Young, Bobby Young, Ciaran Hill, Rachael Brown, Andy Halley, Iain Martin, and my wife, Elaine Holmes, for her usual, unstinting support. And to all those who allowed me to use their photographs.

And, as always, my publisher: Paul Camillin, Jane Camillin, and the terrific team at Pitch Publishing.

Foreword by Connor Goldson, Rangers FC

AS A footballer, you go into every season hoping that come May you're still in with a chance of lifting silverware. This one was no different. The motivation is ever-present, but success is a marriage of many different factors. As an individual, and as part of a team, you have no control over fate – so you get on with your job, you train hard, you live right, you listen to the manager and the coaching team's instructions, and your motivation, drive and desire are with you every time you cross that white line.

We've received lots of plaudits this season for the manner in which we've defended, created and attacked, but it's almost three years to the day since I arrived at Ibrox and what you see on the park on matchday: all the components that go into defending a set piece, playing free-flowing football middle-to-front, or scoring from a well-worked move, are all things we've been working on day in, day out since my first day at the club. There is no magic formula; it's good organisation and hard work.

The gaffer has worked tirelessly to put together a squad that would give us a chance of being successful, and it was fantastic to see certain things pay off the way they did. Apart from winning football matches the big buzz for me is to see something you've worked hard on pay dividends.

We started the season well and had seven successive clean sheets in the league. That gave us a solid foundation to keep building on, and every time we managed to keep a clean sheet, we wanted another. We defended really well as a team, and the ability to play a settled side most weeks was a bonus.

We decided early on that the mantra would be 'one game at a time', and we meant it. We didn't ever get too far ahead of ourselves and it stood us in good stead.

Playing in empty stadiums was bizarre at first, but we soon got used to it, and instead of having 50,000 behind us at Ibrox, we knew it was down to us and the coaching staff. We were well aware that our supporters were watching on from home every week and we were determined not to let them down. When we beat St Mirren 3-0 to all but clinch the title, the natural thing was to celebrate with the supporters, but sadly the stadium was empty. Still, it was a great feeling knowing that when we'd needed it, we had come up with another commanding performance. That was very satisfying.

Winning the league with Rangers has been incredible. You dream of moments like this when you're a young lad playing with your mates, but the reality is very different.

It has been well documented the amount of football I've played this season, and that means so much to me as I've had my ups and down in the last few years. When I signed for Rangers I was well aware that the club hadn't won the league for a few years, so our first was always going to be special. But more than anything, we're all delighted that we managed to deliver this one for the supporters. It was an important season, for a variety of reasons, so there was a lot of pressure on the players and everyone at the club, but we've come through it well, and getting our hands on the trophy was the culmination of a long, hard season.

We've learned so much this term; we've also achieved so much, but the journey isn't finished. Rangers is such a special club and winning the league gives you the appetite to win more. We may have been playing in empty stadiums, but we knew that our supporters were still with us every step of the way, and this one is for them!

Introduction

SCOTTISH PREMIERSHIP champions!

Let's take a moment to soak it up and consider the significance of title number 55.

It would be so easy to take the fork in the road marked 'karma', but let's not become bogged down in retribution; let's focus on the positive, or at least the facts. Celtic didn't lose the title, Rangers won it. Ten in a row only ever existed in the ether region. Fifty-five always trumped the ten.

It's a bit like the movie that's building up to a thrilling climax: there are disappointments before the big bang, but the good guys win in the end.

Or maybe that's being too simplistic. How about making the correlation between the events of Friday, 6 March 2015 and this season's title, because without one, perhaps you don't have the other. Without Dave King, John Gilligan, Paul Murray and the other guys securing such an important victory at the EGM, maybe the club takes the fork in the road marked 'mediocrity'. In fact, there's no maybe about it. Profit before players.

Perhaps it's significant that the decisive win of the season, 3-0 over St Mirren which all but clinched the title, took place six years to the day from that astonishing boardroom success. So it's important to remember that while Steven Gerrard, his backroom team and the players have performed heroics this season, we will forever owe a debt of gratitude to those who worked so fervently behind the scenes to ensure our great club was rescued from the clutches of individuals who did not have the best interests of Rangers at heart. The consequences of failure that day are too frightening to contemplate.

So let's now enjoy this one. And speaking as someone who has watched Rangers win many championships, it truly was special. From day one, when we travelled up to an empty Pittodrie and secured the points with a fine goal from Ryan Kent, to mid-January when Celtic were making the headlines for all the wrong reasons in the UAE, to the first weekend in March when we beat St Mirren at Ibrox and our nearest rivals slipped up at Tannadice, it has certainly been quite a season.

The stakes were sky high for both halves of the Old Firm from day one. Apart from the perennial struggle for superiority, both clubs had a clear incentive, and this particular two-way battle had the potential to eclipse everything that had gone before it.

In the Blue corner, a side risen from the ashes of a near-fatal demotion to the fourth tier of Scottish football following catastrophic mismanagement but, like Arnold Schwarzenegger, we were back and challenging for top spot.

In the Green corner, the noisy neighbours; chasing an unprecedented tenth successive title, despite many claiming the ninth should be accompanied by an asterisk.

In the early 18th century US president Benjamin Franklin coined the phrase, 'No pain, no gain,' and it seemed appropriate as we patiently awaited the restocking of our trophy room. Another popular saying is, 'Good things come to those who wait.' And they certainly do. The euphoria which accompanied the winning of the 2020/21 Premiership was nothing short of cacophonous.

When Gerrard landed the big job, there was a sharp intake of breath. He had been in charge of Liverpool's under-18 side, so did he really have the experience to lead such a big club? A one-club player of great note prior to finishing his career in the USA, he had given sterling service to Liverpool and played 114 times for England. He was a born leader, and while it's often lazily assumed Rangers supporters demand instant success, the majority had no problem giving Gerrard time to bed in and accumulate the necessary experience. It wasn't too long until we started to think, 'Hey, he might just be the guy to sort this team out.'

There was a ridiculous gap between Celtic and Rangers. Not only in terms of points, but financially the clubs were as wide as the River Clyde. Celtic had taken full advantage of Rangers' years 'downstairs' to supplement their bank balance with a haul of Champions League cash. The shrewd appointment of Brendan Rodgers was another major factor.

Gerrard not only had to steer the Rangers ship in the right direction, but would have to do so while working under the constraints of financial disparity. Full credit to the Rangers board, though, as they backed him as far as they could financially.

The first two years of Gerrard at the helm produced many positive signs. Prior to his appointment, Celtic would have thought nothing of coming to Ibrox and scoring a few, but Gerrard put a stop to that. He began to challenge Celtic's domination of Old Firm games. Up until May 2021 he had presided over 12, and won seven to Celtic's four. The 2019 Scottish League Cup Final was as one-sided as these games get but a clear offside goal gave Celtic a victory they barely deserved. Fine margins, but Gerrard flipped this fixture on its head and made his players believe that second best was for losers. The Scottish Cup fourth round win at Ibrox in April offered another case in point.

Gerrard has also given us back our Continental swagger, while impressive runs in three successive Europa League campaigns helped swell the coffers and keep the treasurer happy.

Not bad for a man who was described by a sports journalist as looking quietly terrified at the size of the job which lay before him.

The careful recruitment of his backroom team has been excellent: hand-picked from his time at Liverpool, as well as other areas. They come across as close-knit, with all pulling in the same direction.

The players identified and brought in this season were positive additions to an already-talented squad. Each one makes the group stronger. Equally, Gerrard realised there were those who were surplus to requirements, and we said goodbye to stalwarts such as Andy Halliday, Wes Foderingham and Jason Holt, guys with around 300 appearances between them. But the desire to free up space at the club trumped individual need.

One got the impression that after two years at Ibrox, Gerrard was preparing for the big assault. He knew exactly the strength of his squad and recognised the need for cover in certain positions. There was also a requirement for more creativity so he tied down Ianis Hagi on a permanent deal at the end of May. Fine tuning for a title tilt had started in earnest.

Calvin Bassey joined from Leicester City at the beginning of June. He would provide cover on the left-hand side – and the centre of defence, if required – and, crucially, he was just 20 years old. Allied to 21-year-old Hagi, Gerrard was conspicuously building for the future as well as the present.

Experienced Scotland international goalkeeper Jon McLaughlin arrived to push the evergreen Allan McGregor for the coveted number one jersey. McGregor enjoyed one of the best seasons of his career. A masterstroke by the gaffer.

Matt Polster returned to the USA in the first week of July, and a couple of weeks later, experienced German-born central defender Leon Balogun arrived from Wigan Athletic to bolster an already-strong defensive department. The 32-year-old Nigerian international brought experience of playing in Germany and England.

It was soon time for the pre-season exertions, and for starters, Rangers were invited to take part in a prestigious invitational tournament in Lyon where victory over the host side, as well as Nice in the second game, proved a fine start. This was followed by victories over Motherwell and Coventry

City at Ibrox. Opponents picked for tactical reasons. Ten goals scored and zero conceded.

With the opening league match at Aberdeen successfully negotiated, the need for extra firepower had supporters speculating as to who might arrive at the club. Alfredo Morelos and Jermain Defoe were our only recognised senior strikers and it was clear that reinforcements were required.

Three days after the single-goal victory at Pittodrie, supporters had their answer. First through the door was Kemar Roofe, a Midlands-born striker with just a single season behind him at Anderlecht after joining the Belgian side for a reported £7m. The 27-year-old had first caught the eye by scoring some sensational goals during a three-year stint at Leeds United. Roofe, who had come through the ranks at WBA, signed a four-year deal, tying him down until his 32nd birthday; a great piece of business.

He was followed later that day by Cedric Itten, a 23-year-old product of the excellent youth setup at perennial Champions League entrants Basel. The talented Swiss international was undoubtedly one for the future, but his incredible will to win would soon endear him to supporters.

The transfer merry-go-round continued with Ross McCrorie (Aberdeen) and Greg Docherty (Hull City) leaving the club, but despite all these comings and goings Rangers continued to perform admirably. From the first seven league games came six wins and a draw with zero in the goals against column. It was a huge statement. McGregor, Goldson, Balogun, Helander and Barišić were playing as though they'd known each other for years.

There was one other player, though, who had started his Ibrox tenure in the latter stages of the lower-league journey; a man who had been installed as captain by Gerrard shortly after his arrival. It was a role he slowly grew into, and while never the loudest on the park this dignified Yorkshireman seemed the perfect fit.

Fittingly, James Tavernier had scored the goal that clinched promotion back to the Premiership in 2016. He has become part of the furniture at Ibrox and it's difficult to see him finishing his career at a club other than Rangers. Watching Tav return from injury to lift the Scottish Premiership trophy was one of those moments which tugs at the heartstrings, and who would bet against him doing it again next season?

Gerrard is another we hope might remain at Ibrox for another few years. He has clearly come to love Rangers and the guy who arrived in 2018 to take up his first managerial position has steadily grown into the job. Just as he was a fearless leader on the park, so he has become a similar type of character from the dugout. Not one to shout and scream from the sidelines, he isn't afraid to show his emotions when the time is right.

The manner in which he defended Alfredo Morelos at Livingston, and Glen Kamara on the night he suffered racist abuse against Slavia Prague, was outstanding. A manager who cares for his players. And it has been mirrored in the way his players fought for him throughout the season.

He was criticised for 'over-celebrating' the December 2019 win at Celtic Park, and throughout the season just finished he was on his best behaviour at the side of the pitch. But he's a winner, and winners like to win. His outpouring of emotion when the title was secured was empathetic towards those locked out of stadiums due to COVID. To see the manager celebrate with his players in the manner he did was wonderful. For one day only, he was one of the lads.

The Premier League title is once again the domain of the world's most successful football club, and boy how we enjoyed it. The 4-1 win over Celtic at Ibrox at the beginning of May wasn't just the icing on the cake, it was the strawberries and cream, and it was delicious. Now read on for a unique look at the 2020/21 campaign, seen through the eyes of Rangers supporters from all walks of life.

One final question, though. How did you celebrate?

Jeff Holmes
June, 2021

From the Boardroom

Dave King

Former Rangers chairman
South Africa

'ON THE eve of the EGM, I was still very apprehensive about the outcome. Along with Chris Graham, I had done my homework on the votes and as long as certain key shareholders voted with us, or abstained, we should have succeeded but I was concerned that one of them might change their mind and tip the balance in favour of the incumbent board.

'The fact that James Easdale and the chairman had already stepped down gave me some confidence that they were anticipating defeat. We had come a long way and I was desperate that we didn't fail at the final hurdle – too much rested on our success.

'At that time I was solely focused on regime change.

'The moment I knew we'd been successful, there was an immediate release of the pent-up anxiety and emotional energy that had been building up in the weeks and days leading up to the EGM. Without success at this EGM we were doomed to be a second-rate club.

'The supporters were key. Without the boycott of the season tickets and of Sports Direct, the incumbent board would have been in a position to survive for a prolonged period to the point that the damage might have been irreversible. When this season's title was officially won, I was completely overwhelmed with emotion. It is the benchmark for everything we have done since regime change and marks the official end of the dark days that we had all endured. We wanted to become the number one club in Scotland again – and we are a clear number one at the moment.

'I've witnessed many successes as a Rangers supporter, but I put this one at number one, because of the starting point. The club was never at a weaker point, across all activities, than we were at regime change. We have come such a long way in a relatively short period.'

Paul Murray

Former chairman and board member Portugal

'WE WERE all feeling the pressure of the EGM, so when we knew we'd secured the vote the relief was palpable. Mind you, there was still work to do before it was confirmed. As Rangers was listed on the stock market, the vote had to be recorded, and at that time supporters were talking more about NomAds than Kris Boyd. The NomAd is the nominated adviser, who advises the club or company on the stock market, and he had to sign off on the result before releasing a statement to the stock exchange explaining how it had gone.

'While Dave awaited his fit and proper clearance from the SFA, I was chairman so I had to put my name to this document. There were around seven resolutions, all of which were important, so the NomAd and I sat in an office in Argyle House and double checked them.

'My heart was beating so fast, and I'm trying to go through it properly, but quickly. We checked it one final time, and he asked if I was happy. I said yes: he pressed a button to send it to the stock exchange and, I kid you not, 30 seconds later there is this massive roar outside Argyle House. All these supporters had been on their phones waiting for this statement to be released by the stock market. It was so emotional. The NomAd and I looked at one another and just said, "Wow!"

'We went downstairs and Dave King, John Gilligan and I walked out the door and into this huge outpouring of human emotion. Supporters were crying openly. That moment will live with me forever.'

John Gilligan

Former Rangers director
Ayr, Scotland

'THINGS COULD have been so different had the takeover bid failed. Mike Ashley was waiting in the wings to give the club a £5m loan, and in exchange he would have taken security over the stadium. The club and the property would have been in the hands of another company. Imagine we had lost control of our own stadium, and Rangers had to rent it back to play there. It beggars belief.

'After we gained control, and got down to business on the Monday morning, it was a mess. The quality of the building, the infrastructure; it was awful. There hadn't been maintenance of any note done in a long time, and it showed. Staffing levels were around 30 per cent of what they had been. It all represented big problems for us, but not as big as they were for the folk still working at Ibrox under awful conditions. People were only there because they were working for Rangers FC. It wasn't the money; they didn't want to desert a sinking ship. It must have been hard for these employees to keep their heads up during really tough times.'

Mark Walters

Solihull, England

Aberdeen 0 Rangers 1
Scorer: Kent 21
1 August 2020

There is a moment during the Hearts v Rangers match at Tynecastle in 1988 that is frozen in time. Goalkeeper Nicky Walker has, as a backdrop, thousands of Rangers supporters packed tightly like sardines on the Gorgie Road terracing. With the ball in his hands he bounces it a couple of times before launching it deep into enemy territory. It veers out to the left, like a wayward drive off the first tee, where Hugh Burns is keeping a close eye on Mark Walters. Not close enough, though, because as the ball comes in their direction, Walters somehow flicks it with his right heel, behind his body and off he goes, bearing down on the Hearts goal, where only a smart Henry Smith save prevents Walters from scoring. Like everyone else, Burns is completely bemused, and still wondering how the hell Walters pulled off such an audacious piece of trickery. Frankly, it was almost more Cruyff-esque than the legendary Dutchman himself.

During the late 1980s and early '90s, there were few greater sights than Mark Walters on the ball, tricking his way past defenders before sending in a killer cross. He was the undisputed wing king of Scottish football. He had few equals, and his fantastic array of skills – which included the awesome double shuffle – made him the footballing equivalent of David Copperfield.

For almost four years Walters was revered by Rangers fans, and he also knew the quickest way to goal, finishing 1990/91 as the club's top league scorer. He's up there with Paul Gascoigne and Brian Laudrup as one of Rangers' most talented and influential signings of the late 20th century.

Exactly 30 years after leaving Ibrox, to join Graeme Souness at Liverpool, Walters still catches as many Rangers games as he can – and that's a lot. He watched most of the 2020/21 games and marvelled as the Light Blues forged a clear path to the title. Without fear of contradiction, one can say that no one was happier than the Brummie-born England international that Rangers won the Scottish Premiership. No one.

He still has three Scottish Premier League (as it was known in his playing days) winners' medals in his collection, but insists the club's latest league honour is extra special. When he checked the fixtures before the start of this season, one game stood out from the rest: the first, Aberdeen at Pittodrie. Walters knew it would either get Rangers off to a flying start or they would be playing catch-up from day one.

He settled down in his Solihull home to watch the game and admits to being pleasantly surprised at what he saw. Watching the build-up brought back memories, many of them not too pleasant, of previous matches against Aberdeen up in the north-east.

He said, 'When I was at Rangers there always seemed to be a real edge to these games, a bit like the matches against Hearts at Tynecastle. These are two fixtures I remember as being harder, certainly mentally. Not quite to the same tune as the Old Firm matches, but a real undercurrent of something dark going on. It wasn't usually a nice atmosphere. You expect games against your big rivals to be feisty and tight, but this was something else. In the dressing room before these games our boys would be pumped up and buzzing to get out on the pitch.

'It could have been something to do with Sir Alex Ferguson's time at Aberdeen, and how successful they were, or the game I played in, in which Neil Simpson had that horrendous tackle on Ian Durrant, but there was definitely something there.

'I was convinced that an empty Pittodrie would work in Rangers' favour as I know the Aberdeen fans have a bit of a reputation for giving Rangers a hard time when we go up there. In the season just finished, the away teams definitely had an edge in certain games, and I think that was reflected in a lot of the scores we saw.

'So, going to Pittodrie was always going to be a tough start, especially with all the pre-match talk of Alfredo Morelos and his on-off transfer to the French team Lille. In my experience, speculation like that *would* affect a player, especially if he wanted to leave. If you know a team is interested, and it's a move that excites you, then it stands to reason you're not going to be in a good mental state during the game. It can play with your emotions. But the flip side is that if you don't want to leave, and the club that's interested isn't as big or ambitious as the club you're currently with, then it probably isn't going to affect you too much.

'And let's be honest, Lille certainly don't have the stature of Rangers. They aren't as big a club as Rangers, and although they did incredibly well this season they still aren't as big a draw as my old club. I could perhaps see the attraction if it was a team like PSG, but even they don't have the history of Rangers. They can pay more money, but that isn't everything.

'Perhaps it was financial, though. In that case the player might want to move. I like Alfredo Morelos as a player. I don't like his temperament, but I like his goals and his link-up play. I've watched games where I'm genuinely thinking, "Is he going to last the 90 minutes here?" We all know that any player, during any moment in a game, can snap and do something stupid. My breaking point was if an opponent spat at me. That was a red rag to a bull, and whereas I wouldn't just knock him out there and then, I would take revenge at some point in the game.

'When I was playing I can't remember anybody who was as likely to get into trouble during a game as Morelos, but as we moved into the second half of the season there was definitely a sign that he was curbing his temperament. He is a really good player, and the fans adore him.'

One man who did impress Walters in the game at Pittodrie was Ryan Kent, the £7m man from Liverpool. The 24-year-old wide boy scored the only goal of the game midway through the first half when he latched on to a perfect Morelos through ball and beat Joe Lewis with consummate ease.

Walters said, 'I really like the look of Kent, he has two good feet and the only thought in his head is to get forward. He is very attack-minded, and that's exactly what you need when you play for a club like Rangers. He likes to drift into the centre and therefore sees a lot more of the ball. Perhaps it's because James Tavernier and Borna Barišić get forward that much that it narrows the pitch for guys like Kent.

'Still, Rangers have benefitted enormously from him coming inside. It's something I liked to do during my career but was more or less prohibited from doing so due to the barbaric tackle from behind. Now that referees clamp down on that sort of brutish behaviour from defenders, creative players have more freedom to express themselves.

'I call guys like Kent "mobile" players, as they can drift from area to area in their bid to influence the game. One of my favourites was my old team-mate at Aston Villa, Brian Little. What a player he was.

'The days of the traditional wide player staying out on the wing have all but gone. And that's good news for guys like Kent because he now has many more opportunities to make his mark. He is only 24, and definitely still has time to improve even further. I'd like to think that in a couple of years he would have aspirations of playing for his country. At the moment he probably isn't consistent enough, and there are quite a few ahead of him, but he has the talent to be a future England international if he keeps improving. To achieve that, though, he needs to be performing at a high level week in, week out for Rangers, and also doing well in European competition. He should now get an opportunity to show off his skills in the Champions League after Rangers' great title win.

'I thought Rangers were comfortable at Aberdeen. It may just have been 1-0, which doesn't suggest they were in complete control, but I thought they controlled the game for the biggest part of the afternoon. The new lad, Leon Balogun, slotted in beside Connor Goldson with ease, and it looked like they had been playing together for years.

'I was willing them to get another goal or two because we've seen all too often what happens at grounds like that when you're protecting such a slim advantage. One free kick into the box, a corner, a punt, and it can be down the road with two points dropped.

'It's so easy to look back and say that Rangers looked like definite title contenders that day, because we've now seen exactly how everything has played out, but they have grown steadily with each game and improved week on week. By the end of January, Rangers had amassed an incredible 23-point lead. Okay, so Celtic had games in hand, but we saw that they could only manage one win in their first five matches of 2021, so games in hand are only relevant if you win them.

'Going into February, it was difficult to see how Celtic could ever catch Rangers. For one they were in complete disarray themselves, seemingly imploding after coming back from their misguided trip to Dubai, which played into Rangers' hands. Not that we needed a helping hand, of course.'

Rangers were doing fine on their own, although the east-end sideshow perhaps prompted Neil Lennon to take his eye off the ball. Meanwhile, over at Ibrox, Rangers were going about their business in a professional manner, with everyone buying into Steven Gerrard's one-game-at-a-time mantra. The years-old saying was being put to good use, and after the way Rangers had imploded following the winter break of season 2019/20 it seemed the sensible route to take.

But Walters had only to look at the way so many of Gerrard's top-team stars were performing week in, week out to know that Rangers had a real good chance of landing the title. He said, 'When you have so many players giving you at least seven-out-of-ten performances each week, then you have something special on your hands.

'You had guys like Tavernier, McGregor, Goldson, Jack, Davis etc. playing consistently well in almost every game, and that's hard for opposition teams to handle. That's championship-winning form if you can keep that going for the biggest part of the season. The amount of form dips most teams experience during the course of a season would scare you, but somehow Rangers managed to continually turn in really good performances.

'I don't suppose anyone would have predicted the type of crash Celtic would experience. I certainly didn't expect to be so many points in front, but, as I've said, that was more down to Rangers' consistency than bad play from Celtic.

'Now that I get *Sportscene* down south I am able to watch a lot of highlights, and one of the games I caught was the Celtic v St Mirren match at Celtic Park, and I genuinely couldn't believe how awful Celtic were. Some of the individual performances that day were nothing short of horrendous, and I wasn't in the least surprised when Lennon hooked two of his players at half-time. They hadn't looked interested, never mind just off form. Players lose confidence for any number of reasons but there is no excuse not to give everything in all games. Sometimes it's the only way to regain your confidence.

'Some of their players weren't very humble when they won the league last year, with the way they celebrated at times, so perhaps it was karma coming back to bite them.'

Walters was impressed by most Rangers players throughout the season, but none more so than the old warhorse himself, Allan McGregor, who defied age at times to pull off some great match-winning saves. 'He has been superb most weeks,' Walters said. 'In the 2 January game against Celtic he had a few great saves and we won 1-0, but there have been many times when Rangers have been so far on top, with like 75 or 80 per cent of possession, and he has had little to do, and then he pops up in the 89th minute with a wonder save. That's what top-class keepers like Allan give you. You might have Roofe and Morelos scoring match-winning goals at one end of the park, but if you don't have a guy like McGregor making match-winning saves at the other then these goals often count for little.

'Tavernier's goals have also been an important feature of the season. What a fantastic return for a full-back, albeit one that gets up the park as much as he does. I really like him; he contributes so much, like that free kick at Dundee United. That was a real wow moment for me. He might not be as much of a shouter as others, but he knows what it means to play for a club like Rangers, and that's important. I met him after a game once and he was saying he had played alongside my nephew Reece Wabara at Wigan, so we chatted for a while and I was very impressed with the lad.

'I've also been impressed with the way Steven Gerrard has been working the transfer market. Gone are the days when you bring someone in just to fill a jersey, as just about every player Rangers have signed in the past 18 months or so has improved the team, or at least made the man in possession of the jersey realise he can't take his place for granted. When I was playing, that was the biggest motivation for me to play well every week. The guy in the stand, sitting there, waiting on me dropping my standards so that he could replace me.

'Rangers are in a good place at the moment, but they need to keep working hard. No resting on their laurels, no saying, "Right, we've finally won the league so we can relax a bit." No way, the hard work needs to continue and under a winner like Gerrard I'm sure it will.

'Celtic were going for ten in a row, although I'm a firm believer that at least four of them didn't count as we weren't in the top league, but you would expect them to come back hungrier than ever next season and that means a different type of challenge for Rangers.

'But one look at the stats for the season just gone, with so many clean sheets, so few goals conceded and you have such a great base to start from again. Seven goals conceded in their first 24 games is fantastic in any league. New players on pre-contracts were added during the season, and that alone tells you that Gerrard isn't happy with one title. He wants more, and I wouldn't bet against him achieving it.

'When I'm watching Rangers games in England, there is still that condescending attitude about the Scottish league, although they do take notice of Old Firm games and especially with an England legend like Gerrard in charge. But one way Rangers can really make them sit up and take notice is by doing well in Europe. I know we've done well in the Europa League recently, and beat some very good teams, but the next step must be to push on and start making semi-finals and finals. That would really give them something to talk about down here.

'I genuinely thought Rangers were coming good at precisely the right time in 2019/20. Going into the winter break – which came at exactly the wrong time! – we were in a great position, but it all went to pieces the moment the season restarted.

'I had a feeling that when Gerrard went into management, he wouldn't accept anything less than a genuinely ambitious club which mirrored his own wants and desires. Let's be honest, if he wanted he could sit on a beach for the rest of his life sipping cocktails. He probably has the means, but he is a fiercely ambitious young man, driven by success.

'He was a great player with a great mindset, and he has brought that to Ibrox. He was a fantastic choice of manager for Rangers. People might have laughed at the club for appointing an "academy coach" in 2018, but who's laughing now?

'Management, like any other job, is a big learning curve. Sure, he was a great player who worked under several great managers, but that counts for little until you get in that dugout and do it for yourself. You learn by your mistakes, you take stock, you sort things out, but real winners get there eventually.

'Who knows what the future holds for Steven. Who knows what Steven wants to achieve in his managerial career. He might want to manage Liverpool eventually, I'm sure he does, but he will know that if he had failed in Scotland then he wouldn't have got anywhere near the Liverpool job.

'Steven's time will come. First, though, he has to be consistently successful in Scotland. Regardless, he will feel he still has a lot more to achieve at Rangers, which is good news for supporters.'

Walters revealed his only real brush with Gerrard came when he was playing for Liverpool. Gerrard was a highly promising youngster but had suffered from injury quite a bit in his formative years. Walters said, 'I was out with a knee injury and I was sent to the English FA rehabilitation centre at Lilleshall and Steven was there. We chatted for a while and even at a young age you could tell how ambitious he was. He was a nice lad and I was really pleased to see him go on and have a fantastic career with Liverpool.

'He has obviously taken a lot from the managers he worked under, folk like the late Gérard Houllier, and nowadays you can see that he is continually improving players. He has assembled a really strong coaching team around him, and guys like Gary McAllister will prove a great sounding block for him.

'But all these guys will know that retaining a title is often tougher than winning it for the first time, so they will leave no stone unturned in preparation for next season. I would love to see Steven stay at Rangers for at least the next two or three years. At the moment, Rangers can help him fulfil all his ambitions, and if he can prove to be a consistently good and successful manager up in Scotland then the world will be his oyster.'

And the talented winger is hoping he can get back up to Glasgow next season to see how things are progressing, as the campaign just ended was a bit of a washout as far as live football was concerned. He loves nothing more than watching one of his old teams in action on a Saturday afternoon. Whether that be Aston Villa, Rangers or Liverpool, he's willing to travel for the privilege. But in this COVID-hit campaign, he managed just one live game – although what a game it was.

He explained, 'I've been doing a bit of TV and radio in the last couple of years, and I still think there is nothing better than a live game of football on a Saturday. But the season just passed was a bit of a nightmare. Everything was scaled back, and that often meant me giving my opinions from the house via Zoom. Not great when you love the thrill of live football.

'But I did manage to get to one game, which was a little bittersweet. Aston Villa 7 Liverpool 2. What a game it was. Villa had little more than seven shots on goal, and each one seemed to go in! At the end of the game I took a pic of the electronic scoreboard, just in case I woke up in the middle of the night believing it had all been a dream.

'Everyone thought Liverpool would romp that one but Villa were fantastic, and it was just a shame the ground was empty. Or perhaps the fact it was empty helped many of the Villa players with their confidence. It's a perfectly plausible train of thought.'

Marco Negri

Bologna, Italy

Rangers 4 Dundee United 0
Scorers: Kent 13, Tavernier 39, Roofe 68, Arfield 87
12 September 2020

'"Once a Ranger, always a Ranger" are the words our supporters like to hear, so thanks to the channel Sky Sports Italy, which is covering Scottish football this season with a game every weekend, it is now easier to "be there" despite being so far from Ibrox. I am very happy to watch live of course the Old Firm and some other games.

'Being a regular viewer, the standard of the Rangers side hasn't surprised me. We were almost there in 2019/20, and after the first three months I could see a team which was very solid, aggressive and very physical with a clear development of the play, perhaps just needing three or four players that could make the difference and change a single game.

'I was sure, especially after the Old Firm win at Celtic Park, that the gap was finally closing and of course the battle for the title was open. I believed it was 50-50 for the championship. Then the Dubai trip happened for Rangers and on their return so many points were dropped, but the direction was clear and both the gaffer and the board knew perfectly how to improve the weakest parts of the team.

'Thanks to the great job of the manager and his backroom staff, the level of the squad has this season been raised, but most importantly, I believe, mentally Gerrard has pushed every player to a new level of confidence which is very high. He has turned the tables on Celtic by using that confidence to apply pressure on his rivals, and they didn't handle it very well.

'The manager is working so well on the defensive side of the team, and the mentality looks like we don't concede a goal and then, with 60 or 70 per cent of possession of the ball – most of that in the offensive half – we offer something special going forward. We also have some talented players that can take an opportunity from set pieces, which now means for sure the team will find a goal from somewhere.

'I really love the mentality around the team taking just "one game at a time, three points and one less game to go". It worked very well throughout the season, with Rangers only interested in their next game, and their own performances, while also giving young players a chance to impress in the team.

'The big switch has been Dubai. Joke apart, Rangers are totally focused on doing the right thing at the right time, just like a great penalty box player, they know that it is a strange season: coronavirus, no fans at the stadium, ten in a row, but never improvising and one great example could be how the club solved the Morelos bid in the summer. That means doing things more with the head, and with the emotions always in control, and you can watch the game on the pitch when the team is playing.

'It is all about pressure. Pressure can be a force that can kill you, letting you feel confused, unsure and uncomfortable, pushing you into having a negative reaction, or making a bad decision, but on the other side pressure can be the force that helps push the bullet in the air with an exceptional speed and allows you to overcome every stumbling block which is in the way of you achieving your goal.

'You can clearly see it on one side, Celtic, and then there is Rangers.

'"Nine in a row, one more to go." I am still hearing this chant in my head, thousands of fans singing and bouncing every single game. It remains the biggest regret of my professional life, that I was not able to make the dream of every single Rangers supporter become a reality.

'Believe me, I fully understood the value of that title and I can tell you that you could feel the pressure every single day. It was tough mentally, like I imagine it was this season for Celtic. But unfortunately, too many things happened a long time ago to make sure it didn't happen, like my bizarre eye injury, Gazza's departure to Middlesbrough, the last dance for Walter Smith, still thinking we were the strongest side in the league, but I'm a sportsman and always accepted the truth of the pitch.

'I was one of the players that let the fans down that season. Believe me, the pain is still there, and if I could I would give up every single honour and every single goal I scored if only we could get that title. Believe me, please, for this is the truth.

'But we move on, and what can I say about Gerrard. He was a winner when he played the game and this is an aspect that lives with you forever, also when you become a manager and in a team sport like football you know that the more you pass this way, the more chances you have to win.

'I remember I met him at the training ground last season, before the legends game when I was part of the Rangers team to face Liverpool. After a training session we were in the same dressing room and he was blaming a member of the staff about a performance in a small game which he had organised to prepare himself for the legends game. It was so sweet to see him still have that belief that every single thing was about winning, even for a game which was like a friendly. He was not in the mood to accept second best, and I liked that quality.

'He is so successful because he is not behaving like a boss but like a leader. Of course he doesn't know everything but the key factor is that he wants to keep on learning. He doesn't look to answers but to the solutions, he listens more than he speaks, he encourages more than he criticises. He also takes the blame when it is necessary, and he is always asking for more from his players because he knows that the results will only come if the performances are exceptional.

'That is why players love him and the fans adore him, and I consider him one of the best young managers in the world right now. He is in the right place to show everyone that he is the best, which is why this was exactly the right time to bring a trophy home to Ibrox. The sowing season must be followed by the harvest.

'For sure I hope Steven Gerrard can stay at Rangers for a long time, because he has so much more to offer the club. He has been their most important signing of recent times.

'The football style of Rangers has changed so much in the past few years. It now starts with the goalkeeper having possession of the ball and playing it out from there; not all the time, but a lot. You definitely attack with 11 players and defend as a team when you don't have the ball. This is something I wasn't so good at during my time with Rangers. Our side was very solid; it was a group of men and friends, playing together for a long time, with an amazing winning mentality, while perched high on top of the cake we had some incredible individual talent like Gazza and Laudrup – two complete geniuses on a pitch who could solve the mysteries of a game in one incredible move. That is why I was swimming like a shark in and around the box, because I knew that some "good chocolates" could come at any time, from my special team-mates. But to be fair I would love to play in the present-day side that Steven Gerrard has built so carefully.

'I don't underestimate also the great job done by the board and the coaches who work behind the scenes. In the last couple of seasons they have made some amazing and important signings. They seem to be watching players all the time, and if they see someone they like then they watch that player many times, just to see if that player has the right mentality and profile for the manager and the club. They have brought in many talented players for relatively small sums of money; guys like Morelos, who have proved their worth to the team.

'Two season ago, I was working at the Serie A club Udinese. I was on the staff of the first team, working on the development on the pitch with the strikers. At the time I had spoken so many times to the scouts and to the board about buying Morelos. I could see exactly what he could offer. But now that I'm not involved at Udinese any more, I am more than happy that they didn't listen to me going on about him (but did nothing about) because now he is still free to score goals for Rangers!

'And then, of course, there is that young goalkeeper McGregor. It is amazing to think that I played with him all those season ago, and he is still there, flying to his right, and to his left.

'Balogun and Roofe, another moody one that doesn't smile after a goal, have so far proved to be excellent signings, but the player that has impressed me the most is Glen Kamara, a universal midfielder, so clever and tactical, with an enormous future in front of him, and bought for £50,000. That's right, £50,000. But I truly believe that after the Euros some very good bids will be offered to Rangers and it might just prove a bit too difficult to say no.

'Goals bring smiles to the faces of supporters, and maybe some extra money to the treasurer, but a good defence can bring a trophy or two to a club and if you want to see that happening then you must start building a great back line. This must compose of two centre-backs, who have to play simple football and focus mainly on defending their goal. They will be directed on the pitch by McGregor, and that is like having a manager behind your back. Their mentality has to be to concede as little as possible, and to leave the majority of the build-up play to the rest.

'The fantastic runs in the Europa League over the past couple of seasons have been an eye-opener for many. For the results, of course, but most importantly for the confidence of the team. It showed that if the team got a specific identity, that it would work against any opposition, regardless of whether in Scotland or in Europe, because what matters most is your approach to a game and how good your football style is. Not the opponent. During TV interviews you often hear a manager talking about how they will let the opposition worry about them. That is possible when your team has a strong identity.

'I was very confident about this season, for what Rangers could perhaps achieve, but most of all for the experience the Europa League competition can bring to every single player. Europe is an incredible shop window, but forgetting the players for a moment, it is also the perfect opportunity for the fans to head across to the Continent, and to stay away from their wives for a few days, but this will only ever be achieved again when we manage to resolve the issue of coronavirus!

'During my time, to have my team-mate at right-back as top scorer would have been a very bad issue for a striker like me. I don't know if I could have accepted that, for sure it would have asked me many questions, and for sure I will not let him take so easily the penalty kick – but Tavernier is different.

'He is the perfect modern defender; talented, skilled, can play the ball with precision, always prepared for the offensive development, without missing the defence, ready to close the space in the box when the ball is on the feet of the left side (thanks also to the instructions of the manager and the "pushing pushing" style of the play he prefers), taking penalty kicks and able to take extremely well all set pieces. In modern football you score around 70 per cent of all goals from free kicks, set pieces, etc.

'And don't forget he is the captain of the club, a great role that can earn a player legendary status, but can also put you under the spotlight and add very big responsibilities. I couldn't wait to see him raise to the sky that Premiership trophy, and see Tav's infectious, beaming smile. It is my hope that he will wear the blue jersey for a long time, and also that one day he will get a call-up for the England national team. But while he is at Rangers we will enjoy him, and it shouldn't be too long until we are looking at James Tavernier in the Rangers Hall of Fame.

'One of the games I watched this season was the match against Dundee United at Ibrox, and it brought back to me so many happy memories. Rangers played very well, won 4-0 and collected three very important league points. One thing I noticed was the four different goalscorers – Kent, Tav, Roofe and Arfield.

'When I played against United back in the day, I liked to score them all myself (only kidding). But like a bull who sees red then gets crazy, I like to say when I caught sight of that tangerine colour I scored a lot of goals. My numbers against Dundee United were comparable to Messi!

'I've been in touch through social media with Sieb Dijkstra, the former Dundee United keeper, and often he blames me for him having had a nightmare that season, and asked me if I was trying to end his career. In fact, five goals in a single game, which was made up of a header, a lob from distance, right foot outside the box then inside, and a penalty is something that still allows me to smile and think about a very personal love affair with Rangers.

'And when I watched Rangers beat easily United this season, I soon realised that Steven Gerrard and his men were on to something special. When you score a lot of goals and concede very few then you are sure to be on to a good thing. Not only did Rangers achieve these two football fundamentals, but they also played very well that day.

'I am also very very happy about the way things are going at the club right now. The team is playing well, the results are coming, and we now have a trophy as a result – but I know that things were not always so easy.

'It has been like the fall-out from an earthquake with everything at the club destroyed. But fans, and those who had much love for Rangers, didn't cry for long, they immediately started the job of rebuilding the club with their bare hands, and in a real team effort the house has once again been rebuilt.

'I remember when we were asked to buy into the future of the club. Club 1872 were looking for supporters and ex-players to buy stock so that they could have a voice in the boardroom. I contributed because I wanted to help, do my small bit, and thankfully many others did too. They also wanted to take the fight to the guy in charge at the time who thought more about money than the team. There was a walk to Hampden with thousands of fans, the Oceania Rangers Supporters Association and North American Rangers Supporters Association conventions around the world, to which I was invited, and where former players and legends like Richard Gough, Mark Hateley and John Brown told the gathered supporters in no uncertain terms that the club would be back very soon, and where it belongs.

'This is the past, but I wanted to let you understand that these words weren't just hollow words. The club is now back at the top thanks to the love of the fans, who followed their team through the tough days of the lower leagues, and the loyalty of so many legends, former players and of course the professionalism and talent of the current manager and his staff, and their players, who have given everything to bring success to this famous old club.

'So many people have pushed so hard in the right direction, and I am so proud and honoured to be considered one of the Rangers family. You have no idea how much that means to me. So you could say that title number 55 has been a win from the ashes. It has been a title that has come from not just on the pitch, but from people planning season after season, for the fans that took part in the rebuilding of their club, and who always had faith that they would get back to the top.

'On the pitch, of course, has also been very important. So often it is the best team in the Old Firm who wins the league and this season there has been no doubt about that. Which team has been 20 points ahead, or 23 points at times? The standard Rangers have set has been incredible. There is only one team this season who has deserved the title.

'And now it only remains for me to say one more thing. I hope that everyone ordered their helium balloons with two number fives in plenty of time, because when the trophy was presented in May, it was impossible to find them!

'Ciao everyone, and congratulations to Rangers Football Club. Big winners of the league, and very deserved.'

Lisa Swanson

Coatbridge, Scotland

Hibs 2 Rangers 2
Scorers: Morelos 45+1, Arfield 57
20 September 2020

Is it any wonder that all Lisa Swanson ever wanted to do was play football? From the moment she could walk, she had a ball at her feet. In her first school picture she has the full uniform on – and a flyaway football in her hand!

She played football with her pal in the street, and the pair would scour the regular haunts in Saltcoats looking for a game to join in. And then on her first visit to Ibrox, she 'met' her two footballing idols on the same night. Her fate was sealed.

She explained, 'My dad used to take my brother and sister, Billy and Amanda, to the games, and then he started taking me. My first game was Rangers v PSG at Ibrox in the Champions League. Most supporters get to see run-of-the-mill Scottish league games or friendlies on their first visit to Ibrox, but not me, I was so fortunate.

'Watching the likes of Ronaldinho and Mikel Arteta was amazing. Ronaldinho was my hero – but I also met my "other" hero that night. We had just arrived in at Central Station from Saltcoats and who was walking past but Ally McCoist. He came over to chat to us so what a great start to the night.

'We drew 0-0 with PSG, and it was the same in the return game, but we beat them on penalties to go through to the next round. I'm sure that was the first time we'd ever won a penalty shoot-out in European competition!

'We were walking up the steps from the concourse to our seat in the Broomloan front and the moment I saw the pitch and the floodlights, wow! My dad said, "You'll remember this moment for the rest of your life," and he was right.

'The Primary One photograph sums me up best. I'm four years old and I have my wee school skirt on, and this football in my hands. As I got older, as a kid, and if things weren't going well in my life, football was my escape. My best pal Mark, a big Celtic fan, and I would play football every day. Me v him; Rangers v Celtic. All summer, every summer. We would also play two v two with older lads in the street.'

But Lisa, these days the longest-serving Rangers Women player, soon outgrew street football and was looking around for a team to join. However, 1990s Saltcoats was like most other places in Scotland; it wasn't exactly awash with women's football teams, especially for those starting out.

She said, 'The first team I played for was Saltcoats United, a boys' team. A number of the boys in my class were going along for trials so I tagged on more in hope than expectation. I was in Primary Seven at the time, but I got in! Sadly, we were the worst team in the league by some stretch, and would get hammered nine and ten nil. We won a single match that season and the way we celebrated you'd have thought we'd just won the league!

'Stephanie Breen and I were the only two girls in the team, and we both went to Kilmarnock together, and then Rangers at the same time.'

Lisa also reflected on her formative years, 'When I was growing up, my nana was a massive influence. I was so close to her and she was always the first to throw a protective arm around me. I remember telling her it was so unfair that I couldn't play for Rangers through no fault of my own. It was around the time of my 11th or 12th birthday, and she immediately booked me on one of the Rangers Soccer Schools. It was magical, and it took place on the small pitch across from Ibrox. My nana was amazing.

'I was at a Scotland trial as a kid and had played really well, and scored from around 30 yards. But when I discovered I wouldn't be asked back I was really down. My dad took me home to Saltcoats and dropped me at my nana's. She told me not to worry, that everything would be fine. And it was, because I got a call that night from an unknown number. Thinking Scotland had reconsidered, I called back, but it was John McMonagle, a guy who was taking over women's football at Rangers. Rangers were starting a girls' team, and then a women's side a year later. He said, "I'd love you to come and train with us. Can you meet me at Anniesland at ten o'clock tomorrow morning?"

'I agreed, came off the phone buzzing and said to my nana, "That was Rangers. They want me to train with them, at a place called Anniesland. Where's that?" I'd never heard of Anniesland! The furthest I'd been from Saltcoats was Ibrox, so I was straight on to Google to find out how I was getting to Anniesland for 10am next day to meet this total stranger who said he was from Rangers!

'It was a six-week trial, but each week the numbers would be reduced until they had identified the best players. Stephanie and I trained every day, and thankfully we were both picked for the girls' team, and also the following season, 2008, when the Rangers Women team began. It was the start of a great journey.

'Of my entire 11 years at Rangers, I was most nervous when we drove through the gates at Murray Park for the first time. I had watched the programme *Blue Heaven*, which followed young players like Bob Malcolm and Chris Burke as they tried to make the big time, so the training ground was instantly recognisable.

'We signed our registration forms at Murray Park, and that was another buzz. We had played for the under-17s for a full season but now we were in the women's side. Once I'd signed my name on that form, I thought to myself, "I'm a Rangers player" – and my nana was so proud.'

When she moved to Rangers, Lisa switched from the right wing to central midfield, and eventually ended up a striker. She explained, 'A number of players left to sign for clubs like Glasgow City, Hibs and Spartans. We needed a striker, so I volunteered to play up front and it worked out. I still don't understand why so many chose to leave. Everyone was in the same boat at the time. No one got paid. As a Rangers supporter, it wouldn't have crossed my mind to leave. Being in the starting 11 was all that mattered to me.

'My coach described me as an old-fashioned striker, a target player, and not many in the women's game were that type. Even now, there aren't really that many target players around. It's all about coming short, getting in behind defenders, speed, etc., but if I got a chance, I would score. I adapted to my new position quickly.

'We went through hard times at Rangers so that others could reap the benefits, but I went from a wee kid who couldn't play for Rangers through no fault of her own to someone who played for the club they loved for 11 years. I wouldn't change that for anything.

'Even when I'd been at Rangers seven or eight years, my team-mates would laugh as I said, "I can't believe I'm a Rangers player!" They would all say, "You've been here for ages," and I'd reply, "So!" But it went in really quick. Eleven years, just like that. I'm glad that I was one of the players who never took it for granted. I appreciated every moment.

'I didn't drive, so it was quite a trek getting up and down to Milngavie from Saltcoats. It was two trains there and the same back. It would often be 1am before I got home from training, because we had to wait until the boys were finished before we could get on the pitch, and then it would be the last train home. I switched colleges to tie in with training and playing in Glasgow. Sometimes I would be at training two hours early, so I would do my course work while I was waiting. Some folk might say it was total dedication, but it was my life. Every job I had also had to suit my football. I'm 29 now and at last I'm in a career that I actually wanted! Football dictated my life, but that was my decision.'

As Rangers Women's longest-serving player, Lisa has many highlights – but recalls only too fondly the 2010 Scottish Cup semi-final against Celtic at Toryglen. She said, 'It was a feisty game, as you can imagine. Our manager Scott Allison was red-carded, and then one of our players was sick, so she had to go off. Turned out she was pregnant!

'Everything seemed to be falling apart, but the tie went to extra time, and then penalties. I was desperate to hit one, and got the nod for the last one. The manager said, "It's down to you, Swanny!"

'There were loads of Celtic supporters there, and they were booing me as I walked up to take the kick. Between me and a place in the Scottish Cup Final stood Nicole Andrews, an ex-team-mate when we were kids at Killie. In those days, I would turn up to training in my Rangers top, and Nicole her Celtic shirt. Thankfully I managed to give her the eyes and I scored. We were through to the final and I ran more during my celebration than I had during the match!

'Old Firm games were also special, at least in the early days, but latterly many of the players on both sides were pals so it took an edge off it. Personally, I wanted the rivalry to be intense, and more often than not the manager would say to me before the game, "Don't let the occasion get the better of you." They knew what it meant to me as a massive Rangers fan.

'We went through a season and a half where we failed to beat them, and that was hell. When we eventually won you can imagine how we celebrated. We had "Simply the Best" on in the dressing room, but the manager told us to turn it off as it was disrespectful. I thought those comments were over the top.

'If the players we lost to Glasgow City had stayed at Rangers we would have challenged their domination of the women's game. We would have been more than capable of winning trophies, but too many players left. We were the first team to take points off Glasgow City, and finished second to them in the league, so it was frustrating.'

Surprisingly, Lisa didn't get the chance to represent her country, although she was invited to train with the Scotland Elite squad. She said, 'I enjoyed it, but when their training nights clashed with Rangers there was only ever going to be one winner. I had just broken into the Rangers team and didn't want to lose my place. I decided that if I was good enough, they would come and get me through time. I was young enough. I don't regret my decision. I took part in a few "A Squad" games, but it was quite an insulated setup.'

But when an opportunity arose to play abroad, Lisa remembered her nana's words, 'If you get the chance to travel and play football, take it.'

Lisa said, 'A football agent asked if I wanted a move abroad to play professionally. I had been at Rangers eight years and said I would consider it once I got to ten, so I put the idea out of my head. When the time was right, I was grateful that an opportunity was still there. It was the second half of the season in Scotland and a Finnish team, Aland United, wanted me for the last three months of their season. They were desperate to avoid relegation and wanted a goalscorer. I had to check with both Rangers and my work, to ensure that I would be able to go back to both, and thankfully I was given those assurances.

'Playing abroad, and professionally, was a great experience, although I was forced to learn quickly after being sent off in my first game! I was supposed to play six games, but I was given a one-match suspension. I played up front for three games and scored in each one, and we stayed up. Mission accomplished.

'Finland was great, but the travelling was unbelievable. We were was based in the Aland Islands, which is between Sweden and Finland, and travelled to every game on cruise ships, but it was five hours to mainland Finland then we had to travel for hours to get to the venues. I'm so glad I did it, though, because it was a great experience.

'While I was away, my nephew Frankie was born, so I had that to look forward to when I got home. I have another nephew, Freddie, and I love them both.'

But things would quickly take a turn for the worse when Lisa arrived back home in Scotland. She remembers, 'When I returned from Finland, I felt that Celtic were miles ahead of us, mostly in the way they were treated by their parent club. Dave King had said much the same. The straw that broke the camel's back was when our new manager introduced pre-match huddles. I told the manager I didn't think we should be doing that, and I got the big speech. I was told it was an attempt to bring the clubs closer together, but I said it would have more of an impact coming from the men's team. I had loads of messages on my phone, which I showed the manager, and soon found myself on the bench. It became quite clear I wasn't getting back into the team so I went out on loan to Kilmarnock. It was dropping down a league but I played eight games and was the top scorer. I did well and was the league's player of the month for September. I also scored the goal of the season, so it was a successful stint.

'I believed I had proved myself and headed back to Rangers for a meeting and, I hoped, back into the team. I was told that what I had achieved would have been expected of me because it was a league lower!

'To be honest, as soon as I sat down for that meeting I more or less knew my time was up. That was a tough time for me, personally. I had lost my wee brother and my nana, and Rangers brought my mental health into it, which was bang out of order.

'It was decided I should move back to Kilmarnock, and while I was reluctant to leave Rangers I knew it was for the best as I couldn't be around that person. I had stuck by Rangers through the worst of times, but sadly that wasn't reciprocated. I certainly didn't want to leave.

'It was strange playing for other clubs after being at Rangers so long. It's different with Kilmarnock, because I played there as a kid. Hearts and Motherwell didn't feel the same, but I always did my best, and I loved the girls at Motherwell.

'I'll always have an emotional attachment to the Rangers Women team. At the moment I'm on loan to Killie from Motherwell, and I'm playing in the Scottish Women's Premier League 2. I've moved to Coatbridge, so it's a bit of travel again for me, but it made sense as I get on really well with the manager, Stewart Hall, and he has a lot of belief in me as a player.

'When I knew I was going back to Kilmarnock I asked for the number 13 squad jersey. It was Ally McCoist's number at Rugby Park, but it was also personal as both my nana and wee brother were born on the 13th. Moving to Killie definitely helped me fall in love with football again.'

And while Lisa also fell in love with the majority of Rangers' performances during the championship-winning season, there was a hint of frustration as she watched the Bears on their visit to Easter Road way back in September.

She said, 'After the game, Steven Gerrard said it was two points dropped and I would agree, especially as we had come from behind to lead 2-1. It's always disappointing to lose a lead, but Hibs are a good team and games against them this season were tough.

'It was our eighth league game, and the first in which we'd conceded, which was staggering. You don't usually know what you'll get early in the season, but as soon as it became apparent that the defence was solid, it quickly became the norm, and anything which fell below the line was deemed unacceptable.

'Performing in empty stadiums must have been strange for the players, especially as they are so used to a big crowd driving them on. In women's football we don't get big crowds, so you wouldn't notice a big difference.

'It's just a personal preference, but I prefer watching Rangers away from home. There is usually a better atmosphere at games.

Ibrox can be bouncing for Old Firm games, or big European matches, but for standard league games it often resembles a library. This season, though, we were forced to watch from home, and it shone a different light on following the team.

'At Easter Road, Alfredo equalising on the stroke of half-time was so important and would've given the players a huge boost. Scott Arfield then got us in front with a great goal, and it would have been a worthy winner, but sadly we lost a second goal, and that's probably what disappointed the gaffer the most.

'Hibs were one of the better teams we played, but that didn't surprise me. They have good young players and always raise their game against us. It's the same for most teams we play. When I was at Rangers, and we were playing Celtic, we would raise our game. Whether or not you're aware of it, or it happens subconsciously, I'm not sure, but it is a thing.'

Lisa insists there would have been an enormous amount of pressure on the players throughout the campaign. 'Until we won the league, it was always going to be the case for any players representing Rangers. It's been so long, but so rewarding.

'I've seen people suggest Celtic threw it away, but what about giving Rangers some credit for what they've achieved? The number of games we've won, goals conceded, undefeated for so long, etc.

'When it comes to listing our main performers you could literally go through the whole team. Connor Goldson's contribution has been awesome. People talk about him playing every game, but I prefer to focus more on his consistency. Mind you, to have played every game means Steven Gerrard has the ultimate trust in him. Folk maybe thought Allan McGregor would get the nod [for the captaincy] if Tav was injured, but the manager has obviously given it to Goldson for a reason. He's the right type of player: a leader on the park, and he never shuts up. He's a different type of person than Tav. I heard Andy Halliday say on a podcast that Tav was a brilliant captain. He said Tav was great in the dressing room, and in a more personal way. That doesn't make him any less a captain than anyone else, just a different type of captain.'

Lisa has been impressed with the qualities Gerrard has brought to the job, such as discipline and man-management. She added, 'I also like the way he defends his players, which in turn means he will get the best out of them. It means so much to a player to know the manager has your back. I've been there, and when you have a good relationship, it's a joy going into training.

'Steven Gerrard has backed Alfredo Morelos to the hilt, and what a difference in Alfredo during the second half of the season. He was rarely getting involved in anything nasty. He has repaid the manager's trust in him, although I think the "reputation" Alfredo has is wholly undeserved.

'When you're a striker and up against a few big defenders, or not having the best game yourself, you might try to provoke a reaction by nicking their heels; something to mix it up. I know I'm getting done next but it helps you get back into the game. You can only really appreciate it if you play that position.'

Last time Rangers won the league, the season climaxed in an unforgettable afternoon at Kilmarnock as the team romped to a 5-1 win. Kyle Lafferty grabbed a hat-trick and Lisa was one of thousands of joyous supporters inside Rugby Park. She said, 'Great day, but it seems a lifetime ago. I was sick of seeing Celtic win the league, so this title was a welcome break from that. It was overdue and I had been looking forward to it all season, especially as we had been in command from day one. Sadly, the circumstances weren't ideal due to COVID, but we've made the best of a bad situation.'

There was never any doubt which team Lisa would support, with the majority of her family big Rangers fans. She continued, 'Both my nana and dad were Rangers daft. My nana had the nine-in-a-row DVD box set and I watched them all so many times, so I got to know all the players from that era. Ally McCoist was just such a legend – and a lovely guy. He chats to you like he would chat to one of his mates. Kris Boyd was also a great striker, so he is another of my favourites.'

Lisa will never forget winning a newspaper competition. 'I was a kid at Kilmarnock and there was a soccer skills competition in *The Sun*, which my dad put me forward for. I used to watch videos of Ronaldinho and practise his skills, so I was delighted to take part in it. Five boys and five girls would win a five-day trip to Barcelona. When I got the phone call to say I'd been chosen I was delighted, and I decided to take my nana. She was my go-to person when I was a kid, so this was payback. Then my dad and all the family decided they would make a holiday of it, so I had everyone with me!

'Murdo MacLeod coached us, but on the last day of filming Giovanni van Bronckhorst and Henrik Larsson turned up and we got to chat to them. They joined in with the training and when I told Gio I was a Rangers fan, he gave me the biggest smile ever! Henrik Larsson was listening and said, "I suppose we're all still human!" We were then asked to take penalties and I scored past Larsson, so I had the last laugh!

'Rangers is such a special club. Our history, values and tradition set us apart from the others. We have fans in every part of the world. When we were in the lower leagues our supporters stood by the club in their thousands and ensured our eventual return to where we are today.

'Rangers means so much to so many. My uncle Billy received an MBE for services to the Army, but the day I signed for Rangers my nana likened it to Billy's achievement! That's how important it was to her. Whenever we were out, and bumped into someone, she would say, "This is my granddaughter Lisa, she plays for Rangers!" I would pretend to be mortified, but really I was made up!'

Return of the
Rangers Men

Paul Murray

Former Rangers chairman and director Portugal

MR SINGH'S was busy on the evening of Thursday, 5 March 2015, as it is most nights. It's a popular eatery close to Glasgow city centre and has a well-earned reputation for serving fine Indian cuisine.

So anyone who spotted three guys enjoying their meal probably wouldn't have given them a second glance. This was no ordinary group, though, and it's fair to say the prospects of a safe future for Rangers Football Club were enhanced greatly that night. Because as Dave King, John Gilligan and Paul Murray enjoyed their meal, they were putting the finishing touches to their plans for the following day's EGM at Ibrox.

Murray explained, 'Dave is a big fan of Mr Singh's and because he isn't over here that often he always wants to go when he's back in Glasgow. When we asked him where he wanted to meet, he answered, "Let's go to Satty's!" Satty kindly gave us the side room, which is partitioned off with a curtain.

'It gave us the opportunity to chat, and as we hadn't met face to face for quite some time, it was important to get together before the meeting. We were pretty confident we were going to win, but there was still an apprehension.

'The evening also served to calm us down a little, and we managed to enjoy a social get-together before the big one the following day. Dave had his trusty spreadsheets with him and seemed quite confident about the outcome of the EGM, and, in turn, that made me confident too.

'But until the votes are cast and counted, there is always a worry that things might not go your way. But anyone who knows Dave knows he is a meticulous and detailed guy, and when he gets into something he is like a dog with a bone and completely focussed on what he's doing. He was keeping his spreadsheets on who was voting what way, and he was all over it every minute of every day. I never actually saw this spreadsheet but it was talked about a lot!

'We were all phoning round the shareholders we knew and had met, and on the basis of that he was building up this picture of how it might turn out. We worried it might be like a General Election; you know, someone comes to your door and asks if you're going to vote for them, and you say, "Oh, absolutely," but you don't know what they'll do once inside the polling booth.'

Murray had organised a takeover exercise in December 2013, along with three others, but it came up short. He said, 'I think I got to 34 per cent, which was about a third of the vote, although insufficient to carry the resolution. But we knew the key people and we knew the way they were thinking. We maintained dialogue with them, so we were confident of winning, although we didn't expect to get 85 per cent!

'The pressure on us was enormous, and you felt it every day. I always maintain that the big difference in March 2015 was that everyone who got involved was a Rangers fan.

Myself, John Gilligan, Dave King, Douglas Park, George Letham, George Taylor. Our only interest was to help the club move forward. Sure, we made mistakes, but they were made by guys who had the club's best interests at heart. We did our best and everything we did, we did for Rangers. We were emotionally, financially and intellectually engaged with the club.

'On the day of the 2015 EGM there was probably around 1,000 shareholders in the stadium, and it was very encouraging to get a round of applause as we walked out towards the stage. That was a good feeling. We kind of knew at that point we would win, because Derek Llambias and Barry Leach, who were on the board, had already left the building.

'One of the first guys I called after the EGM was John Greig, and I asked him to come back to the club as honorary president. He is my hero; the guy I identify as the head of the Rangers family. John said to me, "I don't want to be involved on the board." I replied, "We just want you to come and be John Greig, nothing else." And he seemed really happy about that.'

Following the successful takeover, the three new board members headed up to the training ground at Auchenhowie where they met Ian Durrant and Kenny McDowall, the management team at the time, and the players and staff. They wanted to keep everyone up to date.

Murray said, 'By about 6.30pm, we were all absolutely exhausted. The emotions of the day had taken over. But I still had to drive back to Edinburgh, as my son had a play on at school. When I reached Harthill I had to stop for a coffee. I was sitting alone at a table looking out of the window, and I could feel this presence at my shoulder. The guy must have been mid-70s, and he said to me, "Mr Murray, I'm sorry to bother you, but I'm so pleased at what happened today." The guy was crying, and he gave me a bear hug, and I could feel the raw emotion. He said to me, "Thank you. This is a great day." And that's when you realise exactly what it means to people.'

The following day, Rangers drew 0-0 at Cowdenbeath, and it was down to earth with a bang after the euphoria of the successful takeover. Murray recalled, 'That was the reality of our situation. Hearts had thumped Cowdenbeath 10-0 a couple of weeks previous, so it was absolutely dreadful, and we're thinking, "What have we done here?"

'But six years later – to the day – we were champions. Dundee United and Celtic drew 0-0 at Tannadice, 24 hours after we'd beaten St Mirren 3-0, and it was all over. People had been talking about winning the league at Parkhead, but I always felt it would happen when it did, and the whole symmetry pulled it together.

'I had sat on the board previously with Dave King when David Murray owned the club, so I was involved before the Craig Whyte episode. In those days, apart from David Murray, no one knew who the directors were. Everyone knew who Dave was, as he'd put in £20m, but the other board members were virtually unknown. Directors were basically just guys behind the scenes, and most of the questions at the AGM would be about Walter Smith and which players we were buying, and what was happening to the team, etc. All football-related stuff.

'And suddenly, from 2013 onwards, the football became irrelevant and it was more about what was happening in the boardroom. We all became well-known people for the first time, so whereas these things had always been dry and boring, they were now interesting because there were boardroom disagreements, takeovers, etc., so it was a really unusual period in the club's history.

'When we clinched the league earlier this year I was very emotional. I'm not afraid to say it but I had a tear in my eye. I know it had been looking likely for some time, but there are always concerns at the back of your mind that there might be some last-minute collapse or something. I refused to talk about it until it was mathematically certain.

'I watched the game against St Mirren on Rangers TV on the Saturday, at home in Portugal, and after that I felt it was over. That 3-0 win all but brought the title home. The following day's game between Dundee United and Celtic merely rubber-stamped it. I felt a real pride in the club. We had been battered for ten years. People across the board having a right go at us, and I think just to get our pride back was so important.

'John Gilligan is one of the biggest Rangers fans I know, and he makes a great point when he says it was important not to lose a whole generation of Rangers supporters through failure on the park. If we'd lost these guys, we could've had a serious problem.'

It was perhaps ironic that Rangers all but clinched the title with the win over St Mirren, as Murray admits he could easily have been a Saints fan. He explained, 'I'm from Paisley originally and my dad was a big St Mirren fan. His dad and his brothers all supported Rangers, so he kind of rebelled a bit. Dad and I used to go to Love Street a lot in the early 1970s.

'But although Dad was a Saints man, he definitely had a soft spot for Rangers. St Mirren were in the Second Division so I watched them play the likes of Berwick Rangers in front of 500 folk. But then Rangers came to town and it changed everything. It was a Scottish Cup fourth round tie in 1972, and the crowd was 29,000. It was jam-packed. I'd never seen anything like it. We used to stand in the home end, but for some reason we were in the Rangers end that day. I was only seven, so obviously I couldn't see. We were at the back of the terracing and I was up on Dad's shoulders. The crowd was unbelievable and that got my interest. Rangers won 4-1 and Tommy McLean got a couple of goals. I was completely mesmerised, and that was the starting point for my love of Rangers.

'After that, we would go to see St Mirren one Saturday, and Ibrox the next. I remember Dad going to all the home games the year we won the European Cup Winners' Cup. I asked if he would take me to the semi-final tie against Bayern Munich but he refused as there would be 80,000 there. He told me I could watch it on TV but I was distraught, and having whetted my appetite with the cup tie at Love Street, I was then forced to watch the biggest game of the season on TV!

'As I got a bit older, I started going to the Rangers games on my own, although I still had a soft spot for St Mirren as they were my hometown team.'

Murray first became involved with the club when he and a group of others invested in the Rangers Youth Development Company. He explained, 'I knew David Murray through business and when I came back up from England in 2003, and moved to Edinburgh, I re-engaged with David and a few of his guys. At the time the club was looking for fresh investment, so I joined the board of the development company. John Greig and Sandy Jardine were on the board, so meeting both guys for the first time was great. From there I was asked to join the main board in 2007, and I left when the club was sold to Craig Whyte.

'When we took control on Friday, 6 March 2015, we had the initial burst of euphoria but the harsh reality of our financial predicament soon kicked in. John Gilligan and I were trying to sort out this incredible mess when the phone rang. It was Colin Stewart, a director of the Rangers Youth Development Company, and he said he had a cheque which he had refused to give to the old board. He would regularly say to them, "Oh yeah, don't worry, it's coming." Colin added, "But now that you're here, the good guys, I'm giving it to you." It was for £150,000 and it was such a big help. It showed just how much of a Rangers man Colin was. And that's part of the reason we are where we are today, because everyone who is now involved at Rangers has the club's best interests at heart, and long may that continue.'

Josh Holmes

Neilston, Scotland

Motherwell 1 Rangers 5
Scorers: Tavernier 12, 37; Jones 28, Itten 75, 80
27 September 2020

Josh will never forget Helicopter Sunday. He will never truly remember it either, for he was just three months old when Nacho Novo scored the vital goal for Rangers at Easter Road. Meanwhile, 34 miles west, Scott McDonald was bagging a couple for Motherwell to destroy Celtic's hopes of landing the title on the final day of the season. That was Helicopter Sunday.

A couple of days after Josh was born, Frenchman Gregory Vignal and Novo, again, scored the goals that gave Rangers a 2-0 win over Celtic at Parkhead. The win contributed significantly to Rangers wrestling back the title they had lost so disastrously to their Old Firm rivals the season previous.

But despite the Helicopter Sunday triumph being among the most sensational in the club's history, by the time Josh was old enough to start going to the games he would be brought up on a diet of visits to Airdrie and Albion Rovers, wins at Elgin City and Brechin, and cup losses to Alloa Athletic and Raith Rovers.

Fast forward to May 2018, and Josh was one of 7,000 supporters who took their place in the West Enclosure to hail the arrival of the messiah.

He explained, 'That was one of my best days as a Rangers supporter. Celtic fans were always banging on about having

Brendan Rodgers, but as far as I'm concerned Stevie G was on another level. He is probably the best England midfielder of all time – and then there is the "Miracle of Istanbul". That Champions League Final has to be the most exciting ever. To come back from 3-0 down – with Gerrard scoring Liverpool's first goal that night. Wow!

'I was only three months old when that game was played but I've watched it on YouTube so many times. It was incredible. AC Milan were three up at half-time. No team should have been able to come back from that, especially against such a talented Milan side, but Stevie G dragged his team back into it, and within six second-half minutes they were level. They went on to win a penalty shoot-out – with Gerrard probably down to take the fifth and final penalty, although he wasn't required. It was Liverpool's fifth European Cup win and Gerrard was named man of the match. That's how good he was. His determination won the Champions League that night.

'When he was appointed as our manager I was really pleased. How did we manage to get this man to Ibrox? We are a massive club, but being there to welcome him to Ibrox will live with me forever. I can't remember if we were officially off school that day, or if I had a "dental appointment", but I wasn't missing it for the world. Up until we won the league that was my best moment as a Rangers fan.'

One game really stood out for Josh during the season as marking Rangers down as the real deal – the day we thumped Motherwell 5-1 at their place. He said, 'For as long as I can remember we've never had it easy at Fir Park, so I didn't think this one would be much different. No one was happier than me when I was proved wrong. Not many teams scored five at Motherwell last season so it was a great result – and a good one to get ticked off the list.

'When I saw our team that day I was a wee bit more confident and predicted a 2-0 win. I know Motherwell usually sit in when they play us so I didn't think there would be a lot of goals in the game. Once again, I was way off the mark.

'The draw we had against them at Fir Park later in the season was much the way I had predicted the earlier one to go – only with a happier outcome!

'Jordan Jones scored a great goal for us, his first for Rangers, and right there and then you saw why the manager had signed him. It was a top move, and a peach of a goal. The curve he put on the ball was amazing. I also liked the way he cut across the defender, so any contact and it would have been at least a free kick, or a penalty once he was inside the box.

'I'm sure it was his first start for us, and he looked like a player, so it's a pity the way the whole thing with him and George Edmundson panned out. Both were put out on loan in January, which was annoying as it was down to their stupidity and could easily have been avoided. After the game, Stevie G praised Jones and talked about his potential. Hopefully there's a way back for him, as Nathan Patterson proved after he was also involved in a COVID-related incident.

'Jones is a Northern Ireland international, so he's one that Gerrard might have been relying on throughout the season, so I can only imagine how frustrated the manager was. He did well for Kilmarnock, which is obviously how he got his move to us. He scored against us at Rugby Park when I was there. I didn't know an awful lot about him before that but that goal made me take notice of him. I remember the Killie fans singing "We are the People" when he scored! He's a good player with a lot of pace so hopefully he still has a future at the club.'

Jones wasn't the only player to make a positive contribution, as Cedric Itten came off the bench and scored two beauties. Both were different types of goals and added a touch of gloss to an already impressive score.

Josh said, 'I think Itten is a class striker. He is another one I hadn't really heard of before he signed, but I checked up on him and he scored plenty of goals in Switzerland. He got 29 in one season, which is fantastic.

'At Motherwell that day, he took his first goal superbly. When the pass came through to him he flicked the ball up with his first touch and battered it into the net. No goalkeeper would have saved that one. It was a great finish.

'For his second, he reacted quickly at a corner to prod the ball home. He was the most alert player in the box. To have scored four goals against Motherwell this season is brilliant. I thought he also played well when he started at Hamilton, but he didn't get much service from the likes of Aribo, Kent and Hagi. He seemed to be up against the entire Hamilton defence, but I definitely think he will be a good striker for us.

'Such a comprehensive win would have sent out a message to the others in the league. It showed we weren't just a major force at Ibrox and that we could score goals anywhere. Even the goal we conceded was a late own goal from Edmundson, which was actually a great finish. Just a pity it was in our goal!

'It was three welcome points, but far too early in the season to start talking titles. I'm with the manager on that one. If there are lessons to be learned from the last nine or ten years it's that it isn't over until it's over. I thought we might win the league last season, but look at the way that went. Although when you go to a place like Fir Park and score five it's only natural to start thinking you're good enough to be up there challenging for the title. When you see how far we've come since the dark days, it's okay to let yourself believe, as long as that belief doesn't turn into complacency.

'It's strange, but it seems as though the players have been playing with a lot more freedom this season, and of course there are no fans in. I wonder if the two are linked. Football fans can be critical at times. Some will scream for a player to shoot if he's on the edge of the box, and when he does, and it goes over the bar or the keeper saves it, they scream at them again, "Why didn't you pass it?" Sometimes the players can't win.

'Take Tav, for instance; he has had the season of his life but maybe that's because he doesn't have anyone shouting at him for a misplaced pass! And because there are more Rangers fans in the stadium than just about every other team, it stands to reason that the players will hear the frustration from the stands when something goes wrong. Being told you're rubbish can't be good for their confidence. Nobody likes to be criticised but I get that fans become frustrated, because everyone just wants to see their team doing well.

'But then you look at the Braga match the season before last. I don't think we would've come back from 2-0 down if it hadn't been for the fans roaring the team on. If that match had been played behind closed doors I think we might have lost.

'Talking about Tav, it's ridiculous to think that our right-back could have scored a hat-trick that day at Motherwell, but he took a cracking free kick and only a great save prevented it from going in. Tav has been one of our key players this season, and has been in the opposition box just as much as any of our strikers. It's fine if he scores, or doesn't cause any goals to be lost, but the late equaliser at Hamilton came from his side, and I just wondered why he had to be so far up the park when there were only a few seconds to go. But overall, Tav had a great season, and was one of our most influential players. I was gutted when he got injured in Antwerp.

'Clean sheets were definitely the foundation for our league success. If Celtic had been closer, it might have gone down to goal difference, and we could potentially have had another Helicopter Sunday on our hands. Thankfully we didn't, as good as I'm led to believe Helicopter Sunday was!

'At one point in the season – around the middle of February, I think – we had a +60 goal difference, and Celtic were about 20 worse off, so while we were scoring a few, our defence was more than doing its job by keeping so many clean sheets.

'Connor Goldson was probably our most consistent player. It seemed he had learned from a lot of the silly mistakes he had been making in the previous two seasons. He was such a mainstay in the defence and really did lead by example. The defence contributed massively to the title.

'He even scored eight goals, which is good for a defender, and I will never forget his two at Parkhead. The big man was brilliant for us, as was Borna Barišić. He seemed to do his job quietly, and always tried to make sure he was back in position after a Rangers attack. He and Tav have great energy levels.

'Although it has been all about the team, we've also had some great individual displays, and if we're talking player of the year, there would be four candidates. I know it's difficult to pick so few, but I really liked Tav, Goldson, Glen Kamara and Kemar Roofe. Roofe was a great signing and probably our best striker over the course of the season. He's so good with the ball at his feet.

'The season, in my opinion, was too much of a stop-start affair for Alfredo Morelos, although he still managed to chip in with some really important goals, and he was asked to play a different role from normal, where he was out of the box more and linking up play. He was involved in Goldson's second at Parkhead.

'I thought he was outstanding against Antwerp at Ibrox. He was unplayable that night. Imagine he played like that most games, he would be worth an absolute fortune – but priceless to us! Jermain Defoe is still one of my favourite players but he didn't get as much game time as he normally does as he was injured quite a bit, and Itten was mostly used from the bench, but proved really effective when he came on.

'We had four different types of strikers and it certainly worked in our favour.

'But our main man was Stevie G. He brought success back to Ibrox. This is his first managerial job and he has been brilliant. He has had to learn on the job but he has so much determination that he was always going to be a success. I can't imagine Stevie G failing at anything.

'When we clinched the league title, I was so emotional. I'm not frightened to admit that. I had only ever seen Rangers win an important league title or trophy on YouTube, so to see one in the flesh (I hate you, coronavirus!) was unbelievable.

'I had only missed two home matches in four years (and one was parents' night – but I watched the game on my phone while I was waiting for my appointment!) and I love going to the games.

'My season ticket is in the Broomloan Road front, and me and my dad sit quite near the away fans. It's a brilliant seat – when we win! The atmosphere is usually really good in that corner so it helps you get right into the game. I missed the games millions last season, but winning the league definitely made up for the disappointment of not being able to be there.

'We played some great football, and one of our biggest plus points was our strength in depth. The players on the park know that if they're not doing the business then there are a load of good players waiting to come on and replace them.

'If the opposition are defending deep we can take Kamara off and bring Arfield on, and there's little change, or we can push Aribo further up the park, or bring Hagi on if we need some extra firepower. Our squad gives the manager so many different options. We also have so many players who are flexible and can play in different positions.

'A couple of years ago you would look at the bench and there wasn't really anyone who could come on and change the game. Thankfully that's not the case now. We've moved on from the days of Ian Black and Nicky Law "running" the midfield!'

The question of who to support was never an option for Josh, and he credits his dad and grandpa with his love for Rangers. He added, 'It's all about family. Normally, you go with who your dad supports and thankfully that was Rangers! I reckon you're born a Rangers fan.

'One of my pals supports Man City, and his dad is a Man Utd fan. That's not good!

'My first game was a pre-season friendly against Newcastle United at Ibrox [in August 2013]. My grandpa took me and one of the first things I was amazed by was our stadium. I believe I was inside it once waiting on the team coming back from an away game where we had just won the league. But it was so different being at a game there. It might just have been a friendly, but it was my cup final. My first ever game. I was only eight years old but I remember virtually everything about it. We scored early on through Lee McCulloch and were winning up until about five minutes to go, when my grandpa said it might be a good idea if we left early to beat the traffic. We did, and I got home thinking we had won 1-0, but Newcastle equalised in the last minute.

'We were in League One at the time and I went to a couple of matches during the season. To be honest, that was all I knew. I didn't know Rangers as a top-league team, although I knew all about our history of course, as I'd covered it for a school project.

'I've also been to loads of away games, including St Johnstone and Kilmarnock, and an Old Firm game at Parkhead, which was unbelievable. Sadly we lost 5-0, so it wasn't a great afternoon.

'My favourite away game was Progrès Niederkorn in Luxembourg. There is something about travelling to a foreign country to watch your team. The banter with all the fans was first class, as was the general atmosphere the whole time we were away. It was my first time abroad watching Rangers but it definitely won't be my last.

'But you can't beat your own ground, and so as much as I love supporting my team on our travels, I really look forward to going to Ibrox, regardless of the opponents. And now that we haven't been allowed in for so long, I'll be doubly looking forward to going back. I'm even missing the steak pies!

'My first ever favourite player was – and still is – Alfredo Morelos. I love his swagger, his goals, in fact just everything about him. He didn't get as many goals as last season, but he did score at Celtic Park, which was a magical moment. When he ghosted in at the back post – bang!

'I also really liked Martyn Waghorn and Jason Cummings, the latter more for his swagger than his talent, although he was a good player as well.'

When it comes to recalling his favourite ever game, there is no competition, as Josh explained: 'That's an easy one. The home match against Braga. Not many of us in the stadium that night believed we could come back from two down against a very good Portuguese side, who had Francisco Trincão on loan from Barcelona. The atmosphere was off the scale. Hagi was amazing and scored twice. The Braga fans didn't take it too well. We were right next to them and there were a few sweary words thrown our way. At least I think they were sweary words!

'But although that's my favourite one-off game, nothing will come close to the day we clinched the title. It meant everything. Years and years of getting slagged off some of my pals, and listening to them singing about ten in a row. I've honestly not heard a peep from them for ages now; it's great!

'This is my first big success as a Rangers supporter, and so I now know how my dad and grandpa must have felt when they were growing up watching us win trophy after trophy. It's just the first one, but it won't be the last. I was always kind of used to us being okay, but this has been such a massive step up.

'Things are going to change in Scottish football. There will probably be a lot of players leaving Celtic in the summer, and new ones coming in. And we are continuing to sign new players as well, but Stevie G definitely has the upper hand so I'm hoping we can build on this and go on and win more trophies. Maybe this is our first league title of ten – I want us to be Celtic's worst nightmare!'

John Wallace

Southampton, England

Celtic 0 Rangers 2
Scorers: Goldson 9, 54
17 October 2020

Jock Wallace led Rangers to the Scottish First Division championship in 1974/75. It was a significant success as it prevented his great rival Jock Stein clocking up a tenth successive league title for Celtic. When Colin Stein scored the vital goal at Easter Road to give Rangers a 1-1 draw in front of almost 40,000, there was none prouder than Wallace. Legendary status at Ibrox was assured and Wallace's stock was never higher.

Celtic didn't even manage second place that season. That minor accolade went to Hibs, with Jock Stein's broken side one place back, 11 points behind the champions.

There are clear similarities between Wallace's Class of '75 and the squad which has just lifted the title, not least Rangers regaining the upper hand in Old Firm league matches.

The 1970s title was the last time clubs in this country competed for the old-style Scottish First Division, with the 18 clubs playing each other once home and away during the league campaign.

Rangers had edged a three-goal thriller at Celtic Park in the first Old Firm game of the season, with goals from midfielder Ian McDougall, and centre-half Colin Jackson. In the return on 4 January the Light Blues cruised to a 3-0 win with the two Dereks, Johnstone and Parlane, scoring either side of wee Tommy McLean. It was a comprehensive beating which contributed to the title being secured with four games to spare.

The Premier League was in place the following season and Wallace won that as well. The top ten clubs in the country – the elite – facing off against one another four times in league competition. Back-to-back titles put Wallace up there with the great Rangers managers.

Now a certain young man is celebrating Steven Gerrard halting a second Celtic bid for the holy grail of ten in a row. But John Wallace isn't just any young man; he is definitely a chip off the old block, and the grandson of the great Jock Wallace. He has Rangers in his DNA.

Despite being brought up in Spain, he has only ever supported one football team. Since the day his dad, also John, took him to Ibrox for a Rangers v Manchester City pre-season friendly, he was hooked.

He recalled, 'I was only eight or nine but that day was fantastic. I loved everything about it. Walking up towards the stadium was such an awe-inspiring experience in itself. The crowds, the buzz, the programme sellers shouting at the top of their voices, the guys selling flags and scarves; it was magical and I drank in every single moment.

'And then you see the stadium. That's when you realise just how big a club Rangers actually is. The red-brick facade, the front door; everything about Ibrox Stadium is class.

'I had been looking forward to going to a Rangers game for ages and the scene inside the stadium was everything I had dreamed about. There was just over 35,000 there that day, and I lapped it up from start to finish. In fact, I didn't want to leave. I know it was only a friendly but we won 3-2 and Nacho Novo, Kenny Miller and David Weir scored for us. From that day onwards, Rangers have been in my heart and each time I get to Ibrox I cherish every moment.'

Like every other member of the huge Rangers support during lockdown, John, who is 22, longs for the day he can get back inside Ibrox. He is based in Southampton, where he is attending university on football studies duty, and playing semi-pro for Winchester City.

His aim is to make some sort of career in football, although he is well aware of the percentage of folk who are fortunate enough to progress full-time in the game.

He said, 'I love playing football, but I'm also smart enough to know that it's so tough to make it in the game these days. I've not long turned 22, so I still have a little time on my side, but it'll soon be make or break time for me.

'Relocating to Southampton from Spain was a big change but I'm enjoying the experience and that is one of the most important things.'

While in the south of England, John has been glued to the TV each time Rangers are on. What he witnessed in the season just finished was beyond even his wildest expectations. 'Achieving 55 was everything. We've been singing about it since we came up from the Championship, but to actually do it now is unbelievable. Let's be honest, it was never going to happen overnight. Celtic had years on us while we were in the doldrums and we needed to build up our strength – and finances – just to get challenging again.

'I always believed Steven Gerrard was the man to guide us to 55. I also wanted him to succeed so much, and I'm delighted that has been the case.'

John admits it has been a nervy watch, although he concedes that's down to him and not Gerrard or his team. 'I normally watch the matches on my own as I've been a bag of nerves this season. Getting our 55th title and stopping Celtic's ten has been huge. But we've done it and I couldn't be happier.

'Being unable to get to Ibrox this season has been tough, so the next best thing has been to watch us win almost every week on TV.'

And one of the matches John enjoyed most was the early-season victory at Celtic Park. A 2-0 win in the east end of Glasgow was probably a fair reflection on the day's play, although with the home side failing to have a single shot on target all afternoon, it meant an easier ride for those of a blue persuasion.

'I was still extremely nervous,' said John. 'I watched the game in a pub in Southampton and there were quite a few other Rangers fans there as well. I remember seeing one Celtic fan sitting in the corner and he didn't look as though he was having a particularly great afternoon!

'We really laid down a marker. I was so impressed by the team that day; the whole team, mind you. I know big Connor Goldson scored both goals, and he was immense, but to a man the players did us proud. We were on the money from the first whistle and played the game exactly the way Celtic have done against us so often in the recent past.

'I'm always hopeful when we get a free kick anywhere on the right-hand side because James Tavernier is so deadly. We were only nine minutes in when he put in a great cross and big Connor glanced home a header. What a moment.'

But when Mohamed Elyounoussi robbed Goldson moments later, and saw his chipped effort clear Allan McGregor's crossbar, John and his fellow Rangers fans watching in Southampton could breathe a little easier.

'These games are always torture. Sometimes it doesn't even matter if you're dominating play and possession because you're always aware that football matches can turn so quickly. But while we were full value for our slender half-time lead, I'm sitting there thinking Celtic are getting a bollocking from Neil Lennon and are gonna come out all guns blazing in the second half and put us under intense pressure – but it didn't happen.

'After about ten minutes of the second half we got the crucial second goal – and what a goal it was! Glen Kamara, Alfredo Morelos and Scott Arfield played a couple of neat passing moves and the ball ended up with Scotty Arf just outside the box. He fired over a low cross which Connor prodded home. He had initially side-footed the ball against Shane Duffy – his ex-Brighton team-mate – but poked it home at the second attempt. I went berserk, and so did all the other Bears in the pub. It was amazing, but only what we deserved after being on the front foot the entire game.

'Probably for the first time ever, I felt comfortable for the last half-hour of an Old Firm game. Sure, there were still nervy moments – which there are in every football match – but from the moment Connor left Duffy lying on the turf to score the second, I was as calm as could be. I knew we were about to land back-to-back wins at Celtic Park for the first time since the mid–90s.

'And we should have had a third goal. Borna Barišić crossed for Ryan Kent but somehow big Ayer managed to block his shot. It was going in, no doubt about it, but I was much less stressed than I would've been had the score been 0-0!'

It was Rangers' ninth win in their opening 11 games, and with just three goals conceded, things were looking bright. It might just have been the middle of October but with such a bold statement made at the home of the defending champions, and some tremendous football played to boot, many supporters dared to dream. John wasn't one of them.

'No chance. After what we'd been through in the past nine or ten years I was keeping my feelings close to my chest. I wasn't getting carried away. There was still a hell of a lot of football to be played.

'Yes, we had just dominated our rivals, in their own back yard, and yes, we had a decent lead in the table – and were conceding very few goals – but we all know that football has a nasty habit of biting you on the bum when least expected. So, no chance was I thinking that way.

'It's not a nice thing to say but I think we all know that Steven Gerrard had to win something this season. I think he's fantastic, and love the way he sets up his teams, but the bottom line at a club like ours is trophies. That's what all Rangers managers are judged on and Gerrard is no different, so I'm delighted he has brought home the title in his third season. He has learned quickly and most of the players he has brought in have done a great job for us. He is definitely a clever guy.

'This was always going to be a huge season for us, but I'm so happy with the way it has turned out. We now have something concrete to build on and I hope we can go on and achieve further success.

'The gaffer has done so well in the Europa League in each of his three seasons; beyond our wildest dreams, if I'm being honest. We've had some great European nights and that's all down to Steven Gerrard. Next season we will be able to test ourselves in the Champions League, and that's a great thought.'

It's all a far cry from one of John's favourite days out at Ibrox: Rangers v Falkirk, 30 January 2016. It was a chilly afternoon, but as he made his way down Broomloan Road there was an extra tingle in his spine as he caught sight of Ibrox Stadium.

He takes up the story: 'I had flown over from Spain for the game and had been offered a seat in the directors' box by John Gilligan, who was on the board at the time. John is a lovely guy, but I had to decline his offer as there was only one place I wanted to be that afternoon – BF1!

'I made sure I was in the ground nice and early and lapped up the atmosphere that was building from just after 2pm right up until kick-off. The stadium was packed and everyone was hoping we could win a fifth straight league match (Falkirk being the last team to beat us, at their place), but it was a tough game, and we struggled every time we got anywhere near the Falkirk goal.

'Andy Halliday had been in superb form leading up to that game, but had been sent off the midweek beforehand for celebrating a goal at Cappielow the night we beat Morton 2-0. I'll never forget that. He was in the middle of the park and when Barrie McKay scored, Andy raised his fist in salute – like he did every time we scored – and the ref sent him off. Couldn't get my head round that one.

'Anyway, we pounded Falkirk, and the Union Bears were in great voice. We sang from start to finish but it was nothing compared to the scenes in injury time when we got a free kick just outside the box and Billy King smashed it into the back of the net. Everyone went wild.

'The whistle sounded not long after that and the fans filed out of the ground. I stayed behind for a few extra minutes as I wanted to enjoy every last moment of being inside Ibrox, as I don't get many opportunities to be there. I love the place!'

But John's day was far from over. He was to meet John Gilligan at the front door after the match to be shown up to the players' lounge, where he could grab some pics and autographs.

He said, 'John is a lovely man. When I first met him, he said to me, "Any grandson of the great Jock Wallace is always welcome at Ibrox." What a lovely thing to say.

'He took me up the marble staircase and the first person we bumped into was the chairman, Dave King. He was great and we got a photograph taken. Next it was into the trophy room, and I replicated a pic I'd taken before that friendly match with Manchester City all those years ago.

'John Gilligan then introduced me to the Rangers historian, David Mason, and he took me in to see the manager's office, and I sat in the chair that my grandfather would've used when he was in charge. Another poignant moment arrived when we walked through the door which joins the manager's office and the Blue Room. It was packed full of directors from both Rangers and Falkirk, visiting dignitaries and legends such as Richard Gough and Mark Hateley. It was at this point I thanked my lucky stars I'd chosen to wear a tie, because you aren't allowed into the Blue Room on a matchday if you're not wearing a tie!

'And then David introduced me to one of the Falkirk directors. His name was Alex Totten and he had been my grandfather's assistant during his second spell in charge at Ibrox. Wow, that was quite a moment. Mr Totten told me all about his time at Ibrox with my grandfather. I could've listened to him all day. It was such a great honour to meet him and have that type of conversation.'

From the Blue Room, David Mason took young John along to the players' lounge; it's expressly out of bounds to most on matchday, but not to the grandson of a Rangers legend. It's a long and winding room where the players and their families can relax after a game and have a drink or two while chatting in a closed environment.

'That was the highlight of my trip,' said John. 'It's a difficult thing to say, because I met so many great Rangers folk that day, but ultimately it was the players I wanted to meet, so it was perfect. I had photographs taken with Barrie McKay and Danny Wilson, and then Andy Halliday walked into the lounge. Nothing was too much trouble for him and we chatted for ages.

'I also had really good conversations with Dominic Ball – who was on loan to us from Spurs, and who had a great game that day – and Tav, who was also impressive. I was really nervous but both guys quickly put me at ease and I enjoyed chatting to them.'

But John's day of surprises wasn't quite finished and as he headed back down the marble staircase towards the front door he spotted assistant manager David Weir, the former Rangers and Everton defender. He was delighted when Weir agreed to pose for a pic and sign his shirt.

John asked if Mark Warburton was around, and Weir said he would give him a shout.

Moments later, out popped the Rangers manager, and John was made up. He said, 'He was another gentleman. I told him who my grandfather was and his face lit up. Mark had played under granddad while he was a player at Leicester City so we had a good chat about that.'

With a long but satisfying day over, John headed back to his digs to reflect on the people he'd met, and chew over a day with the Union Bears; another three points for Rangers, and one step closer to ending a four-year hiatus in the lower leagues.

And it would be in the Premiership that John would next see Rangers in action at Ibrox. The opponents were Kilmarnock, and goals by Lee Wallace, Andy Halliday and Joey Garner gave Rangers a 3-0 win.

That afternoon, John did accept a seat in the directors' box, and he was sitting beside two very special people – his dad and his gran. They were in Glasgow to celebrate Jock Wallace's inauguration into the Scottish Football Association's Hall of Fame.

John explained, 'In many respects it was a hush-hush trip. We were asked to keep it quiet, but I was delighted when I checked the fixture list and saw that Rangers were at home that day. I contacted the club and they invited us to sit in the directors' box. I was really happy for my gran because it was a lovely touch, and a moment she cherished.

'We went to the inauguration on the evening of the match and it was lovely to hear my grandfather spoken about in such reverential tones. We were all very proud when he was added to such a pantheon of Scottish football greats. It sealed a great trip to Scotland.

'The link between my grandfather and Rangers will always be there; it's an unbreakable bond, but my love for the club is now so strong in its own right, and this season has been incredible. We might not have been able to be at Ibrox for any of the games, but that doesn't make the achievement mean any less.

'Scottish Premiership champions. Now doesn't that sound just perfect?'

Sammy King

Heckmondwike, England

Kilmarnock 0 Rangers 1
Scorer: Tavernier 19 (pen)
1 November 2020

Imagine visiting Ibrox for the first time. You're walking along Edmiston Drive, a few hundred yards from the ground, and the sun is splitting the sky. All around you fans are walking towards the stadium, attracted like a magnet to this magnificent structure.

The closer you get, the more detail you notice: the magnificent red-brick frontage, the letters spelling out Rangers FC high above the grand entrance to the magnificent marble staircase, which you will see very shortly. The low-slung, arched windows and a crowd of supporters, decked out in red- white-and-blue scarves and jerseys, hanging around the main door, desperate to catch a glimpse of the many former players who use the entrance to go in and see the team they once represented. Others are happy to chat to mates before the game. It's an incredible sight, and you can't wait to get inside, although a small part of you is happy to remain outside a little longer just to soak up this wonderful atmosphere.

And then you hear it for the first time. Thousands of supporters singing a song that's very familiar to you, and very dear. Your signature tune; your song. 'Penny Arcade'. The song you wrote for the great Roy Orbison. It's one of those moments you experience very occasionally in life.

It's now time to step inside the beating heart of Ibrox. You're welcomed at reception and shown upstairs to hospitality. It's the beginning of a wonderful day.

Sammy King had been invited up to Ibrox in 2011 as recognition for allowing his song to be used in a fundraising drive for Erskine, the veterans' charity. He recalled, 'It was such a special moment, and one I will never forget. Hearing the fans sing "Penny Arcade" as I walked towards the stadium was unbelievable; one of those moments that stays with you forever.

'I'm a lifelong Huddersfield Town supporter, and really only took an interest in Rangers when my song became popular up at Ibrox, but that interest quickly developed into something far more special and I now have many friends who are Rangers supporters. I have a genuine love for the club now.'

King had received a phone call from a friend a few months earlier to say that he was watching a Rangers match live on Sky Sports and that the supporters were singing 'Penny Arcade'. He said, 'My friend asked why the supporters were singing my song, but I didn't have a clue, and I still don't know why they latched on to that particular song, but from the word go I was both proud and honoured in equal measures.

'That was the moment I started to take an active interest in Rangers – how could I not? My friend – a lifelong Rangers supporter – helped me form a love of the club, and it has never waned. I've now heard the supporters sing "Penny Arcade" many times on televised matches, and it never diminishes in effect. It's marvellous. In fact, let's go a step further. For someone who loves football as much as I do, to have stepped on to the hallowed Ibrox turf and led 50,000 fans in singing a song I wrote has to be the high spot of my career. For me, the history of Rangers and Ibrox epitomises Scottish football (although I do admit to being a wee bit biased).'

Quite a statement considering that King's band appeared on the same bill as The Beatles! But the talented singer/songwriter admits his life changed forever when he wrote 'Penny Arcade' in 1969. He recalled, 'The inspiration for the song came to me when I was camping in Anglesey, North Wales. I was sitting relaxing with a beer one very dark night and I noticed some coloured lights being switched on across Trearddur Bay. That was the "light shone in the night" line from the song. I got this little riff in my head and I worked on it further when I got home.

'Later that year I was at the Batley Variety Club, in West Yorkshire, a well-known venue which had attracted so many big stars in its heyday, including Louis Armstrong, Tom Jones and Neil Sedaka. Roy Orbison was on that night. He was a true gent, so I asked him for an opinion on some of my songs. I played him a couple, but the one song I didn't play was "Penny Arcade" as I didn't think it was his style!

'The tape I had included six songs, and "Penny" was the last of them. He asked if he could take the tape and play it to his producer in Nashville. Of course I agreed, and about a month later I received a really nice letter saying Roy had recorded four of my songs and that "Penny Arcade" would be his next single. I was staggered. He also arranged for me to sign with a top publishing company and I received an advance on royalties.'

This was music to King's ears, because after suffering a breakdown due to overworking he had been struggling to get back on his feet. He said, 'Little did Roy know that I was on my uppers due to being skint after my breakdown. The man saved my life and for that I will be eternally grateful to him.

'Everything changed after that and I was soon back on my feet. The name Orbison certainly opened many doors for me, including those beautiful ornate gates of Ibrox! I was happily retired when the phone call came and before I knew it the Bears were buying my version of "Penny Arcade" and it stormed into the charts. The veterans' charity Erskine were also really grateful for the money it raised.'

'Penny Arcade', by Sammy King, entered the UK charts at number 47 and also at number nine in the Scotland-only charts. King, who was 69 at the time, became one of the oldest artists ever to make their UK chart debut.

And then the song was chosen for a starring role in *T2*, the follow up to Danny Boyle's *Trainspotting* movie. 'It was nice to get a credit at the end of *Trainspotting 2*, which was a surprise. I thought the scene it was used in was very funny.'

King has a lifelong affinity with our armed forces, so he was delighted when 'Penny Arcade' was able to raise funds for Erskine. He said, 'I had uncles in the Royal Navy and who served aboard the aircraft carrier HMS *Ark Royal* during the Second World War. They also saw active service aboard HMS *Hood* and also HMS *Prince of Wales*.

'I had other relations in the Royal Tank Regiment, which is part of the Royal Armoured Corps, and the Royal Electrical and Mechanical Engineers as well as infantrymen. My father had only partial sight in one eye and failed an army medical, but still served as an air raid warden during the Blitz in London.

'It's well worth mentioning that my brother and I were born as a result of a "mixed" marriage. My father was an Irish Catholic and my mother a Liverpool Protestant. We were brought up to understand there is good and bad in all walks of life and were never aware of any sectarianism. Sadly, I lost my only brother recently but neither of us were religious so in retrospect I'm so glad Rangers adopted "Penny Arcade" and not another team. My family have also been staunch royalists, so I have many things in common with the Rangers family.

'Since 2011 I have been up to Scotland on many occasions to help the Rangers Supporters Erskine Appeal with their fundraising and I was extremely proud when I was made an honorary patron of Erskine. That was such a nice moment.'

Just 12 months after experiencing the joy and jubilation that 'Penny Arcade' brought to legions of Rangers supporters, King couldn't believe it when the situation at Rangers took a turn for the worse and the club was forced into administration.

He remembered, 'Along with the fans I was gutted at what happened with administration. It was an awful time for everyone connected with the club. But they continued to sing

"Penny Arcade", although when the club was at its lowest ebb, I had a request from Rangers supporters to write and record a new song for the club, and I came up with "The Legendary Rangers". I was very pleased with it as it seemed to hit the mark with a lot of fans. It's a general Rangers anthem about the club's proud history and the great players who have served the club well.'

And when asked who he would want to win if his beloved Huddersfield Town played Rangers in a friendly, he answered, 'I would settle for a draw! My first introduction to the excitement of a proper live football match was at t'Town and as you know, once you're hooked, that's it! But Rangers are my Scottish team and that will never change.'

King's introduction to music arrived after a promising football career was cut short due to injury when he was in his teens. That was it as far as football was concerned. He said, 'I spent nearly two years in traction and missed the latter end of my schooling due to being hospitalised. As a result of the injury I ended up with no qualifications.

'What to do as a career was the big question. I joined a skiffle group, as they were really popular in the UK in the 1950s. I then progressed to a rock group, The Voltairs. We had a fair bit of success without ever really becoming a household name. In June 1963, we supported The Beatles at the Queens Hall, in Leeds. I recall the poster said, "Returning by Popular Request!"

'They were undoubtedly good days, but being in a band took up so much of my time. There's no doubt it was fantastic to be part of such a great music scene in the 1960s, and on reflection I couldn't have wished for a better time to be young. My parents had backed me all the way in my choice of career, but inevitably due to the constant toil I ended up having a nervy [nervous breakdown] so it was a scary time.

'Once I got back on my feet, on the most part due to Roy Orbison and "Penny Arcade", I had a thoroughly enjoyable solo career until retiring. I have been to so many different places but without ever really seeing them, if you know what I mean. Many's the time it was bed, work and bank. There never really seemed to be any time for sightseeing. It soon becomes just a job.'

But along with music and Huddersfield Town, Rangers are now a big part of Sammy's life and he watches as many games as he can. In the 2020/21 season he managed to see Rangers play on many occasions. He knew, virtually from the off, that there was something special about this Rangers side, and he looked on from West Yorkshire as they quickly moved into pole position in the Premiership table – and remained there the entire season.

He said, 'Rangers were a joy to watch this season, and I was delighted when they won the league. It was a fantastic achievement given where they had been not that long ago. During the past ten years my wife Linda and I have made so many wonderful friends among the Rangers family. We were both rooting for the Gers all season – and that includes loads of my mates at the Hudders. My influence has spread among my friends at the John Smith's Stadium, so we have even more members of the extended Rangers family now!

'I'm truly made up for Rangers, and Stevie Gerrard deserves every accolade he received for such a wonderful achievement.'

But while King enjoyed most of the Rangers games he watched, he admits he wasn't too enamoured with the games they had to play on synthetic surfaces such as at Livingston and Hamilton. And that includes the match at Kilmarnock's Rugby Park on Sunday, 1 November. Rangers might have won it thanks to a James Tavernier penalty but King simply can't take these surfaces seriously.

He said, 'Yeah, it was a tough game on a tough surface out the way, but I don't think there is a place in professional or amateur football for artificial surfaces. I don't think they should be anywhere near top-flight games. Perhaps for five-a-side football, or maybe even training, but football was invented to be played on grass, and we should stick to that.

'I also watched the Hamilton Accies v Rangers match at the beginning of February [2021] and that was the same. It just doesn't seem like real football, but while these pitches are allowed, teams like Rangers will just have to get on with it and handle it the best they can.'

The win at Kilmarnock put Rangers nine points ahead of Celtic after 13 games but their big rivals had two games in hand, and King admits it was far too early to be talking in terms of winning the league. At the post-match press conference Gerrard was asked if he would smile when looking at the league table, but he answered, 'I won't be looking at the league table. It's not the stage of the season to be looking at the league table – but I will analyse our performance as always.'

King said, 'I thought Rangers handled a potentially dangerous situation very well. They started positively and had an early chance or two, but the goal eventually came about when Borna Barišić's free kick was headed by Connor Goldson on to the hand of Ross Millen and referee Andrew Dallas had no hesitation in pointing to the spot. Tav stuck the penalty away very well.

'He was a major player in the title-winning season and contributed both offensively and defensively. Mind you, in my day full-backs very rarely crossed the halfway line. In the modern game they are wingers who can "tackle a bit". Tav's a very good player and a team man – and he's from West Yorkshire! Interesting to note though, that over the years a lot of the best penalty takers were also full-backs!'

King was reluctant to be drawn into who should have won the club's player of the year award as so many first-team stars can rightfully claim to have played their part in the season's success. One player, though, stuck out just a little more than the others. King explained, 'I did see a lot of games through the season, but probably not quite enough to have an out-and-out favourite player but at stick and lift I would say Allan McGregor, as any time I saw him play he would inevitably make one or two fantastic saves. Goalkeeper is one of the hardest positions to play, as for starters you're the last line of defence and the consequences of "letting one in" can be dire. But also due to the fact that as the team are dominating possession in the biggest majority of games, then McGregor isn't seeing an awful lot of the ball, so his concentration levels have to be spot on. He appears to be a master at keeping his levels extremely high.

'But I've been impressed overall by the way the team passed the ball during the season. Their movement off the ball was also fantastic. There always seemed to be a spare man to receive the ball – usually Steven Davis – but it was a real good trait the team possessed. Steven Gerrard would have brought good habits with him from Liverpool. He was schooled in good habits and it was great to see Rangers benefitting from them, and their new style of play.

'Football is a simple game, made complicated by tactics, but the brand of football Rangers played was usually easy on the eye and I'm sure they won a whole new army of fans with the way they went about their business this season.

'Of course, not once did anyone from the club come out and say it was all over until the day it was mathematically impossible for Celtic to catch them. Any competition is only over when "the fat lady sings" and I never take anything for granted.

'It was a wonderful season and I'm just so happy for all the many friends I have north of the border – and in many other parts of the United Kingdom, too – and who support the famous Glasgow Rangers. It was a good season to be a Rangers supporter and all we can hope for is more of the same in the coming season.

'The hope is that supporters will soon be allowed back into stadiums and that they can watch their team in action. I know that for a lot of Rangers fans, missing out on one of their greatest title triumphs was a negative in a season full of positives. It was a great shame, but we're back now and title number 55 meant so much to so many people.

'Come on the Glasgow Rangers – we truly are the people!'

'The Legendary Rangers'

All along the walls, of the Ibrox halls
Are picture of Legends of old
Making history, for the world to see
The stories of glories unfold

We are the Legendary Rangers
We wear the Legendary Blue
Today, forever and for always
We are Rangers through and through

Well the Legends come, and the Legends go
But Rangers they've hung just the same
For a new one's born, when the blue shirts worn
And we all remember their name

We are the Legendary Rangers
We wear the Legendary Blue
Today, forever and for always
We are Rangers through and through

And there is no doubt, what we're all about
When we face the World and say
Bring it on some more, cause you'll know for sure
That we don't do walk away
That we don't do walk away

We are the Legendary Rangers
We wear the Legendary Blue
Today, forever and for always
We are Rangers through and through

We are the Legendary Rangers
We wear the Legendary Blue
Today, forever and for always
We are Rangers through and through

Written by Sammy King

Ambassador Chris Sainty

Lisbon, Portugal

Benfica 3 Rangers 3
Scorers: Goncalves 24 (own goal), Kamara 25,
Morelos 51
5 November 2020

The gentle notes of the pleasant melody float through the open window and out into the adjacent neighbourhood. It's early evening, and the faint sounds grapple with the more aggressive thumping of rain on to the deserted Lisbon pavements. It's not a tune that many inhabitants of the Portuguese capital will be familiar with; in fact, one might have to travel around 1,800 miles, say, to the south side of Glasgow, before finding someone capable of adding lyrics to the tune.

'I've sailed the wild Atlantic crossed the broad Pacific Shore
I've sailed around the stormy Capes and heard the Forties roar
I've plied the Indian Ocean, I've sailed the China Sea
But there's a sea back home in Scotland more than all the rest to me ...'

The song has been a firm favourite with Rangers supporters for more years than I care to remember, and can regularly be heard during games both home and away, although during lockdown – and the title-winning season – it was strictly canned chants only.

So, why are tunes such as 'Blue Sea of Ibrox', 'Four Lads Had a Dream' and 'Every Other Saturday' filling the evening air in Lisbon? The answer, of course, lies with Her Majesty's Ambassador to Portugal, Chris Sainty, who has once more taken to playing the piano to help with a different type of blues – those associated with lockdown.

He explained, 'My association with Rangers happened completely by coincidence. Rangers have enjoyed a couple of successful years in the Europa League and in that time have been drawn against their fair share of Portuguese sides. I have been the ambassador to Portugal for around two and a half years now so I've been in office while Rangers have come up against the likes of Porto, Sporting Braga and Benfica.

'And I have to say they have done ever so well, unquestionably getting the better of Porto and Braga, and almost Benfica, although I'm sure the neutral would agree that Rangers should have won the tie in Lisbon.

'I'm a long-standing Liverpool fan, and like most of my fellow Reds I'm a huge admirer of Steven Gerrard. He is an Anfield legend, so I was always going to take an interest in how he was doing after his playing career was over. I must admit, it's great to see him enjoying success in Scotland.

'When Rangers played in Porto at the end of 2019 I was an interested observer and watched the game on TV, likewise when they were in Braga in February of last year. I would like to have gone to that match but Braga is quite some distance from Lisbon. Rangers were fantastic that night and turned in a really gritty performance to win 1-0. It was an impressive win against a very good Braga team.

'I tweeted my congratulations to Rangers after the game and a lot of supporters were amused at the British Ambassador showing such an interest in their team.'

But then coronavirus struck and the world as we knew it changed forever (or at least until a suitable vaccine could be developed, manufactured and distributed!). They didn't have it easy in Portugal, suffering three different waves of the virus which had killed almost 17,000 people up until the end of April.

Mr Sainty racked his mind to think what he could possibly do to help lift the mood in Portugal, and also back home in the United Kingdom. 'When coronavirus struck, and we were all plunged into lockdown, it was so tough for a lot of people here in Portugal and in the UK, so I decided to do something I hadn't done for a long, long time – and that was to start playing the piano again.

'To my great surprise it started to garner a lot of attention in Portugal, and in the media. It was mostly Portuguese songs, and it was really just to try and keep morale up and bring a little light into what was a really dark time for a lot of people. Once the media picked up on it I was soon being asked to play requests.

'Posting my videos on social media was also a small way for me to say thank you to the health services in the United Kingdom and Portugal for the way they were handling the pandemic, and the great job they were doing of looking after us all. So many people were praising their bravery in such trying circumstances which, I felt, was a nice thing to do.'

And then a single request came in asking the ambassador to play something, well, quite different. Mr Sainty explains, 'A Rangers supporter called Alan Kerrigan got in touch to ask if I would play a couple of Rangers tunes, as he felt it would cheer up the supporters. I was actually quite tickled by the idea, so I looked up some Rangers songs on YouTube and found that the likes of "Four Lads" and "Blue Sea of Ibrox" were set to beautiful tunes.

'So I set about learning them and one by one I got the hang of the tunes and started posting the videos on my Twitter account. The response was extraordinary. My phone was buzzing for days, and I soon had more than 50,000 views (which is ironic, as that's the capacity of Ibrox Stadium – in other words, the entire Blue Sea of Ibrox!). It was great fun, and simply reinforced what a great bunch of supporters the

Rangers fans are. In fact, I believe I am now an honorary Rangers fan.

'I love football, but in my job I don't really get involved with any one team in particular. The thing is, Portugal is such a football-mad country, and it's really nice when British clubs are drawn to meet Portuguese clubs in European competition. I enjoy that very much.'

And then Rangers came out of the hat in the same section of the Europa League as the giants of Lisbon, SL Benfica, twice winners of the European Cup and forever associated with Eusébio, one of the greatest players to grace a football field. It was a glamour tie, no doubt, but one in which they would start second favourites due to the money Benfica had spent on constructing a formidable team. The draw excited most Rangers supporters, and definitely caught the eye of the ambassador.

He said, 'When the draw was made for the group stages, and Rangers and Benfica were drawn into the same group, it was very exciting. I was really looking forward to Rangers coming to Lisbon, but then there was sadness as it became apparent that COVID would mean there would be no supporters in the Estádio da Luz, and for such a big game.

'I had been looking forward to seeing a big, noisy Rangers support in Lisbon, having a great time and enjoying the game, but sadly that couldn't happen. It was a huge miss for everyone.

'On the day of the game the weather was foul. It rained constantly and it was very cold, which isn't the type of weather we normally get in this city. Then I thought to myself, "This might work in Rangers' favour as it apparently rains in Glasgow quite a lot and the ground conditions may suit them more than Benfica!" This might just go Rangers' way." Of course, it was a long shot.

'Like thousands of other Rangers supporters I watched the game on television and it was such a thrilling game. There is no doubt that before kick-off, Rangers were underdogs. Benfica have such large resources and really it should have been no competition. Of course, Benfica – and their manager, Jorge Jesus – would have been well aware that Rangers were having a great season, and wouldn't have taken them lightly, but I'm sure they would still have assumed the result would go their way.

'The game was played on Bonfire Night, and that normally means a barbecue at the ambassador's residence, but even if it hadn't been for lockdown, that would have been completely out of the question due to the weather.

'I was incredibly nervous before kick-off (I was taking my new-found status as an honorary Rangers supporter very seriously indeed!), and the team got off to probably the worst start possible when Benfica scored the opening goal inside the first minute. I could imagine heads going down all over Glasgow.

'My heart sank. I thought, "Oh dear, is this going to be the story of the night?"

'Benfica were on top for the first ten minutes or so, but Rangers managed to fight their way back into the game and started to put some really good moves together. And then the turning point. The moment Benfica were reduced to ten men when the Argentine defender Nicolás Otamendi was sent off. Ryan Kent was going through on goal and could possibly have scored so the decision was the correct one, and I don't think even the home supporters would have complained.'

Rangers really pressed home their numerical advantage and roared into a 2-1 lead before half-time thanks to an own goal by Gonçalves (repaying the favour after Connor Goldson had put through his own net to give the hosts the lead), and Glen Kamara calmly edging Rangers in front. And just six minutes after the break Alfredo Morelos scored to make it 3-1 to Rangers. Game over?

Mr Sainty said, 'At that point, I'm sitting at home thinking the game is now beyond even Benfica because Rangers appeared to be in complete control, and while Benfica are still a very dangerous team, Rangers seemed to have it sewn up.

'But in football we should know that you never say never and near the end it seemed that many of the Rangers players had perhaps lost their legs. They had put so much effort into the game and that was something which Benfica capitalised on. They got one back with about 20 minutes remaining, but it was the goal in stoppage time that broke so many hearts. It must have been a huge disappointment to Rangers supporters back home, but in the cold light of day it was still a fantastic result and I'm sure 99 per cent of supporters would have accepted a draw before the match began.'

The ambassador has yet to take in a game at the Estádio da Luz, but insists it's definitely on his post-COVID to-do list. 'Sadly, I haven't managed to get there yet. When I first arrived in Portugal I was stationed in the north of the country, in Porto. I was there for a short time and managed to get to a couple of games at the Estádio do Dragão, so I suppose because of that I had an early affinity with Porto.

'When I moved down to Lisbon, where I have been ever since, staff at Sporting Lisbon got in touch with the office and invited me along to a game at the José Alvalade Stadium, and I've since been to a couple of games there, which I enjoyed immensely.

'The grounds are quite close to one another, probably just under two miles apart. I've driven past the Benfica stadium often and I would love to attend a game there once things get back to some semblance of normality. The Benfica mascot is a rather ferocious-looking bald eagle, while the Sporting symbol is a friendly looking lion!'

The ambassador looked on curiously in the summer of 2018 as Steven Gerrard was announced as the 16th manager of Rangers. 'There are never any guarantees that a great player will become a great manager,' he said. 'It's almost like they are starting all over again. It's yet another learning curve for them, but he has done ever so well in Glasgow. He was indeed a great player for Liverpool and England, and it looks like he has taken some of that winning mentality up to Glasgow with him.

'I don't think anyone expected him to go straight into management with Liverpool, but the job at Rangers is huge and comes with a lot of pressure so he really does deserve a lot of credit for what he is doing at Ibrox.

'Altogether he has done a fantastic job at Rangers, but the club must also take a lot of the credit for that, especially as they had the foresight to appoint him to the position. Steven Gerrard has made a massive contribution to the success Rangers achieved in the season just finished. As a result of this, the future is very bright for the club, and that also has to be a good thing for Celtic as it's healthy for Scottish football to have two really strong clubs challenging for honours. Having one club dominating isn't so good for sport.

'But Rangers are finally in a position now that they have won the title, and become a force in Europe again, where they can continue to improve and grow season on season. And it's also great to see Scotland's coefficient getting stronger as a result of Rangers' resurgence.'

Like most football supporters, Mr Sainty is well aware that the links Gerrard has with Anfield almost certainly means the pair will become one again in the future.

He said, 'Liverpool have had a lengthy list of charismatic managers and Jürgen Klopp is right up there with the best. He is an amazing character and you really can't help but love him. He has such an amazing infectious passion for the game and that rubs off on everyone around him, from his players and coaching staff to the supporters.

'We were badly hampered by injuries last season – particularly to the centre of our defence, with Virgil van Dijk a huge miss – and we seemed to lose a lot of our confidence as a result of this, but he has so much credit in the bank and I look forward to seeing him at Liverpool for many years to come.

'Steven Gerrard, manager of Liverpool? One day, hopefully. It would be a dream to see Steven successfully managing my team – and his – but I don't see it happening any time soon.

He is doing a great job at Rangers and I'm sure they would love him to stick around for a while longer. It's great to see him doing well at Ibrox and having such a high-profile figure there is surely a win-win situation for Scottish football.'

Hopefully that means we can look forward to many more piano solos from the ambassador, and that classics such as 'Blue Sea of Ibrox' and 'Every Other Saturday' will remain part of the repertoire at his residence.

Mr Sainty said, 'I learned the piano as a wee boy growing up in London. For four years it was my favourite thing in the world and I absolutely loved playing. It gave me so much pleasure, but then the dreaded teenage years were upon me and for some reason I just gave it all up.

'I had barely played in 30 years until this year, when COVID struck, and that was that. The second and third waves of the virus in Portugal were particularly awful for a lot of people so we all needed something to cope with lockdown, and so I hit on the idea of reviving my piano career. I was a bit rusty at first but soon got back into my stride.

'Once again it gave me a lot of pleasure and I thought about trying to give some of that pleasure to others. I'm glad I did as it has been a lot of fun, but with a slightly serious side to it.'

Mr Sainty revealed that he's half-Scottish, as his mother was born in Fife, so perhaps his new selection of tunes shouldn't be considered too left field.

'The Rangers fans sing many traditional songs with lovely tunes. I wasn't familiar with most of them but Liverpool supporters have been singing "Every Other Saturday" for a number of years now, although to my knowledge it was first sung by Rangers supporters.

'"Blue Sea of Ibrox" and "Four Lads Had a Dream" are another couple of really lovely songs which I listened to on YouTube, and once I had learned them I was happy to post a couple of videos on Twitter. It was a lot of fun trying to play them and I was particularly taken by the lyrics of "Every Other Saturday", as many of them are very Glaswegian. That was why

I chose "Wae Ma Wee Pal Joe" for a hashtag. It was a line that particularly stood out.'

For the next couple of years, Lisbon will be home to Mr Sainty, and it's a city he's very comfortable in. He explained, 'I've been here just over two and a half years now and I really like living in Lisbon. It isn't the biggest city in the world, with a population of around half a million, but it's a lovely place to live and work. Portugal is a great country and the relationship with the United Kingdom is a long-standing and historic one – an alliance that goes back well over 600 years. We work well together and long may that continue. Our shared interests include climate change, the environment and pollution. Portugal is also very good on oceans, which shouldn't be too surprising given we are right on the Atlantic.

'In my line of work you can never be quite sure how long you will stay in a country but I hope to see out my four-year tenure in Lisbon. Sadly, like so many others around the world, we haven't been able to get out and about and see the city at its best these last 16 months or so due to lockdown, so when we eventually return to normality it will be such a relief.

'Meanwhile, I will certainly continue to take an interest in how Rangers are getting on and I'll be hoping they can win more honours under Steven Gerrard – and I will definitely get over to Ibrox to see a game some day.

'Winning the league was a great moment for everyone connected with the club, especially after what they have been through in the last few years, and I couldn't be happier for them.'

Don MacLean

Georgia, USA

Rangers 8 Hamilton Accies 0
Scorers: Arfield 16, Roofe 18, 54, Aribo 19, 36, Barker 62, Tavernier 65 (pen), 69
8 November 2020

Don MacLean didn't smile or celebrate on Helicopter Sunday. He didn't dare. He was in a packed Irish bar in Atlanta, Georgia, and the regulars weren't too enamoured with Scott McDonald, Motherwell, Rangers, or anyone who might have a liking for red, white and blue. So Don was silent as he supped his Guinness, which just happens to be his favourite tipple anyway.

Thing is, there weren't many bars in Atlanta showing the Scottish games that day, so beggars can't be choosers, etc.

He recalled, 'Helicopter Sunday was one of the greatest days of my life. It was all set up for them to win the league, but they "Hibsed" it! I watched the game in this rough-and-tumble Irish pub and I could barely see the TV with all these crazy folk standing up and shouting and bawling. They were going bonkers, so when the game finished and we were declared winners, I finished my pint and quietly slipped out a side door. What I felt inside definitely didn't mirror my expressionless veneer. The moment I was safely outside I punched the air with delight!'

So when Rangers won title number 55, Don made sure he was safely tucked up at home watching the action on the club's

Filip Helander has enjoyed a fantastic season

Our captain, James Tavernier

Allan McGregor: The safest hands in soccer

Glen Kamara was a mainstay in the title-winning team

Kemar celebrates 'Roofe style!'

*Steven Gerrard brought
the title home to Ibrox!*

Tower of strength: Connor Goldson celebrates another goal

Steven Davis: A Rolls Royce in midfield

*Borna Barisic -
no nonsense, but
effective*

*Joe Aribo
celebrates against
Dundee United
at Ibrox*

Blues Brothers: Nathan Patterson and Scott Arfield

The irrepressible Alfredo Morelos grabs his first goal against Celtic

Ryan Kent was on fire
throughout the season

Ryan Jack was enjoying
a fine season before
injury struck

Ianis Hagi with the goal that clinched the title

Jermain Defoe adds the icing to the cake against Celtic at Ibrox

Victory at the EGM: John Gilligan, Dave King and Paul Murray at Ibrox in 2015

Mark Walters shows Celtic's Chris Morris a clean pair of heels

*Mark Walters with fellow ex-Ranger,
Mark Hateley*

*Marco Negri celebrates another
Rangers goal with team-mate Brian
Laudrup*

*Marco scored FIVE
times against
Dundee United*

Lisa Swanson: Rangers Women's longest-serving player. Pic by Lorraine Hill

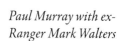

Paul Murray with ex-Ranger Mark Walters

Josh Holmes with his young brother Zac at Ibrox

Rangers-daft John Wallace with Jeff Holmes outside the Bristol Bar

Sammy King sporting the colours while belting out Penny Arcade

Ready for a tune: Chris Sainty at home in Lisbon

Flying high: Don MacLean has a flag day at home in Georgia

Proud Ranger: Chris Mayhead in the home dressing room at Ibrox

Tour guide: Chris Mayhead with Aussie duo Annmargaret and Aaron

Fraser Aird takes the applause of the Rangers faithful. Pic by Willie Vass

Signing on: Derek Johnstone with Jock Wallace

Tale of the tape: Stephen Millar with 'part' of his Rangers collection

Andy Cameron celebrates Helicopter Sunday with Alex McLeish

Stephen Purdon salutes Ally McCoist in the Legends game. Pic by Willie Vass

excellent TV channel. 'It made quite a difference in terms of being able to celebrate appropriately,' he laughed.

'I watch some of the games in a local pub, which is in Milton, funnily enough, a home from home. There is a guy from Fife who works in the pub, and he tries to get the games on the big screen for me. It doesn't always work out, so I often have to head back up to the house to watch it on Rangers TV. I like watching the footie in a pub, but Rangers TV is a great fall-back.

'When we moved to the area at first, it was quite rough. They film [Netflix crime drama] *Ozark* here, which gives an idea of how it was! But it has changed so much and it's a great place to live.'

In a season full of high points, Don decided to run the rule over the home match against Hamilton Accies – and boy did he have a ball watching a festival of goals. Eight was the least Rangers deserved that day.

He said, 'It was the day everything clicked into place. We'd lost 1-0 to Accies six months previous and that game more or less put the final nail in the coffin of our title hopes. It was probably a big turning point for Steven Gerrard and his team. I reckon it was when he started to question why his players hadn't turned up, and why things weren't going according to plan. We had a good squad but it seemed to be lacking an important ingredient. Whereas teams last season were playing a certain way against us, which normally meant sitting in and defending for their lives, some had noticed our vulnerabilities and were having a go.

'Just a few days before the defeat to Accies we lost 1-0 to Hearts at Tynecastle in the quarter-finals of the Scottish Cup; another disappointment, so it was a difficult period for us.

'Six months later, and whatever the manager had been searching for he'd found it, as we were playing some great football and scoring for fun. Our stats were fantastic. Our pass success rate was up in the 90 per cent bracket. And all this with virtually the nucleus of the squad who had lost so disastrously to Hearts and Hamilton. It was the second week in November, and everyone knows titles aren't won so early, but that game gave us a sense of "you know what, this could be our year", because this team who had come to our place previously and won had just been massacred.

'There were still a lot of nerves around, because we wanted so much to win title number 55, and to stop the ten, etc., but we knew after that game that if we could just carry on the way we were playing, especially into the New Year, then perhaps [it might happen].

'Our passing and movement was on point. In fact, it was glorious. The opposition wasn't important, because I felt we would have destroyed any team that day. Get your opponents running around and they will tire, and the stats proved that. The pass success rate was in the low 70 per cent in the first 15 or 20 minutes but as the game wore on that stat grew exponentially, so our fitness was already paying off.

'The boys had a swagger, but not an arrogance. You could see they were having fun but complacency was nowhere to be seen.'

Once again the goals were shared around, although Kemar Roofe, Tav and Joe Aribo managed two each, and that delighted Don. He said, 'I always felt Roofe was an okay player with Leeds United. He had his moments, some really good moments, but he has bought into everything the gaffer is trying to achieve at Rangers and has really gone for it.

'Joe Aribo is another one. His laces are tied to the ball; he has such brilliant control of the football. What a talent, and he's as cool as a cucumber. I didn't know an awful lot about Aribo before he pitched up at Ibrox. The same with Glen Kamara, who was literally sitting on the bench at Dundee.

'It was exhibition stuff against Hamilton at times. We hit our stride early on and kept it up. The way we played, no one would have lived with us. Accies were simply the unlucky ones. And we played virtually the full 90 with that intensity. There was little let-up, and that's impressive. Gerrard has instilled this relentlessness into the team which the supporters have been craving for years.'

The game against Hamilton was our 14th league fixture of the season, and despite being less than halfway through the campaign there were supporters who were starting to believe. Don said, 'Yes, I get that, definitely. We all had good feelings; we weren't conceding goals, we were scoring a few, and it was a completely different feel from previous seasons. The way we were playing proved how important the work the guys were doing on the training ground is. It's crucial. In the past, when the team wasn't quite gelling we seemed to lose, but this season you could see the result of all those hours at the Rangers Training Centre because we were still finding ways to win games.

'I get the impression that when Steven Gerrard isn't happy after a game, and he's speaking to the press, he isn't just wheeling out the old clichés. Unlike other managers, he absolutely means what he says. There is never any talk of "we move on to the next game", etc., which is something Rangers, as a club, has been lacking for many years. Proper direction and leadership.

'The way Gerrard has the team set up, Tav is a vital cog in there. In the league we know that if we lose a game then there is time to make it up, but Europe is a different animal. There are a lot of knockout ties played so we have to play every game to win, and press high up the park. Tav is a master at that. He has taken some stick when he gets caught up the park, but it's a gamble the manager seems willing to take, and it has often paid dividends. He's very skilful, takes players on, he controls the ball well under pressure, and is generally one of our best players. He has certainly proved a lot of the doubters wrong, and I'd be happy if he finished his career at Rangers.

'I'm not sure how much of Tav being captain has gone into making Rangers the team they are. That team doesn't need an awful lot of on-field direction, and anyway we have McGregor blowing a gasket in the 18-yard box and Connor Goldson pulling the strings in the centre of defence. John Greig was a great Rangers captain and seemed to play that role perfectly by taking games by the scruff of the neck. Nowadays I think the captaincy is little more than a coin toss and the armband. And that's not in any way, shape or form a criticism of Tav, who I love. I think it says more about the team and coaching staff that the players know exactly what they're doing before every game – and just get on with it.

'A great team performs most weeks. It is far more than just individuals. A great team rather than great players; a collective. This is a new way of playing for us – a new style – and every single one of our players has bought into it.

'I reckon our impressive defensive record is a product of our attacking strategy just as much as our defensive one. The opposition are on the ropes that much they don't have time to attack, therefore they aren't creating as many opportunities against us, and as a result, we supporters don't have the same knot in the stomach we once had!

'I don't think there's a Rangers supporter out there who would've put money on us being 18 points clear at the end of February. It was a shock to the system, but a welcome one. I looked on after the Old Firm game of 2 January at the utter chaos surrounding Celtic. Neil Lennon decided to get his players out of Glasgow and take them to Dubai to see if he could re-energise a failing squad. Their fans were going mental and I suppose he just wanted to get them out of the firing line. Little did he know he was lining his players up against a wall. It was a PR disaster, and it soon became evident that something major was wrong at their club. Of course, he was gone by the end of February.'

The Lisa Stansfield song 'All Around the World' could apply to Don as before moving to the USA, he lived in South Africa for many years. All a far cry from growing up in the east end of Glasgow.

He said, 'I was born in Haghill, which was a good start as it was mostly Bluenoses who lived there. I went back a few years ago and the majority of football shirts were still blue, so perhaps not a lot has changed since I left. As the crow flies it's only a mile north of Celtic Park, but still light years away. It's near Dennistoun, and that was always a Rangers stronghold.

'My dad was originally from Maryhill, but he wasn't a big football fan. If push came to shove I'm sure he would've chosen Rangers but he didn't bother much. He was born in 1938 and was good pals with Bertie Auld. They went to the same school.

'We moved from Haghill to Milton, and I attended Miltonbank Primary School, which was predominantly Rangers with a few token Celtic fans. No one really had football shirts in those days but we all knew who was what! We all had scarves knitted by our granny and wore them to the football. When I was seven, I took a brick to the head because of my scarf. Obviously somebody in Milton didn't agree with my choice of team. I was taken to hospital, where I received a few stitches, but the most important thing was mum washed the scarf!

'We had a neighbour who cut the hair of most kids in the street. He was a bus driver, but to earn some extra cash he would sit this stool over his sink and hoist you up on to it before chopping off your beloved locks. He was also a big Rangers supporter. I palled about with his son and he would take the two of us to Ibrox now and again, which was a huge thrill for me. It was the early 1970s and I got the chance to see John Greig, Tommy McLean and Willie Johnston.

'It was all men at the games in those days; there were very few women. The men seemed like giants. They would be shouting and bawling at the opposition, or the referee, but they were great with us. They could see we were the future so they made us feel really special. It was just after the disaster and we would get lifted over the turnstiles. That was my first taste of going to Ibrox, and once you get that taste it sticks.'

And with every great team there is inevitably a favourite player. 'When I was a kid there was no one quite like Derek Johnstone. He was a great goalscorer but also a fantastic player. For a 16-year-old to all but single-handedly win his team a trophy in an Old Firm final at Hampden in front of more than 100,000 supporters is incredible. How did a kid that age handle that pressure?

'DJ was very under-rated, and I was furious when Ally McLeod omitted him from the 1978 World Cup finals in Argentina. I mean, what was he thinking? I also really liked Tommy McLean, who provided so many of Johnstone's goals with his pinpoint crosses, while John Greig and Sandy Jardine were also big favourites.

'Every time I go to Ibrox I get this tremendous feeling of awe. I get that it's an extra-special place for us Rangers fans, but there's more to it than that. It just seems such a special place, period. I've been to loads of impressive stadiums in the United States, but they seem so surgical in comparison. They don't have that sense of history like our place.'

Don's family left Glasgow behind in 1973 and moved to Johannesburg. 'My dad was a joiner in the shipyards, but his yard shut down and he simply couldn't find work. It was awful, and I don't think it has ever been fully acknowledged just what that did to Glasgow. Literally thousands of jobs were never replaced and all these highly skilled workers headed off to countries far and wide to earn a living. It was a great loss to the city.

'Many of these great tradesmen ended up in South Africa, and we lived in a place called Yeoville, a Johannesburg suburb. When I went to school I couldn't believe how many other Scottish kids were there, and while there was an even split of Rangers/Celtic supporters, I seemed to be the only Bluenose in my immediate circle!

'My dad got a job building big supermarkets along with, I'm sure, many of the dads of my fellow pupils. Glasgow's loss was South Africa's gain. I enjoyed going to school there. We transported the Old Firm rivalry to Johannesburg, and although it was rough times in the 1980s, it was mostly gentle ribbing.

'In our school we had just about every nationality: kids from other parts of the UK, Greece, Italy, Jewish kids, etc., but it was a great testament to the Scottish education system that the five who collected the top academic prizes each year were aye Scottish kids. We were the smart ones. Oh, and we started the chess club!

'Richard Gough was also a pupil at King Edward VII School, which was government-run, although he was two years ahead of me so our paths didn't often cross. Later on, I would enjoy a beer with Richard's dad in the Radium Bar, which was in Orange Grove, Johannesburg. We got on well, and while he didn't boast about his son's achievements, he was quietly very proud of him. The great South African golfer Gary Player was also a former pupil.

'I had a brief hiatus from attending school in South Africa when we returned to the UK, Basingstoke, in 1980. But after a year in England we returned to Johannesburg and I saw out my final two years at the same school.

'Whenever we came back to Scotland I would stay with my nana in Milton, and would go and see Rangers as often as I could. I would get the bus to Cowcaddens, and jump a subway over to Ibrox. The Copland Road rear was my stand of choice.

'When I was 15, and we had come back to Basingstoke, my nana had moved to Cowcaddens so any time I got up the road it was only a short hop over to Ibrox on the subway, which was great.

When I was back at school in South Africa, I didn't have much of a clue what I wanted to be, so one day I flicked through the *Yellow Pages* (yes, we had them there too!) and decided I would like to be an engineer. I didn't have any money so I applied for a bursary, and thankfully I was successful. But it was tempered with a change in the law, which meant I might have to do my national service in the South African military. Initially, conscription didn't apply to foreigners, which made the locals unhappy, so the law change meant if you were between 18 and 25 in September 1984, and had been in the country five years, you would have to do a term of military service. I was back in Glasgow at Christmas and when

I phoned my dad, he said, "Merry Christmas, your papers are here!"

'In terms of job prospects, there was nothing for me in Scotland. I had sorted out my bursary and realised my immediate future lay in South Africa. I wasn't too chuffed about the military service but I did my two years. We were based in Ondangwa, south-west Africa, and would fly into Angola for operations. Rangers had just endured a horrendous 1984/85 season, so chances are I was better off in the jungle!

'I received a letter from a mate of mine, Stevie Darroch, a big Celtic fan, and in this "letter" was nothing but a cutting from *The Times* with the headline "The demise of the once great Glasgow Rangers"! It was all good banter, though.

'In 1984 the crowds just hadn't been there. One of the games I had been home for was against St Mirren, and there was little more than 12,000 inside Ibrox. I know Christmas was just around the corner but that was still a pitiful crowd. Heading home that day after the game I had the subway carriage virtually to myself. It was dreadful to see. You got the sense we were impotent. There was virtually no singing and the atmosphere was horrendous. And there wasn't a thing we could do about it. We needed either the management to turn things round or the board to find a way out of this mess.

'It's all so different now (well, pre- and post-COVID) as the fans turn up in their droves, and the walk from the subway to the stadium and up towards the Rangers Shop is one we undertake safe in the knowledge that we aren't on our own!

'In all the years we were down in the lower leagues, we didn't turn our backs on the club. We were there when needed. Others tried to kill us but we stood tall and strong and refused to die. I looked on from Georgia in awe of our great support and it will remain with me until the day I die.

'The way we were treated by the football authorities and the other clubs will needle me for many years. We got to experience genuine bile directed against us. It was crystal clear what the rest thought of us. The first thought of the SFA wasn't to ask,

"How can we help you?" No, it was to organise a sham vote to see how the other clubs wanted to pursue this. It was a cop-out. They cast us aside and left us at the mercy of the baying pack.'

While in South Africa, Don discovered a novel way of keeping up to date with how his club was faring. 'We gleaned most of our info from the late edition of the Sunday papers, but if it was an Old Firm game and we couldn't wait for the papers, we'd walk home after a night out and pop into a Chinese restaurant and ask if we could use the phone to call a taxi. We'd be waking one of the lads in Glasgow, of course. This worked swimmingly until they suspected something and took a closer look at their bills. Last time we went in we received a right mouthful, "No more, no more you use phone to call Glasgow!"

'I soon joined the Johannesburg Rangers Supporters' Club, and we watched the games in a bar in Auckland Park. It was a first-class setup with around 30 like-minded Bluenoses having some great banter, a few bevvies and the chance to watch our team. We would all wear our embroidered supporters' club shirts when the team was playing. Dave King was also a member.

'These were the days before live games on Sky Sports, so we had a guy back in the UK who would record the games on to VHS tape and send them over to South Africa. We paid five bucks to go to the hotel and watch them. We might have been eight and a half thousand miles from home, but it genuinely felt like we were in a Glasgow pub watching the game. Oh, and we had sunshine!

'Every Saturday morning we would go to the Moulin Rouge Hotel to watch the previous week's *Match of the Day*, and *Saint & Greavsie*, on TV. I loved their patter.'

Don switched from South Africa to the USA in 1996 and despite moving almost 10,000 miles, he was still keen to keep in touch with the goings-on at Ibrox. He discovered one or two like-minded Rangers men in Atlanta, Georgia, and a local bar where he could watch some of the games. He said, 'I'm in the process of building a new house, and I'll be including a

Rangers-themed bar in the basement. I'll have a snooker table and a TV so that I can watch the games. That's a priority!

'Kick-off times aren't too much of an issue. We're five hours behind the UK so a 3pm kick-off in Scotland means a 10am start over here. The earliest it gets is a 7am start. It's a big occasion, so I make sure I'm good to go for kick-off, and my Guinness is disguised inside my Rangers mug!

'I love Georgia. The people are incredibly friendly. I've been here 25 years now and couldn't contemplate living anywhere else. And it's a good time to be a Rangers fan. The appointment of Steven Gerrard was a masterstroke. I remember watching a live English match on TV and he was one of the studio pundits. There were all the usual clichés flying about but when it came to Gerrard, he offered a detailed explanation of what was going right or wrong, and was quite clearly a scholar of the game.

'When times were tough for him as a manager, and whenever he lost a game, say, to Hearts in the Scottish Cup, or Hamilton in the league, he wasn't the guy to say, "I'm going home to consider my future." His only thought was how could he improve things and make the situation better. That was the defining moment, when he said, "What am I doing wrong?" and he went home and found the answer.'

Chris Mayhead

Cumbernauld, Scotland

Rangers 4 Aberdeen 0
Scorers: Kent 15, Roofe 29, Arfield 49, Tavernier 53 pen
8 November 2020

Chris Mayhead reckons the title was in the bag the first week in November. It's a bold statement, but he backs it up by citing, as evidence, a completely one-sided demolition job of Aberdeen at Ibrox – and his only regret is that the team took their collective foot off the gas when the electronic scoreboard struck four!

Goals by Kent, Roofe, Arfield and Tav – two in each half – had Rangers on easy street with just a little under 40 minutes to play. But it remained that way until the end, and Chris, although satisfied with the three points, was desperate for Rangers to score more. Weren't we all?

The proud Rangers supporter grew up in nearby Briton Street – a hop, skip and a jump away from Ibrox subway station. In fact, he tells a great story of his earliest memory of Rangers, saying, 'On a Saturday afternoon, my dad and granddad, and the other menfolk of the family would go to the game while the women got on with what they were doing. I would hang out the window watching this carnival of colour roll past on their way to the match. All these supporters with their red-white-and-blue scarves and tammies on, singing their songs and generally in a great mood as they looked forward to another afternoon of excitement watching the Rangers.

'It was an incredible sight, but as quick as it was happening suddenly everyone would disappear and the streets would be deserted, bar a few kids searching for empty "ginger" bottles to return to the newsagent for the deposit, which they would then spend on sweets.

'All of a sudden there would be this tremendous roar, and my granny, without even looking up from her knitting or the socks she was darning, would simply say, "One-nil to the Rangers." I was always so taken with how she knew what the score was simply by listening to a roar. It wasn't until I was old enough to know that the visiting team would bring far fewer supporters than my team, and so they couldn't possibly have made such a noise!'

When Chris was old enough, his dad – who was born in London and a naturalised Chelsea supporter-turned-Ranger when he married into Chris's mum's family – started taking him 'round the corner' to the games.

'My first one was a cracker,' Chris said, beaming with pride. 'Rangers v Ajax in the European Super Cup in January 1973. It was freezing, but that was of little concern. I didn't know the significance of that great Ajax side, Johan Cruyff et al., but I was completely comfortable in my new surroundings. I was in the short-lived Centenary Stand that night and marvelled at the colours dazzling under the floodlights. Rangers in their magical royal blue strip, and the opposition wearing that iconic red-and-white top. We lost, which I wasn't massively worried about because my enjoyment that night was total, and my victory was the beginning of a lifelong love affair. They got me!'

In 1978, Chris – having saved up sufficiently – was able to afford his first season ticket, an £18 Rover brief, which allowed him to move freely around the stadium and view the games from wherever he wanted – apart from, of course, when Celtic were in town.

He recalled, 'I felt ten feet tall when I bought that season ticket. And I had it every year until Graeme Souness arrived at Ibrox to shake up my underperforming club. A guy with his stature was long overdue and, along with the many thousands of Bears, I looked forward to the future with great hope.'

But Chris was a week or so late in reapplying for his season ticket and the upshot was he didn't get one. He was gutted. He hadn't missed a home match in over a decade but was forced to stand outside Ibrox as Celtic visited, and the game ended in bedlam with Chris Woods, Terry Butcher and Frank MacAvennie sent off, later to appear in court on various trumped-up charges relating to this feisty encounter. But what to do about his gut-wrenching personal situation. He felt he had a right to be inside the stadium as he wasn't one of the glory hunters who only tend to appear when the team is winning.

He said, 'I thought long and hard about how I was going to see the games, and I came up with the idea of applying for a job at the stadium. I was taken on by the security firm Rock Steady as a steward. I was in. Or so I thought. For the next home game I turned up full of expectation, only to be told I was manning a fire exit for the next few weeks. I still didn't see the games but at least I was inside the stadium, a foot in the door, so to speak, and serving my club. That was some consolation.'

For the next year or so, Chris continued to monitor the ins and outs at the fire exit. He got on with his job, turned up on time and, keen to make a good impression, always dressed smartly.

He was also being used more in other parts of the stadium, and on non-matchdays, and was eventually asked to look after the prestigious Members' Lounge.

When the club hit rock bottom from 2012, Chris was part of the daily team monitoring events at the stadium but he would become frustrated if visitors, from different parts of the world, approached staff at the front door to ask if they could see inside the stadium only to be turned away.

He explained, 'We are a massive club, known all over the globe, and if people were attracted to the stadium because of what they'd heard back home in Australia, Canada or South America, I didn't want them going home with a negative perception of Rangers, so if I was on duty I would always try and show them the key parts of the stadium, like the marble staircase, dressing rooms and the pitch.

'As a kid I had chosen the history of Rangers as a school project, so I was always fascinated with much more than just what team the manager would pick on a Saturday afternoon. I wanted to know where the wood panelling on the walls of the marble staircase came from, who the architect of the stadium was, etc. I wanted to immerse myself in the captivating history of our great club.

'So I started showing folk around the stadium, and with each "tour" I gave, I wanted to learn more myself, to give folk a better experience. This was eventually noticed by Geraldine Marshall, head of the club's commercial department. She approached me one day about these unofficial tours, and after I realised I wasn't in trouble, she asked how I knew so much about the club. I was then offered a job as a tour guide. It was 2013 and I was given a club blazer and tie. I was made up. As a diehard, it was a proud moment for me, the wee boy from round the corner, given a contract of employment from Rangers FC.

'My grandfather's last words to me in 1975 were, "Take my place at Ibrox Park, son!" I had done just that. My grandfather, Sonny Nicol, was a big Rangers man and had run the Tower Bar Rangers Supporters' Club in Govan for many years. He was a dyed-in-the-wool Bluenose.'

Giving tours to supporters has given Chris years of joy; almost as much joy as those on the tours get from being shown around by a man who clearly has Rangers in his heart. He said, 'When I'm wearing that blazer I like to set my standards as high as those set by the great man, Mr Bill Struth himself. The fans are getting a tour from a fan. I've met so many great people doing these tours.'

But a baptism of fire awaited Chris on his first official day in the job. This was different from all the 'no-pressure, bootleg' tours he had given before being officially taken on as a guide.

He had prepared a running order and script, and when the tour kicked off he set his watch to ensure it would start and finish promptly and on time.

He takes up the story: 'Everything was running like clockwork. At the start of the tour I had been as nervous as hell. Wearing the club blazer and tie brings with it a heavy responsibility, but I had a really nice couple from Holland – whom I still keep in touch with – along with many other very interested parties.

'As we headed down the tunnel towards the pitch, this rather flustered member of the commercial department was heading straight for me. "What have I done wrong?" I wondered. The thing is, this part of the tour was always very emotional for me. I would really build it up, and when we emerged from the tunnel on to the pitch, it would hopefully be an enlightening experience for all.

'So, this girl runs up to me and says, "You need to slow down, stop here [in the middle of the tunnel] and tell them a story. Give me a couple of minutes," and with that she was gone. It was surreal, but I told this completely off-the-cuff story about the wood panelling on the walls. Don't get me wrong, it's a great story, and it goes back to when Ibrox was being refurbished and Bill Struth wanted it to be the best stadium in the world. The *Queen Mary* was being built at John Brown's Shipyards on the Clyde, although work had halted due to a lack of finance, so Mr Struth approached the boss of the firm, and said, "Look, you've got all these talented carpenters sitting around doing nothing, and all this great material. How about you give me these guys and this wood and we will pay for it and keep these guys employed by taking them to Ibrox to work on the interior of the stadium. Once you're back on your feet they can come back and finish your job." Both parties agreed and that's how the interior of Ibrox Stadium still looks so bonny to this day.

'Thankfully this story did the trick and we finally proceeded to the end of the tunnel, just at the dugouts and the beginning of the pitch. There, the girl took over and suddenly this message flashed up on the electronic scoreboard, and a guy gets down on one knee to propose to his girlfriend. The emotional part of my tour just became super emotional! The girl said yes, the couple hugged and everyone started to cheer. What a way to start my career as a tour guide.'

Chris soon became the go-to guy whenever Rangers made a new signing who then asked to be shown around the stadium. He was on hand to give Rob Kiernan and his dad the tour. When they got to the edge of the pitch, Chris said, 'This is as far as I go. I haven't earned the right to cross that white line, but you have, Rob. His dad asked how many the stadium held. I said it was around 50,000 (I did give him the exact number), but added, "You might see 50,000 supporters here on a Saturday, but behind each supporter is another ten friends or family members who can't be here for a variety of reasons, so you'll be playing in front of half a million each home game!" The look on their faces. Rob's dad took a sharp intake of breath and mouthed, "What a place!"

'I also gave Joey Barton the tour, as well as the owner of our sponsor 32Red. And on another occasion my guests were Donald Trump's Marine One helicopter pilots, when the president was over in Scotland. In fact, I drove them around for a couple of weeks, and was at one point part of the president's official motorcade!'

There is one man Chris will never forget. Just once, he made an exception by crossing the white line and walking on to the pitch. It was July 1990 and he was part of Frank Sinatra's Ibrox detail when the legendary crooner appeared at our world-famous stadium. Glasgow was the European Capital of Culture and had lined up some terrific concerts, such as the Rolling Stones and Pavarotti. But the concert of the year was at Ibrox, and Sinatra had 11,000 folk eating from the palm of his hands.

Chris explained, 'I was standing with Mr Sinatra in the tunnel, waiting to go on, and we had a quick chat. I told him

I had never crossed the white line, and he said to me, "You will tonight." We had a chuckle and spoke as we walked on to the park, and when he reached the stage, I helped him up. He thanked me, and shouted, "Hey, son," and passed an imaginary ball to me, which I controlled and scored, naturally! He smiled, and it was such a magical moment. The world's greatest entertainer and I playing imaginary football at Ibrox! Does it get any better?'

Possibly, as in 2020/21 Chris looked on proudly as his team captured an historic 55th league title. As we alluded to way back at the start his story, one game in particular stood out for Chris: Rangers v Aberdeen, Ibrox, on 8 November.

Why that one? 'Because that day we proved just how good we were. We won 4-0, but it was as emphatic a win as you're ever likely to see. And as a Rangers fan around in the 1980s, and one who watched our team suffer many defeats to Alex Ferguson's league-winning Dons, it was a glorious afternoon.

'The stats that day were astonishing. Pass accuracy of 86 per cent, and we had 71 per cent of possession. We played 714 passes and so to have an almost 90 per cent success rate within that is fantastic. You can see I like my stats!

'We got the early goal from Ryan Kent, and then one four minutes into the second half from Scott Arfield, which made it 3-0. The skipper, James Tavernier, converted a 53rd-minute penalty to make it four – and at that point I thought the floodgates would open and we would get eight or nine. Heaven knows, we should've. But the guys stopped the scoring at four, and that was frustrating. Mind you, it's not *Championship Manager*, it's real life, and it gave the manager an opportunity to introduce some fringe players and rest others, especially with a heavy schedule in front of us.

'I was particularly impressed with Kent. Aberdeen couldn't handle him, and his licence to roam paid off. He was out wide, drifting in and going central. He was all over the place and was in the mood to run at their defenders. I know he blows hot and cold, but even the great Davie Cooper had off-days.

'We went 11 points ahead of Celtic after that game and I immediately thought of a statement made by our former chairman Dave King, that Celtic's house of cards would come tumbling down once we proved we were back. Well, the cards started to tumble that day.'

Chris uses the 'jigsaw' analogy to illustrate just how good a job Steven Gerrard has done at Ibrox. 'From the moment he came in, he has been making little tweaks and changes. We've been relatively successful in the Europa League but up until this season we hadn't really achieved anything tangible domestically. As the jigsaw started to fill up, and so that changed. He has been adding little pieces here and there and the completed jigsaw meant 55.

'Everyone has their own favourites, but for me Gerrard's most important signing has been Allan McGregor. The defence has been incredible this season but to know you have one of the safest pairs of hands in Great Britain behind you must be a wonderful feeling. That has helped the likes of Tav and Borna get forward with confidence, also knowing that guys like Kamara and Davis will slot in if they get caught too far up the pitch.

'It's almost like there are no weaknesses in the team, and that's a rarity at any club. Perhaps Alfredo Morelos didn't score as many goals as he normally does, but he still popped up with match-winning goals at Pittodrie, Easter Road and Livingston. High-pressure games. Oh, and there was one at Parkhead!

'Gerrard introduced a great mix of youth and experience as well as competition for places, and that has seen us in good stead throughout the season. At the beginning the pressure was all on Celtic to go and get ten in a row, but that soon shifted, and as the team making the running, the pressure was on us to stay there – and what a great job we made of that!

'From day one at Pittodrie we were so professional, and it paid off handsomely. That first game was a Becher's Brook-style hurdle and we cleared it with relative ease. In the 4-0 return game we showed Aberdeen who was boss.

'We've been building up to this season for the last three years or so. Constructing the spine of the team, the game-day preparation in training, buying in new players, etc. When Gerrard was announced as the new manager, he said he had a three-year plan and naturally you're sceptical as you've heard it all before, but he was spot on.

'But you only have to look at his pedigree at Liverpool to see his class. I remember seeing him being shown round Ibrox six or seven months before he was appointed manager, and the way he carried himself was exceptional. The Rangers job is a massive gig for anyone, but Gerrard has grown into it and become more than comfortable in his new surroundings, and from there has blossomed as a manager.'

And one final question for this dyed-in-the-wool Rangers man. What was more important to you, 55 or stopping ten? 'That's a good question, but an easy one to answer. Winning the league was important for our progression as a club. Fifty-five is proof that we're back. I don't see this as a one-off; 2012 now seems such a long time ago, and it is in many respects, but we started back on the road to redemption a long time ago and hopefully the long-term suffering is over.

'Stopping Celtic's quest for a tenth successive title was important too, but getting 55 wins it hands down for me. I was gutted when we failed to win ten in a row in the 1990s but this has more than made up for it. Now I want to see us go on and dominate Scottish football for many years to come.'

Fraser Aird

Toronto, Canada

Dundee United 1 Rangers 2
Scorers: Tavernier 26, Goldson 44
13 December 2020

Fraser Aird could hardly believe his eyes as he watched the ball travel more than 30 yards before nestling in the back of the net. James Tavernier's incredible free kick had covered just less than a third of the entire length of the Tannadice pitch before beating home goalkeeper Benjamin Siegrist all ends up.

The 25-year-old winger was at home in Toronto, more than 3,000 miles from the action, watching two of his former clubs go head-to-head, and while he enjoyed his time with Dundee United there was only one team he wanted to win.

Aird is back in his native Canada playing professional football for FC Edmonton but hardly misses a Rangers game these days, and he was so glad he tuned in to the match in mid-December. He said, 'I thoroughly enjoyed that game, but it was a tough gig for Rangers. Not long after Tav hit his wonder strike, United equalised, and were playing quite well. My first thoughts were that Rangers were now being tested and I wanted to know how they would react to that. Connor Goldson popped up with another goal just before half-time and Rangers went on to win 2-1, so there was my answer. They found a way to win the game, and when you're chasing the league that's really all that matters.

'Goldson has scored more than a few important goals this season, and his role in the centre of such a mean defence has also been crucial; a huge part of why Rangers would go on to win the title.'

Being in Canada, which means a five-hour lag on the UK, hasn't deterred the talented wideman from getting up at 'the crack of dawn' to make sure he doesn't miss any Rangers games.

'I don't think I missed many games this season. I tried to watch them all as I was really keen for Rangers to win the league. Not just because I was fortunate to be at Ibrox for five years, but because my mum and dad ensured I grew up a Rangers supporter. They are both from Glasgow, and big Rangers supporters, so any football tops I had were always Rangers.

'They used to watch Rangers everywhere; home, away, in Europe, so my pedigree was solid. When they immigrated to Canada, one of the first things I believe they did was to seek out the Toronto Rangers Supporters' Club and become members. They also travelled back to Glasgow many times to watch Rangers – and see family of course!'

Aird watched the match at Tannadice with his brother, and both were delighted to see another three points accrued. December was a busy month with six tough matches scheduled – but six important victories were registered and the playmaker is only too aware of how difficult it is to win any matches at Rangers.

He said, 'Sure, you've got the best players, but it can be so difficult to beat teams who put so many men behind the ball in an attempt to frustrate and stifle such a forward-thinking team. They are hoping to hit you on the break, and the longer a game goes on – like the match against Motherwell at Ibrox – quite often the more desperate a team can become.

'But when you have a player like Tav who can come up with something as wonderful as that free kick at Tannadice then you always have a chance of getting goals from set pieces. We have also seen Borna Barišić do it many times, so Rangers are fortunate to have two such talented free-kick specialists in the team.

'When I was at United, I played alongside Benjamin, and he is a great goalkeeper, so that means Tav's free kick truly was something special. For a good keeper to be beaten from 30 yards out has to be something special, and that one was right out of the top drawer.

'Dundee United have always been a big club, and now that they are back in the Premiership they are desperate to get back to where they once were in terms of league positions, but in many respects this season's games against Rangers were free hits because not many people were expecting them to beat Rangers – and they didn't!

'There is obviously a bit of needle in these games, so it makes it that wee bit tougher for Rangers because the United lads are extra motivated, but Rangers' class told in the end.'

Aird has been mightily impressed by the way Steven Gerrard has taken to the job, especially with his first gig coming at such a massive club. 'Rangers fans demand success, and managers don't often get the time they probably need to build their own team. To build the type of team Gerrard wanted has taken a lot of time; hours and hours on the training field, building all these relationships between the players, as well as the team as a whole.

'Perhaps Gerrard has been given that time because of his standing in the game, which is understandable, but whatever the reason it has paid huge dividends for club and supporters. The type of consistency Rangers showed throughout the season was phenomenal, and something like that isn't achievable overnight. There seemed to be a good feeling about the club that something special was in the offing.

'The backroom team was always going to be extra important, especially with Gerrard stepping into his first managerial job. Guys like Gary McAllister, with his knowledge of the game, was a massive appointment.

'Michael Beale as well, who I believe takes about 75 per cent of training, has had a huge input. The board have backed everything the manager has done and they have shown great vision in doing so. Rangers have improved in each of Gerrard's three years at Ibrox, but the consistency he has achieved in his team has been the key factor. Getting to play virtually the same team week in, week out has paid dividends, and I couldn't be happier.'

Fifteen league wins in a row in the middle of the season, two victories at Pittodrie, and Tannadice, and having the meanest defence in the league were all major contributory factors in the success, and while there were many supporters who refused to accept that the league was won as Rangers scorched a massive 23 points clear after beating Ross County at Ibrox near the end of January, most were secretly looking out the bunting for the title celebrations.

Aird was no different, and said, 'There comes a time when you're watching the team win game after game, and you see Celtic slipping up with back-to-back draws against Livingston, and you allow yourself to believe that it's over. You're not going to publicly say it's over, but in private you know it would take a points swing of monumental proportions for the power to shift back to the other side of the city. You start to dream.'

And dreaming was something a young Fraser Aird did a lot of while still at primary school. With his love of Rangers firmly entrenched within his character, and starting to show real signs of having a special talent for the game, Aird admitted that he dreamed of one day pulling on the Rangers jersey.

He said, 'Before the advent of the Canadian Premier League in 2019, there were two routes that any promising young footballers over here could take in a bid to make the grade. They could go down the road of getting a scholarship in America, or they could try to find a club in Europe.

'I began playing with North Scarborough Soccer Club, and made a bit of a splash there, so with the help of an agent, who knew Tommy Wilson – technical director at the Rangers academy – I had a head start. He sent Tommy some footage of me playing and I was invited over to Glasgow for a week's trial at Murray Park.

'I did well and was asked to stay a further fortnight. I put absolutely everything I had into making the extended trial a success, and at the end of it I was taken into an office and offered a contract – which I signed on my 16th birthday.

'Importantly, the term of the contract was three years, which gave me a great chance to work hard and lay down a marker. It was perfect. Being away from home at such a young age didn't ever cross my mind. I was a teenager just about to embark on a career with Rangers FC. How good was that? So I didn't give much thought to any sacrifices I might be making. I was only interested in making the grade at Rangers.'

It was game on for the football-mad youngster. He worked incredibly hard at Murray Park and it wasn't too long before the coaching staff started to take notice. There were a few injuries in the first-team squad, and after chatting with Wilson, manager Ally McCoist – who was about to celebrate his 50th birthday – drafted the teenage Canadian into the mix for the home game against Montrose at Ibrox.

He was on the bench alongside the likes of Fran Sandaza and Robbie Crawford, and with the game tied at 1-1, and ten minutes of the second half gone, Aird was told to go out and warm up. There was just over 45,000 inside Ibrox, and he said, 'I was desperate to get on. As I was out on the touchline warming up, Lewis Macleod scored to put us 2-1 ahead, and just moments later the bench signalled for me to return to the halfway line. This was it, I was about to make my debut for Glasgow Rangers – the team I had supported as a boy.

'I replaced Barrie McKay and sprinted over to the far side, near the Govan Stand. The reception I received from the supporters was incredible, and that filled me with confidence. The 35 minutes or so I had on the pitch passed in a blur. Further goals by Lee McCulloch and Robbie Crawford gave us a decent 4-1 win.

'Incredibly enough, the win moved us into second place in the table behind Queen's Park, but we would be top before long.'

There was only one thing missing from Aird's Ibrox debut, and that was his parents. He explained, 'They were completely made up for me, and it would've been great to have them there for my debut, but it all happened so fast that they just didn't have time to get across from Canada.

'To make your professional debut for any club is a great achievement, but to do it for Rangers was incredible. I was so happy, and my mum and dad were very proud of me. It's the dream of millions of kids and I achieved it.'

A few days after Christmas, league leaders Rangers made the short trip across the city to face third-placed Queen's Park. In the games sandwiched between his debut and the Hampden encounter, the Canadian teenager had been on the fringes of the team, coming off the bench on more than a few occasions to play his part as the team moved to the top of the table.

He was on the bench again at the national stadium and looked on as Rangers huffed and puffed, especially in front of goal. Twenty minutes into the second half, with the game goalless, gaffer McCoist decided enough was enough and sent him on in place of Ian Black. He was involved immediately, setting up Lee Wallace, but the chance was gone as Queen's keeper Neil Parry saved smartly at the Rangers captain's feet.

You got a sense that a goal was coming but it was a long wait for the 30,000 Rangers supporters, and with time running out Aird picked up the ball on the edge of the 18-yard box then curled a beauty past Parry and into the net. It was a goal of real quality and well worth the wait.

We were already a minute into stoppage time and there was no way back for the amateurs. Fraser Aird had his first Rangers goal, and it was a winner at Hampden.

He recalled, 'I'm sure I read somewhere that the away support that day was the biggest ever for a league match in Scotland. It was unbelievable, just like being at home, so it was a great boost for us, and to score my first goal for Rangers in the national stadium truly was a dream come true. The fact that it was in injury time, and the winner, was extra special.'

Aird will always be thankful to McCoist for giving him his Rangers debut and then sticking by him as the team went on to win the Third Division and League One titles.

He said, 'Ally McCoist was great with me. He is a proper club legend, so to work under someone who had enjoyed such an outstanding career as a striker was important for me. He had been an idol of mine but he was down to earth and always passing on lots of tips to the strikers. He had a lot of time for the kids, and would never pass you in the corridor. He was a fantastic man-manager.

'I loved my time at Rangers; what a way to begin a football career. The type of days you remember for the rest of your life. Sure, we had disappointments too such as losing the cup final to Raith Rovers at Easter Road, which is still one of my career low points, but the good times outweighed the bad.

'I completely get that it wasn't the greatest of periods for Rangers as a whole, with all the never-ending takeover stuff going on in the background, but we just had to try and focus on the football and go out there and win games. It was what it was and we simply had to deal with that.

'My dream would have been to stay at Ibrox my entire career, but we know football – and life – doesn't always work like that. Who knows, though, if I keep doing well over here there might be a wee chance I could return some day. Now that would be something.

'After all the gloomy years, the club is on the up again, and it's a great time to be a Rangers player – and supporter.'

Like all good things, Aird's time at Ibrox came to the beginning of the end in January 2016 when he went out on loan to Vancouver Whitecaps. On returning from Canada, he joined Falkirk for the second half of the season.

'I wanted to play football, it was as simple as that. It's a really short career and I didn't, as much as I loved Rangers, want to sit on the bench every Saturday. I wanted to play, and that was my only motivation to leave the club. It was still a wrench. It was my team, my first professional club, and playing in front of 40-odd thousand every week was a buzz, but it was the right time to leave. I'd had a lot of success at a young age, and working at Murray Park every day was fantastic, but football is football and needs must.

'It can be quite dispiriting to sit on the bench every Saturday. There's also that whole thing about feeling part of a team, and you can only really be part of something if you're contributing regularly. Rangers are the biggest club in Scotland, and one of the biggest in the UK, so it was a step back to go forward again.'

Aird played for Dunfermline Athletic, Dundee United and Cove Rangers before heading back across the Atlantic to sign for Valour in the Canadian Premier League. He has since joined FC Edmonton – who also play in royal blue shirts – and now plays his home games at the 5,100-capacity Clarke Stadium, in Edmonton, Alberta, which really isn't that far from Alaska.

'Yes, it gets pretty cold here,' he laughed. 'It was -27 when I stepped off the plane to sign for the club! When it gets to -30 no one really bats an eyelid. But I'm excited about being here and also for the future of Canadian football. The new Premier League has just started and it will offer a new pathway for youngsters coming through.

'Kids who show real promise can showcase their talents in the new league and those who run clubs in the MLS will be looking on, so now there is a clear route to signing for an American or a European team. That wasn't there when I started but I'm glad to be playing my part in it now.

'My ambition had always been to play in Scotland, at Rangers in particular, and I achieved that. That doesn't mean to say I'm not ambitious anymore, because I am, but we will take it one step at a time.'

Aird played for Canada under-15s in 2010, but when he moved to Scotland he was given an opportunity to represent Scotland at under-17 and under-19 level, which he did many times. He also scored goals but when it came to making a decision about which senior national team he would represent, he thought about it carefully before choosing his native Canada.

He said, 'I was close to being named in the full Scotland squad a few times, but I eventually decided to go with Canada. I made my debut as a substitute against Ghana. It was a fantastic honour and I felt really proud being part of it all. I definitely made the right decision.

'I know I'm half-Scottish, but I was born in Canada, and I've played eight times for my country now and I feel privileged to have done so. I scored my first goal for Canada against, ironically, Scotland, in a friendly at Easter Road. It was a 1-1 draw and that was another landmark moment for me.

'I've been very fortunate to have achieved what I have in my career. I've enjoyed just about every single moment of it, and getting the opportunity to play for Rangers will live with me forever. And watching them lift their 55th title was very sweet, both as an ex-player and as a fan. Let's hope 56 isn't too far away!'

A Ranger Forever

Derek Johnstone, Rangers legend
East Renfrewshire, Scotland

DEREK JOHNSTONE knows a thing or two about winning a league championship. He also knows only too well the pain it can cause when your biggest rival is waltzing off with title after title, and there's not a lot you can do to stop it.

That's one of the reasons he was delighted to see Rangers lift the 2020/21 crown. Another, of course, is much simpler: DJ is a massive Bluenose.

When Rangers won the 1974/75 championship – seven years after Johnstone had signed for the club on schoolboy forms – the Scottish football tide was turning. Celtic had racked up nine successive titles but Jock Wallace had built a team of winners at Ibrox, with Johnstone an integral component.

Signed as a centre-forward, he was now playing at centre-half as much as he was up front, but regardless of where he was deployed he always gave 100 per cent – and he admitted the relief was palpable when he finally got his hands on the league trophy.

He said, 'In those days it wasn't about trying to stop Celtic in their quest for ten in a row, because they were the first team to get nine, and it could've been 15 or 20, so there was no talk about ten in a row as there is nowadays. The only reason ten is a big thing is because both Rangers and Celtic have since achieved nine.

'Jock Wallace had been a coach previous to being announced as manager, and he was desperate to win the league. You wouldn't find a bigger Rangers fan in your life than Jock. He wanted us to win absolutely everything and that was his attitude towards each player that came in. As soon as you signed for Rangers, he would say, "If you're happy finishing mid-table, or fighting relegation, then go elsewhere. This isn't the club for you. We are winners here."

'He got everyone together at the start of that season and told us we'd gone far too long without winning the league. I wouldn't say the fans were drifting away at the time but there weren't as many at games as there should've been. Instead of 50 or 60,000 at Ibrox, there was 25 or 30,000, because we weren't doing well.

'We had ten Scottish internationals in our squad, so it's not as if we were lacking the personnel. We just had to get together and ensure we were firing on all cylinders because one thing you need to win leagues is consistency, and I remember Jock saying before the first game, "Let's get off to a good start. We need to get the fans on side; show them we mean business." We were playing Ayr United at Somerset Park and we drew 1-1, with the late, great Sandy Jardine scoring from the penalty spot. Jock stormed into the dressing room after the game and went through us. We received a stark ultimatum: "Do the job the way I want it done or I'll bring players in who will." We won ten of our next 11 games, with the other a draw at Tynecastle.

'We beat Celtic in both games that season, 2-1 at Celtic Park and 3-0 at Ibrox, which was the first time we'd done that in many years. After the game at Ibrox, Jock said, "They are the champions; the team that's winning this league every year, and we've just beat them again. Does that not tell you something?" And that gave us tremendous confidence.

'We lost just three games that season, and one of them was in the final match of the season at home to Airdrie after the league was won – and there was 65,000 there!'

One game will always have a special place in Johnstone's heart – the league-clincher at Easter Road against Hibs. DJ recalled, 'Hibs were a very good side, and the first team to beat us that season, 1-0 at Ibrox. We had five games left, but a point that day in Edinburgh and the title was ours. It was the old terracing at Easter Road, across from where the teams came out, and it seemed to go on forever. There was 40,000 there that day, and you can guarantee 35,000 were Rangers fans.

'I remember it like it was yesterday. Sandy picked up the ball from a free kick, skipped past two men with ease, about 30 yards out on the right-hand side, and played a lovely ball out to Bobby McKean. Bobby sent in a great cross which Colin Stein bulleted into the back of the net. Colin was magnificent in the air, and as soon as that ball hit the net the whole place erupted. The goal was scored at the traditional Rangers end, but virtually the whole stadium was the Rangers end that day. It was unbelievable. The players went mad, the fans went mad, and everyone in the dugout went mad. Hibs had taken the lead midway through the first half, and then Sandy had hit the post with a penalty, but we knew when Colin scored it was ours.

'At full time, Jock ran on to the pitch and started hugging everyone, which was something he never done. We are talking about a former Marine here. He didn't cuddle men! But it was a marvellous feeling, and Jock told us to go straight over and celebrate with the supporters. We did a lap of honour and you can imagine the outpouring of emotion. It's the same as the present day. Our supporters had been nine years without a title, and that's too long. It was wonderful to be part of such a special day.

'After the game, Jock sat us down in the dressing room and said, "Apart from Greigy [John Greig], that's the first league title you have won at this club. That's what this club is all about, and that is what we expect."

'That was the old First Division, the last one before the formation of the new Premier Division, and we won that as well, so it was great to make a wee bit of history.'

The Rangers side of that era is rightly hailed as one of the club's greatest ever, and the season after the league title arrived at Ibrox there were greater riches lying in wait. Johnstone said, 'When you have ten Scottish internationals, it's fair to say we were a great side. We had the two Scotland keepers, Stewart Kennedy and Peter McCloy, [plus] Sandy Jardine, John Greig, Colin Jackson, Tom Forsyth, Tommy McLean, Willie Johnston, Colin Stein and myself, so we were arguably a better side than the one nowadays. It's maybe easier for me to say as I was a part of that team, but we were a fantastic side and we dominated a lot of games – and we went on to do it the following season as well.

'Jock was always looking ahead, and we bolstered that great side by signing another two Scotland caps in Davie Cooper and Gordon Smith, and Scotland were regularly qualifying for the World Cup finals in those days.

'We weren't a defensive team; big Jock wouldn't have that. We liked to win with a bit of style, and at times we played three at the back. We pushed Sandy and Willie Mathieson up the park, and they effectively acted as wing-backs, the same as we're doing nowadays but 45 years ago! We worked hard because we were very fit. Jock would take us to the Gullane sands every year. He was an Edinburgh man, and the sands were only five or six miles from where he was brought up. It was the hardest training you'd done in your life but you always felt good the next day; your legs were solid and you were raring to go. In those days we won a big percentage of our games in the last ten minutes because we were much fitter than the opposition.

'I'm not saying Jock was the greatest tactician in the world, and he would be the first to admit that, but he set the team up very well. He didn't have to coach us because of the experienced players he had in the side and they knew exactly what was expected once we got out on the pitch. The likes of Sandy,

Greigy and wee Alex MacDonald organised most things on the park, and we just got on with it. Jock's greatest strength was that he got the best out of players, which is the hard thing to do as a manager. A team can have all the skill in the world, but if you're not prepared to work your socks off for 90 minutes then it's no use. Jock got so much out of us. If he didn't think you had worked hard enough in a game, he would let you know. He knew we wouldn't win every game but if you gave everything he would back you 100 per cent. We learned that quickly.'

DJ cited continuity as one of the current team's biggest attributes, and it was also a factor in Rangers' treble-winning side of 1975/76, when Greig, McLean, Colin Jackson, MacDonald and Johnstone himself played more than 50 games each

He said, 'I didn't play centre-forward all the time. We had wee Willie Johnston who sometimes played in a two up front with Colin Stein, and there was Derek Parlane, who had a lot of goals in him, so sometimes I was deployed elsewhere. If we had an injury to Colin Jackson or Tom Forsyth, I would play at the back.

'Derek Parlane was our top league scorer in 1974/75 with 18 goals, and I was just two behind him, even though I played centre-half a number of times. I was still scoring as I was up for corners and free kicks. The way I saw it, my versatility meant I had three chances of getting a game. I could play at the back, up front or in midfield, where I played around 60 games. I would've played anywhere for Rangers, and that's why I played so many games. It's on record that I played 546 times for Rangers but add in pre-season games, friendlies, testimonials, etc. and it's well over 600, and 239 goals. I'm delighted with that.'

Johnstone was a huge favourite with the big Rangers support, but insists growing up in a household with five brothers helped keep his feet firmly on the ground. 'I grew up playing football on the streets of Dundee with my brothers. We had our own five-a-side team, and a sub, so I always had people around me, and if you weren't doing the right things they would let you know.

'The dressing room was a different environment altogether. That was hard because the banter is constant, and you could be the centre of it, so if you weren't prepared to think on your feet and answer back then you might be the one who got picked on. You read about players back in the day talking about bullying, but I don't think it was bullying. It was fun; banter. It helped me grow up quickly. Equally, if you were jumping about the dressing room like Billy Big Time, the senior players would soon calm you down by saying, "Once you've got ten international caps you can start bumming your load." You were brought down to earth very quickly.'

Johnstone sees parallels with many of the youngsters in Steven Gerrard's team, although none have come close to emulating the 16-year-old, barely out of school, when he nodded home the winning goal in the 1970 League Cup Final at Hampden Park against Celtic – in front of 106,000 fans.

He said, 'I'd been at Ibrox several months and had scored a few goals for the reserves. Now and again I would train with the first team, so I knew what it was like to be on the same training ground as these huge international players. Growing up, John Greig was my hero. I wasn't a Rangers fan – I supported Dundee United – but Greigy was the captain of Scotland, and any Scotland captain was good enough for me regardless of who he played for. So to share a dressing room or training ground with people like Greigy, Colin Stein or Sandy Jardine was such a wonderful experience. Learning what the game was all about from guys like that was priceless.

'I remember clearly on the day of the League Cup Final at Hampden, going into the dressing room, and it was about half one. It was a 3pm kick-off but within five minutes I was stripped and ready to play. I had my boots on, the lot. The others started laughing, and one of them said, "Get your clothes back on, we need to go out and have a walk round the pitch!" So I had to get dressed again. That's how excited I was.

'Greigy and Sandy took me aside before the match and said, "You'll be blown away the moment you walk out the tunnel and see so many people. It'll be that noisy you'll rarely hear what we're saying to one another. But the one thing you can't do is stop and look around at all these people on the terracing because you'll lose your concentration. Just keep your eye on the ball and if there's a free kick or someone goes down injured, one of us will come over and have a word with you." And that's what happened every time the game stopped. Wee Doddie [Alex MacDonald] or one of the others would come over and speak to me and give me a wee bit of advice, and it helped take my mind off the occasion and the size of the crowd. That was how I got through the afternoon.

'But the funniest thing is my reaction after scoring the goal. I didn't know how to celebrate properly! It was the stupidest thing I've ever seen. There I am, jumping up like a big woman. Had I not learned anything from playing in the street with my brothers? This was what I'd dreamt of. Whenever I scored I would celebrate like a proper footballer, and it always seemed pretty cool, but here I was ten years on and I didn't know what to do!

'I had only ever wanted to be a footballer, and all of a sudden I was playing for one of the big clubs in Scotland in a cup final at Hampden. That was magical.'

As soon as the players had received their medals, got showered and dressed, off they went into Glasgow city centre to celebrate their success. Not the goalscorer, though. He was having his dinner, some TV and an early night.

He explained, 'I was going away with the Scotland under-18 squad the following morning to Iceland. I didn't have time to go home to Dundee then come back again, so I stayed with John Greig's uncle in Bishopbriggs and he took me to the airport in the morning. I remember all the lads went out for a bevvy, but I was only 16, so I couldn't have gone with them. I sat in the house and had a nice steak and watched the telly.

'Off I went to Reykjavik next morning and the game was on the Tuesday night. About an hour and a half before kick-off, Bobby Seith, the under-18 coach, named the team and I wasn't in it – unlike Graeme Souness – and he turned to me and said, "I'm not playing you tonight as you don't have much experience," and I felt like saying, "Christ, I've just played at Hampden in front of 106,000 and scored the winning goal!" I had been an under-15 international, and I eventually played a few games for the under-18s, and I would also get some Scotland under-23 caps, so I managed the full set. I always enjoyed being part of the Scotland setup, and that particular time was really good for me.'

Included in the 14 major team honours won by Johnstone is the 1972 European Cup Winners' Cup. It was the pinnacle of his 14-year playing career with the Light Blues and still makes him proud to this day. He said, 'If you put it into perspective, Rangers have almost 150 years of history and have won just one European trophy, and I was lucky enough to play in that side. I reckon it's the single biggest game in the club's history. Others will have their opinions, perhaps treble-clinching games, etc., but in Europe you're playing against higher-quality sides. We played nine games to win the trophy, and nowadays you're asked to play a ridiculous number of qualifiers before you even get to the first round, but I reckon if you ask supporters of the three Scottish clubs to win a European trophy the majority would say it was the biggest game in their club's history.

'To go to the Nou Camp, have 99 per cent of the fans there, and to produce what we did for an hour was incredible. We lost the two late goals but I didn't think we were ever going to lose a third as Greigy had rallied the troops and told us all to make sure we played it much tighter at the back.

'The following night we were at Ibrox with the trophy and 30,000 Rangers fans turned up in the pouring rain to see us going round the track in a coal lorry! I think it was short notice and that was all they could get, but no one was complaining as it was just great to celebrate such a magnificent achievement with our supporters. I won a couple of trebles, but the medal I got for winning that night in Barcelona is my most prized possession.

'Colin Stein and Wee Bud [Willie Johnston] were fantastic all through that tournament. They ran defences ragged and scored the goals that mattered. But, for me, the man of the match in the final was Davie Smith. I think it was the first time the two of us had played together, and he said to me, "Go for everything, whether in the air or on the deck. Go for it. Try and get in front of the man if it's on the ground and get your tackle in, because if you miss, and he gets by you, I'll be at your back." That was a great confidence-booster. It meant I could commit myself, because there are times when you think, "Will I make it in time?" but I didn't have to think that way in Barcelona, I just did it. Nine times out of ten I won the ball, and the other time Davie would be at my back to sweep up.

'We also managed to get forward. I had three shots at goal, and Davie set up two of the goals. Moscow Dynamo played a certain way. They didn't really have anyone playing through the middle. Their manager had decided to go with two widemen to try and stifle Sandy Jardine and Willie Mathieson, as they liked to get up the park. He wanted to stop crosses into the box as he knew how devastating Colin Stein was in the air. But it meant Davie and I could get forward more. Davie was outstanding with the ball at his feet; so calm and collected. I would also try and get forward as often as possible and play a few one-twos, and have a couple of shots. I felt confident doing that because I also played in midfield and up front. It was ideal for Davie and I to play there.'

DJ admits he derived just as much pleasure from watching today's Rangers side win the league than he did when he was playing himself. And that pleasure extends back to the day when Steven Gerrard was announced as manager. He said, 'Steven is well respected by an awful lot of people, not just down south but all over Europe. He was a fantastic footballer, and a real leader on the park. Remember the time Liverpool were fighting for the league and he had them all in a huddle on the park. He was the one giving it laldy and trying to drive them on. That is the one thing that is a prerequisite for any successful manager. Leadership.

'He's come to Glasgow with a fantastic pedigree, and the knowledge he has accrued under some great Liverpool managers. He has obviously learned a lot, and has his own thoughts on the game as well, but it was probably still a wee bit of a gamble because he hadn't managed a club like Rangers before. He had been looking after the academy at Liverpool but that's nothing like Rangers; a massive club where we get 50,000 for home games and the pressure to win every week is all-consuming. He would have known that pressure at Liverpool as a player, but he might not have realised the pressure he would be under at Rangers. If he didn't, I'm sure he learned pretty quickly.

'He would know that Rangers hadn't won the league for many years and that he was being brought in to change that. Just listening to him that first day in the Blue Room was fantastic. Here was someone new to big-game management and I thought he handled the press really well. I was thinking, "That's half the battle." If you can't handle the press in Glasgow then you're under real pressure, and ever since then he has been fantastic. Every time he speaks you want to listen, because everything is from the heart and he tells the truth. If his team haven't played well he tells you that. He knows if he comes out and says they did well, when they clearly didn't, then supporters will see right through that, so he is honest with himself, his staff, his players and with the fans. I love that about him.

'It has taken him a couple of years to get things just right, but that was always going to be the case. He would have to learn that it takes a certain type to play for Rangers; someone who can handle the pressure that comes with being a Ranger.

'This season has been sensational. The football we played for the biggest part was a joy to watch. They were scoring goals for fun and defensively they were unbelievable, and when you look at the stats you can see quite clearly why we were so far ahead of the rest. The last time the league was won so early was 1902. The stats don't lie, and that's down to the board giving the manager time to work on his vision for the club. How many managers have been put out the door after a couple of years because it wasn't working? But that was never going to happen with Steven because everyone could see what he was trying to do, and he was constantly improving the team.

'The majority of players coming to our club were doing so because they loved Steven as a player and they wanted to work with him. He now has a fantastic squad with at least two for each position, and it doesn't seem to affect the way the team plays if he changes five or six players. We are still the same team and have that consistency and continuity, and that's vital. Especially when there are games every three or four days, you can't keep playing the same guys. You need to have that quality to change things up, and that's one of the main reasons we won the league.

'When you talk about contenders for player of the year, even though he hasn't been asked to do a tremendous amount of work in each match, Allan McGregor is right up there. And for a right-back, Tavernier was top scorer for nearly half a season, while Goldson has been the heartbeat of that defence, and keeps the team going. And then we have Steven Davis, who runs the show from the middle of the park. If it was down to me Davis would be my player of the year, but realistically it could be any one of six or seven, and that's another reason we're champions.

'That's also why there was such a big gap between Rangers and Celtic. Remember all the chat about how many Rangers players would get into the Celtic team, but let's flip that. How many Celtic players would get into this Rangers team? Not many, I'll tell you. Possibly just [Odsonne] Édouard, for his goals. If we're playing two up front then he would partner Alfredo, but that's it, because we have more than enough quality ourselves.

'When we clinched the league we were 20 points clear. That's the real gap between Rangers and Celtic – a true reflection of how the season went. Twenty points, and that's an incredible achievement – and turnaround. And that's down to Steven and his backroom team, guys like Gary McAllister, Michael Beale, and the others who have been constants on the training ground.

'The hardest thing now for the management team is to maintain these incredible standards. They have reached this level, and that's the level Rangers fans now expect, so it's up to the management and players to keep working hard and keep achieving.

'Players will leave in the summer, but we shouldn't expect a lot of transfer activity because the manager has been building this squad for a couple of years now.'

Title 55 has meant different things to different people, but Johnstone admits that after it had sunk in, his mind turned to those who had started off the journey. 'To be fair, when Steven came in, I heard a lot of Rangers fans say we were back, but I disagreed. We were back the moment we won the title. We are back fighting for and winning titles again, and that's the moment we say we are back. It has been a long journey, and there are plenty of people to thank.

'The first one should be Ally McCoist. On the Wednesday before we played Brechin City in the cup game [in 2012], we had six signed players. That's what he had to deal with. Ally and Ian Durrant, Jimmy Stewart and Kenny McDowall. They took on the job when a lot of people wouldn't have gone near it, and they started it all off.

'Sandy Jardine, God rest his soul, was magnificent. Anything to do with the football club, Sandy was involved. We all remember the fans' walk to Hampden to let the SFA know how we felt about things. When they put us down, Sandy was incredible.

'You look at Dave King, when he arrived with Paul Murray and John Gilligan, and Douglas Park, and the Three Bears who put money into the club, and that was when we started to get a grip of the situation. Steven Gerrard then arrived three years ago and has played a major part in our revival.

'So many to thank, but the most important people who saved this club are the supporters. For us to get 50,000 in the Third Division playing against teams like East Stirling and Annan was just phenomenal. No disrespect to any of these clubs, but to get the crowds we did in those days was simply unprecedented. Our supporters gave so many little towns and villages a big lift and a financial boost, so it was a win-win situation. Lots of folk benefitted from Rangers fans turning up in large numbers. And so it was for them that this title was won; the Rangers fans who stood by their club through thick and thin.

'Personally, I'm just delighted to still be associated with Rangers. There are around 12 of us – all ex-players – who go to the home games and cover the hospitality boxes. Guys who played loads of games for Rangers, some of whom played in Barcelona. We all meet up before the games and have a chat to see what we're doing that day and it's just wonderful. Someone should take a camera and film it because some of the patter is unbelievable.

'I've now been associated with Rangers for more than 50 years. I don't think it's over-egging the pudding to say we're all part of the Rangers family, because when we're in that room before the games, and chatting away, it's clear to see that every one of us just loves the club.

'It doesn't matter where you go in the world, there is always a Rangers supporters' club, and if there are just ten members it's a presence. We all stick together and that's the way it should be.

'Rangers mean everything to me. As a young lad brought up in Dundee, my father died when I was ten, and my mother had to bring up six boys, which was a tough job for her. My mother only ever saw two Rangers games in her life. The first was that League Cup Final at Hampden when I was 16, and she was in Barcelona to see us win the European

Cup Winners' Cup two years later. Willie Waddell had told the players they could bring their wives or girlfriends, but Graham Fyfe and I took our mothers, so they looked after all the young women.

'To be involved with a club like Rangers and win three league titles, five Scottish Cups and five League Cups, as well as a European trophy – and 14 caps for Scotland – was beyond my wildest dreams. I was treated really well at the club and met an awful lot of good people in Glasgow.

When I say the words "I played for Rangers", it still means a hell of a lot to me!

Stephen Millar

Leeds, England

Rangers 3 Motherwell 1
Scorers: Roofe 73, 90+4; Itten 82
19 December 2020

'Seventeen minutes from ruining Christmas.' That's the way Stephen Millar describes one of Rangers' most important victories of the season. It was also a nerve-shredding experience for the legions of Bluenoses looking on from man caves the world over.

Just six days before Santa Claus was preparing to climb down chimneys – wearing a face mask, of course – struggling Motherwell visited Ibrox, bang out of form, and hoping to avoid a repeat of the 5-1 hammering Rangers had meted out at Fir Park earlier in the season.

The match came just three days after a first domestic loss of the campaign – a League Cup defeat at St Mirren – and here was the perfect opportunity for Steven Gerrard's men to get back on track.

Well, that was the way it was supposed to pan out.

'I was really looking forward to the game,' said Stephen, 'like I do every time we're playing, but we were almost halfway through our league programme and everything was going better than we could ever have imagined.

'Before kick-off I'm thinking Motherwell aren't playing too great, we're almost invincible at home, and we haven't conceded a league goal at Ibrox all season. All the ingredients for another three points. And when we go one down in six minutes I'm still not too worried. But with more than 70 minutes on the clock, and it's still 0-1, then I'm worried. I'm actually bricking it. The glass-half-empty guy takes over and I'm thinking that if we lose this one, a second defeat in a row, does the doubt start to kick in for the players and does the whole thing blow up in our faces?

'What made it even more difficult was that Motherwell were defending really well; throwing bodies in front of everything and clearing ball after ball from their box. Jermain Defoe had started brightly, and been unlucky a couple of times, but the visitors seemed resistant to everything. One of those afternoons?'

Christmas was in line to be cancelled, but Rangers these days are a different animal and didn't once resort to lumping high and aimless balls into the 'Well box for Declan Gallagher and co. to routinely clear into the Govan Rear.

Stephen said, 'It might have been different had there been a crowd in, but thankfully the players stuck rigidly to their philosophy and the chances eventually came. Funnily enough, when Kemar Roofe scored our first in 73 minutes, a draw suddenly wasn't enough. I wanted three points.'

And so too did the players, as supersub Cedric Itten scored eight minutes from time, then he looked on as Roofe scored his second in stoppage time to complete a remarkable comeback.

Stephen continued, 'The game reminded me a wee bit of Rangers-Motherwell games in the 1980s, when ex-Ranger Tommy McLean was in charge of the Steelmen and they would come to Ibrox and shut up shop. We all moaned like mad about their style of play, but it seems little has changed since then.

'I lost count of the late winners we would get against them – from guys like Ally McCoist and [John] "Bomber" Brown – but that's probably the best way to "reward" teams who turn up and park the bus. If playing like that is the best way for Motherwell, then fair enough, but I'm watching a game to be entertained, and to see my team win. At least I managed one of them!

'The gaffer brought on Joe Aribo for Glen Kamara at the break as there was clearly no need for two sitting midfielders. Every change Steven Gerrard made was positive. He has been criticised for his substitutions in the past, but not this time. Not like Mark Warburton, who seemed to wait until the 60-minute mark before making changes. Hagi was then introduced to try and carve open a tiring Motherwell defence. We were relentless in driving forward in the second half and you sensed the goal had to come.

'But it wasn't until the third went in that I felt a sense of relief; the first time I had relaxed all day. I was never too concerned about Motherwell as an attacking force but when it's 2-1 there is always the chance that a high ball into our box could cause an issue or two, but with the way guys like Goldson and McGregor are playing these days you're at least a wee bit more confident that we can deal with problems like that.

'After we got the second, our game management was terrific, and to see the likes of Hagi and Aribo take the ball out to the corner flag to waste a few vital seconds was good sense. When Roofe scored the clincher I jumped up and punched the air. My wife said, "Who are you playing?" When I said Motherwell, she just looked at me!

'But it was a massive three points, huge, although the title was the furthest thing from my mind. I thought that if we could get to the Celtic game still seven points ahead then we'd have a chance. Bearing in mind we had St Johnstone (away), Hibs at Ibrox and St Mirren away before then, it was a sensible approach.

'The Celtic game was the big one for me. Even though they had struggled in Europe, up until then they were playing well domestically and seemed to be winning most games, like they had done for years. (P.S. I didn't watch the Old Firm game. My wife had a check-up at hospital and I waited outside in the car. I didn't know the result until my brother-in-law messaged me. You can imagine my reaction!)

'Cedric Itten once again showed his value to the team by grabbing his fourth goal of the season, and most of the team on the day were a steady seven out of ten. But Steven Davis was my man of the match. He just kept the ball moving from back to front. He dictated the pace and used his wonderful football brain to prompt so many attacks.'

Stephen hailed the appointment of Gerrard by the Rangers board as a masterstroke, but was worried in the summer of 2018 because, as he put it, 'We couldn't have dropped much lower.'

He said, 'The 2017/18 season was a nightmare. We lost 4-0 to Celtic in the Scottish Cup semi-finals, and a fortnight later they beat us 5-0 in the league. Five times we played them that season and not once did we win. And to cap it all off we crashed out of the Europa League to Progrés of Luxembourg. Even with what had gone on from 2012 that was a real low point.

'Pedro Caixinha was a disaster, and Graeme Murty certainly wasn't the answer. I think we'd finished the season with Jimmy Nicholl in charge as caretaker. So when we appointed Gerrard I was delighted. He might have come with little or no managerial experience, but we all knew it had to be better than what we'd had previously. There isn't ever a guarantee of success – the previous seven years had taught us that we don't always get what we want.'

Stephen has great memories of being welcomed to Rangers in the 1960s. His dad, Jimmy Millar, made the introduction. It was the days when his dad's namesake was one of the top strikers at Ibrox.

Stephen recalled, 'Dad was a huge Rangers fan, and after he had taken me to my first game – Rangers v Hearts in 1965, a League Cup game at Ibrox – I never looked back. I didn't go to loads of games straight away, but the first I truly remember was a home match against Dunfermline in 1967. Our block in Bishopbriggs was full of Rangers supporters, none more so than future Rangers director John Gilligan. John's cousin Ann married the Rangers player Alex Willoughby, and I remember one Saturday morning seeing Willoughby and his cousin, Jim Forrest, the great Rangers striker, going into the house. I plucked up the courage to knock the door and ask for autographs – and within 20 minutes I was out in the back garden playing football with them!

'I was told Alex Willoughby was playing that day, and dad said he would take me. We were walking up the stairs in the Main Stand, and I remember marvelling at the size and grandeur of our stadium. It was October 1967. The game ended 0-0 and Willoughby did indeed play. There was just over 30,000 there and the atmosphere was fantastic. We remained unbeaten until the end of the season, until we travelled up to Pittodrie and lost 3-2. But the league was lost a couple of weeks beforehand when we could only manage a 3-3 draw at Morton. That killed our title hopes. We had shown a remarkable consistency but Celtic just pipped us to the title, and I think that was the third of their nine in a row.'

But despite losing the title by just two points on the last day of the season, and watching Celtic dominate for the next six years, Stephen was hooked. He said, 'I loved everything about going to Ibrox, particularly the big European games, like Newcastle United and Athletic Bilbao, and even recall the night there was 50,000 inside Ibrox to watch us play Leeds United on closed-circuit television! That was the true passion of the Rangers support. Four giant TV screens set up in the middle of the pitch like a huge cube, and fans watching on from all sides.

'When we were going to Ibrox for the European games in those days, my dad would stop at a pub in his native Springburn, and he would pop inside for one drink with a mate of his. I would be the proverbial kid outside with a coke and crisps! We would then head straight over to Ibrox and he would lift me over the turnstile. I don't think he ever paid for me to get in.

'My greatest European memory is probably the same for most Bears of my age. Rangers 2 Bayern Munich 0. European Cup Winners' Cup semi-finals, 1972. What a night. In my mind, it will never be topped. My team were going to a

European final, MY team! Of course, I wasn't going, but my team were. I was 12 when we reached that final and Rangers were everything to me.

'There were 80,000 like-minded people inside Ibrox that night. It was packed; just a mass of bodies. I was there early, and as it filled up so too did the excitement. It was a nice night, and it was a magical night. I have amazing memories of that Sandy Jardine goal flashing into the net. Going crazy. And then doing it all over again when Derek Parlane added a second. The singing in the second half was something else, and again when we streamed out of the stadium and heard that Dixie Deans had missed a penalty kick across the city in Celtic's semi-final against Inter Milan. That was the icing on the cake. My team were going to a European final!

'In those days my hero – again, like many Rangers supporters, young and old – was Colin Stein. He was magic, and helped by eight goals in his first three games for Rangers after a £100,000 transfer from Hibs.

'The only games I missed out on at that time was the Old Firm. My dad didn't go to them. It wasn't until I was old enough to go myself that I started going. I was supposed to go to the 1971 Ibrox disaster game, but my mum wasn't too keen so I didn't go. In 1971, like many folk from my area, we would watch Rangers when they were at home, and go to see Partick Thistle when Rangers were away.

'My PE teacher at school was Frank Coulston, whose claim to fame is that he was the only forward NOT to score when Partick Thistle beat Celtic 4-1 in the Scottish League Cup Final in 1971. He was a cracking player and I loved having him as my teacher.'

Like most supporters, Stephen didn't own a season ticket until the mid-1980s. He was working with William Hill, and with a Saturday being one of their busiest days, it didn't make financial sense to commit to a season book.

'It sounds crazy but it wasn't until I moved down to Leeds in 1980 that I started to see more games. It was a Monday-

Friday job and I would come home at weekends. When my son Jamie started to get into Rangers we got season tickets for the Broomloan Road stand, and I enjoyed that.'

But if a permanent move for the family to Leeds in 2006 seemed to put the kybosh on his love affair with the Light Blues, it certainly didn't turn out that way. 'I joined the Harrogate True Blues and they ran a 55-seater up to Glasgow for all home games. I was a regular fixture. It was a long day as we got picked up in Knaresborough at 7.30am, and didn't get home until 10.30pm, but it was a good day out. There was a great camaraderie on the bus, and it was well run by Andy Kerr, John Davidson and Les Harrow. We would arrive in Glasgow around 12.30pm and a lot of the guys would go for a pint, but I had the drive home to Leeds from Knaresborough so I didn't drink before the games.

'I'd taken the opportunity of moving down to Leeds permanently and it's something I've never regretted. Even though I'm so far from Ibrox, I don't miss out on much, especially with the internet being what it is. Occasionally I realise I'm 200 miles away, but that's only because apart from family, Rangers is the next most important thing in my life, and if something is happening at the stadium, you can't just "pop over"!'

Stephen has had some great experiences following Rangers, and none more so than his excursions into Europe in the late 1970s and early '80s. 'I went to games in Cologne and Porto, with the Bishopbriggs RSC. The Cologne trip was my first time abroad and it opened my eyes in many ways – like my first experience of unisex toilets in a German pub! "Excuse me mate, where's the gents'?" "Over there", but a woman just came out of there!

'I also saw my first ever Rottweiler, and got the fright of my life – thanks to the Schnapps! What the hell was that I just laid eyes on? They were police dogs, and they were pretty fierce looking. For some reason I don't recall much trouble at that game.

'Outside the ground there were grass pitches, and there was a game going on between fans of the two clubs, but I had just discovered the stein of lager, so I was otherwise engaged. But it was a great experience, even though we had 19 hours to wait on the ferry at Ostend on the way home. It was the first time I had ever been in a pub for so long. But even then, I still wasn't drunk enough to order the horse steak from the menu!'

Porto, in 1983, was another experience altogether. When Stephen was at Ibrox with some mates to pick up their ticket vouchers, they spotted manager John Greig driving along Edmiston Drive – and little did they know he had just resigned. Off they went to Porto, by bus, where they stopped for the night in San Sebastian as it was considered too dangerous to drive through Basque territory after the sun had gone down.

He explained, 'We filled up with flagons of beer and headed off on the marathon journey. By the time we had crossed the English Channel on the ferry, and negotiated the road through France, we docked in the prominent Basque city for the evening.

'We booked into the Hotel Castina, which was on the banks of the river. It was a beautiful city and so we went out for a few beers. There were four of us with two adjoining rooms. We stayed out pretty late, but we had a great time. Not for a second did we worry that the bus was leaving at 8.30 the next morning – on the dot. When we eventually awoke, it was 11.30am!

'First thing we did was check the adjoining room; empty beds. The other two had obviously made the bus but when we flew down the stairs and out into the street all we could see was a couple of old locals sitting enjoying a beer in the mid-morning sunshine. There was also a few stragglers around but the bus was well away.

'There were no mobiles in those days, so we made for the local train station and jumped on a train from San Sebastian to Porto – probably the equivalent of Inverness to Cardiff. It was one of those old-style trains with the passageway running up the side and the compartments which seated around six. Our train was packed, and we had to stand a fair bit of the way, but when we eventually got a seat we were sharing with four nuns!

'We arrived in Porto and headed straight to the stadium to exchange our vouchers for match tickets, and we were in the car park when the bus pulled in. The convenor said, "We thought you were both in the jail!"

'We had a great time in Porto, apart from losing the game, crashing out of the cup and being pelted with everything from hot coffee to bottles and cans.'

Fast forward a few years and Stephen enjoyed the Old Rangers Pics account on Twitter. He would post some of the pics he had, as would some of his mates, and it would inevitably lead to chat about past matches. Stephen had been recording *Scotsport* and *Sportscene* since 1982 and had many hours of footage of bygone Rangers teams, but couldn't upload it on to Twitter as at that time the maximum length of any video was just 30 seconds.

He said, 'Around this time, my son moved out and suddenly I had a room to properly organise my video tapes of Rangers games. It made things much easier to find as opposed to trawling through boxes of tapes. When I mentioned to the guys that I had all this footage, they suggested I start a Facebook page, as you could post any length of video on there.

'I did so and called it The Rangers Archives, more for the 15 or 20 guys who had expressed an interest in seeing the footage of the old games. Beforehand, I had been close to tossing out all the tapes, so it was great having a platform to do something positive with it. It was 2014, and we had around 20 members.'

It has grown ever so slightly since then, and now has 65,000 followers!

'I had no idea how popular it would become. It wasn't the greatest period of our history so it was important to show a lot of our younger supporters that we hadn't always been playing in the lower leagues. This way, loads of people got to see some of our greatest ever players in action. Sometimes these little clips keep the flame burning.'

Stephen's archive now contains between 25,000 and 30,000 hours of footage involving Rangers. There are thousands of matches, features, news reports and more, and over the years he has been lucky enough to meet others with great collections and incorporate much of them into his own.

He said, 'I now have seven external hard drives with four terabyte cards – and they're all full. I have a great filing system and can usually find a requested piece of footage in 30 seconds. I've been taken aback by some of the really kind comments I get from supporters, and completely blown away by ex-players who have got in touch to request a certain game or to say how much they enjoy it.

'I was invited to hospitality at Ibrox by Iain Sinclair, a great Rangers supporter, and had mentioned on the page that I was looking forward to it. Michael Mols said he too would be there and that he would love to meet me. Michael Mols wanted to meet me! I walked into the trophy room and there he was, and he greeted me by saying, "Hi legend." I was utterly gobsmacked!

'I've also had messages from the likes of Richard Gough, John MacDonald and Ian Ferguson, which is humbling. We have members in 60 different countries, and the whole thing is just crazy, but it gives me an enormous amount of pleasure knowing that people love watching the content.

'I get messages every day and it's only then that you realise what it means to some people. I've also heard of some folk using footage to show a relative who has dementia, because that's all they remember, and that alone makes it all worthwhile.

'I don't ever advertise the page as I'm a firm believer in give them good content and they will want to watch. It's a wee bit of escapism for me. We all have one thing in common and that's our love of Rangers.

'You don't realise it, but for a lot of supporters their timeline in life revolves around the club. What game was the day after your stag night? Who were Rangers playing the day you got married?'

Next step for Stephen and his team is a Rangers Archives website, where they will load up match reports and memorabilia from every Rangers game since 1960. Stephen said, 'There will be programmes, tickets and pics from as many games as possible. Guys like Ian Manson and Rick Russell have been assisting and have done a brilliant job. There will be links to footage, where available, and hopefully a page on every player who has played for Rangers in that period, as well as a digitised copy of every *Rangers News*. It is a mammoth undertaking but we do it because we love the club. When we signed up to become Rangers supporters we were making a lifetime commitment!'

Andy Cameron MBE

Glasgow, Scotland

St Johnstone 0 Rangers 3
Scorers: Roofe 23, Kamara 31, Hagi 47
23 December 2020

Rangers have won 30 league titles since Andy Cameron first saw his favourites in the flesh. It was the winter of 1945 and the Ibrox visitors were Moscow Dynamo, opponents still remembered for their poor arithmetical skills as much as their prowess on the football field. During the second half, both teams made a substitution and Rangers' international winger Torry Gillick began jumping around as if he had ants in his pants. He had spotted an anomaly. The Russians had failed to take a player off; they had 12 men on the field, and their red-faced manager was forced to withdraw one of his stars.

Seventy-six years later, and with no sign of any jiggery-pokery, the Light Blues lifted their 55th league title with a points margin the length of Edmiston Drive. And despite witnessing more than half of those championships, Cameron insists this latest success is up there with the greatest he has seen.

He said, 'It was something special. Our first title in ten years and I loved every minute of it. It was always about 55 for me. I wasn't too bothered about the ten. If they'd reached that landmark, so be it. I would've been gutted as we would never have heard the end of it, but rightly so as it's some achievement. They already had four successive trebles, and if that was my team I would've been content. But some Celtic supporters still prefer to talk about Rangers and I'll never understand that.

'We haven't had our troubles to seek in the last ten years, which makes this title all the sweeter. Administration was an awful time, and I still struggle to understand why David Murray sold our club, effectively to a hedge fund, for a pound. These people come into a business, get it back on its feet and sell it on for a profit. It's what they do. Why did Murray give Rangers to Craig Whyte for £1? I get that Murray wasn't really a Rangers fan; he was a businessman first and foremost, and I thank him for giving us Gazza, Laudrup, nine in a row, etc., but we went from that to watching a game in the Third Division where three balls got lost in a hedge!

'It was awful, but real. I was in the directors' room at that first game at Brechin, and the lower-league clubs always presented Rangers with a memento of their visit. That day, chairman Malcolm Murray – who was a Rangers supporter – was asked to say a few words, but Sandy Jardine thought it might be better coming from Charles Green, because regardless of what we thought of him, Green could charm the birds out of the trees. But the bottom line is these guys weren't the people to get us back on our feet, and for the situation he put us in, I will never forgive David Murray.'

Thankfully, Cameron and thousands of fellow Rangers supporters finally had something to cheer in March of 2021 when Rangers clinched the title. Two days before Christmas, though, Rangers faced a tough trip to McDiarmid Park, where a stubborn St Johnstone lay in wait. The two matches prior to the Saints game – a home win against Motherwell, and a 2-1 victory at Tannadice – were arguably our toughest of the season, but six points was a welcome return.

Cameron said, 'The manner in which we won the game was first class. It sticks out as another great victory. We played well as a team that night. The three goals were fantastic but I was particularly impressed by Hagi's effort. He hit the ball first time and it was perfectly positioned at the front post.

I know keepers get stick when they lose a goal at their near post but surely the player deserves a lot of credit for having the confidence and ability to shoot with such accuracy. The goals by Kemar Roofe and Glen Kamara in the first half at McDiarmid Park were both crackers.

'It was the opposite of the League Cup match at St Mirren the week before, when nothing seemed to come off for us. Just ten minutes into the second half in Paisley, I had a feeling it wasn't going to be our night. The attitude of the players didn't seem right, although thankfully that wasn't the norm.

'We've had some great results this season, and the win in Perth was as welcome as the others, but for me, the game which shaped our season was the 3-1 home win over Motherwell. It simply wasn't happening for us that day, and we'd seen that movie before – a Saturday afternoon at Ibrox, up against a team who had all but shut up shop, and try as we might, we couldn't make the breakthrough. In previous years, we would've resorted to an aerial bombardment, but not this time. The players stuck to their philosophy and scored three in the last quarter of an hour. Roofe and Itten were fantastic that day. A lot of supporters reckoned we had one hand on the trophy, but it was both hands or nothing for me.'

There were suggestions on some social media platforms that perhaps Rangers' biggest weapon against Motherwell was the lack of fans inside Ibrox that afternoon. Cameron said, 'A few folk did mention that the team might not have been able to play the way we did had Ibrox been full. There are two sides to that argument, but I remember speaking to big Colin McAdam one day. He was a big warrior for us and nothing seemed to phase him. The big man gave the impression he would have run through brick walls for the club, but the first time I spoke to him was up at Aberdeen, and I asked him if he enjoyed playing at Pittodrie. He said he loved it. He also said he enjoyed playing at Ibrox, but that the majority of our players preferred playing away from home, because if they didn't score coming out the tunnel a lot of fans were soon on their back! I don't miss many home games, but that shook me up a wee bit.

'Years later, I was talking to Walter Smith after we'd won eight in a row. It was the first game of the following season, against Raith Rovers at Ibrox, and the league flag had just been unfurled. Twenty minutes in and it was goalless. The ball goes out of play next to the dugout at the East Enclosure, and Archie Knox goes to retrieve it. As he picks it up, one punter shouts, "Haw, Knox, this is shite!"'

Cameron was born in London in 1940 but was brought up in Rutherglen by his granny. His uncle Joe was a Clyde supporter but took him to many Rangers games, including that iconic match against Moscow Dynamo.

He said, 'When I was a kid I would go to either Hampden, Shawfield or Third Lanark's Cathkin Park to look for bottles (which got me sweets). They were all really close to Rutherglen.

'The match against the Russians is the first I have any real recollection of. It was the most keenly anticipated match in Scotland since the end of the Second World War and I was there, along with 90,000 others. There were reports of supporters queuing for hours to get into Ibrox. My uncle Joe took me and I remember sitting on his shoulders to watch the match. He was wearing his Navy uniform. The world has changed so much since those days and football is very different.

'I'm glad Uncle Joe took me to Ibrox, because I loved the whole occasion and it helped shape my life. When I was 15 I started to take a real interest in the team and the players. I loved the Iron Curtain defence, although Willie Waddell, known as "Deedle", was my all-time favourite player.

'Uncle Joe and I would get the train from Rutherglen to the White City and walk along to Ibrox. He would lift me over the turnstile. I always felt a great sense of expectation going to Ibrox, and I genuinely still feel that today.

'I recall one occasion, when I was nine or ten, and Uncle Joe couldn't go to the game, so I decided to go myself. I skipped on the train and got lifted over at Ibrox. I was quite proud of myself but when I got home my granny went mental. She thought I'd been outside playing and when she couldn't find me she started to worry. I learned a lesson that day.'

Cameron has been to an incalculable number of matches with his friend, Andy Bain, and he said, 'Andy was a massive Rangers supporter, and absolutely hated missing a game. On one occasion he was in hospital to get kidney stones removed. It was a couple of days before the 1992 Scottish Cup Final against Airdrie. The surgeon said, "We need to operate," but Andy told him he had a cup final to attend, and that he would come straight back to hospital after the match and have the op. The surgeon told him if he left he wouldn't be allowed back in, so Andy reluctantly had the operation. It was only the third Rangers game he'd missed since 1945!

'There was the time we were going to Cologne to see Rangers and the bus was passing through Gelsenkirchen. Now, Andy only had one leg. He'd lost the other one during the Second World War. Anyway, the bus is motoring along the autobahn and all of a sudden Andy starts pointing and saying, "There, there, that's where I lost my leg!" And this wee Glasgow wideboy piped up, "You want us tae stoap the bus an' look for it?"

'Andy and I were members of a supporters group called the Dirty Dozen. The group included guys like the impresario Ross Bowie, and Joe Welsh, who had a coal business. Our bus was red, white and blue and one of the first games we went to was the second leg of the European Cup Winners' Cup Final in 1961, when we played Fiorentina. What a trip that was.

'I've been very fortunate that during my lifetime I have seen Rangers achieve great things. The Cup Winners' Cup in Barcelona, the first treble in 1949, and many other great successes, but for some reason I also remember a lot of the bad days. Like the Scottish Cup semi-final at Hampden, when Bill Struth was the manager, and we lost 6-0 to Aberdeen; 111,000 there and we turned in our worst performance of the 1953/54 season.

'Three years later we suffered a humiliating 7-1 defeat against Celtic in the League Cup Final. I went straight home after that game and right to bed. I was almost physically sick. I went in to work on the Monday morning and my tool box was painted green and white, with 7-1 all over it. In those days you argued with your workmates and gave as good as you got, but it was banter and that was that. Look at the Kemar Roofe challenge in the match against St Johnstone. He stretched to get the ball, unfortunately caught the player, and it was then analysed to death on TV and radio for days on end. We are all the poorer for that type of constant analysis. It doesn't help the game.

'I was 15 years old when I started going to the games on Hughie Donnan's supporters' bus. It was a great bus and left from next to Rutherglen police office. Hughie was a character and had great patter. One Saturday we were heading to Motherwell, and had just turned on to Rutherglen Main Street. The fog was thick and the driver could only see a few yards in front of him. Hughie was standing at the front of the bus and turns to the driver and said, "I'll tell ye this, if that fog goes away it'll not be mist." I know!'

Cameron has enjoyed a fantastic career as a comedian and entertainer, as well as the occasional appearance on *Top of the Pops*. It was 1978, and his single 'Ally's Tartan Army' – released to celebrate Scotland qualifying for the World Cup – rocketed into the charts, bringing nationwide fame. He recalled, 'I was 38 years old when I did *Top of the Pops* – it was madness. But the nation was caught up in a World Cup frenzy and I was glad to see the single do so well. Some years later, I was sitting in the house with my three kids from my second marriage, Jennifer, Elliot and Spencer, and we were watching a Terry Wogan show called *Auntie's Bloomers*, and Terry looks at the camera and says, "Remember that time back in 1978 when Scotland thought they were going to win the World Cup?" And it cuts to me appearing on *Top of the Pops*. The kids just looked at me – they had known nothing about it – and one of them said, "I have to go to school tomorrow!" and I got that look!'

Cameron explains how he first got into showbiz, 'I joined the Masons in the 1960s and at the end of our meetings, folk would be expected to do a wee turn; sing a song or tell a few jokes, etc. When it was my turn one night I thought I'd sing "Delilah" by Tom Jones, but I started far too high and completely blew it. I didn't know the words to any others so I started to do a wee routine and tell a few gags. I'd always loved stand-up comics.

'We would travel round other lodges and I was getting asked if I would do my routine for 20 minutes here and there. At one of the meetings I was invited to a stag do at the Rutherglen Glencairn FC social club. I was a guest, but as part of the evening's entertainment folk would get up and sing a song. Someone put my name up, so I did my routine, and it was well received.

'Unknown to me, an agent, Ian Wilson, was at the function, and he invited me to one of his showcase evenings in the Cambusnethan Miners Club. Representatives from many of the clubs in the west of Scotland would be there, and there was a chance of picking up some bookings. I had nothing to lose, so decided to give it a go.

'On the night, I was fourth up, which was tough as most folk would still be sober! But I did my turn, and it's strange how life works at times. Sometimes you just need a break, and that night was mine. I got 21 bookings on the back of a 15-minute slot, and it all took off from there.'

In 2015, Cameron was rewarded for a sterling career, and his charity work, with an MBE. It was a proud entertainer who headed to London to receive his award. He said, 'To go to Buckingham Palace and meet Prince Charles was one of those moments you never forget. It was such a lovely moment.

'I remember Jimmy Logan was putting together a Royal Variety Performance for Charles and Diana and he asked me if I would do my football hooligan routine. When he told me Hector Nicol was also appearing, a lot of folk were like, "Aw naw, no' Hector Nicol," and they were waiting to see just how "blue" he would be. When Hector came on, I was at the side of the stage. Not to get a better view of him, but to see the reaction of Charles and Di. Hector started off with the gag, "Never make love on a stretcher, you're liable to get carried away!" I looked up to the royal box and it was quite clear Hector had won over our esteemed guests.

'After the show, we were all waiting backstage to meet the royal couple, and to this day I'm still proud of a lovely photograph I have of myself, Hector, Una McLean and Charles and Diana. It's a much cherished memento of a great night.

'But fame is a funny thing. I remember being at the Rangers Rally in 1961. I was a bus driver at the time and I was sitting there enjoying the show with everyone else. Next minute, the compere, the great Lex McLean, and our captain, Bobby Shearer, come off the stage and are walking up towards me. Next thing, this woman, shouting and bawling, is heading towards them, so they stop right at my seat. I couldn't believe my luck. The woman rolls up her trouser legs, and says, "Are you Bobby Shearer? Every time my man comes in drunk he says I've got legs like Bobby Shearer!" It was hilarious.

'When I met the great Jimmy Millar, I couldn't wait to get into work the next day to tell everyone about it. And then when I got my MBE I was told that an old schoolfriend of mine had been talking to my mate and saying, "I hear Andy got an MBE. He was in my class at school, you know." And suddenly folk are talking about me the way I was talking about Jimmy Millar or Bobby Shearer. It's a strange thing.'

But when you're having a conversation with Andy Cameron, most roads lead back to one topic – Glasgow Rangers. It's in his DNA. And before you know it, he's talking about his greatest moment as a supporter. 'Like many other Bears, it has to be Helicopter Sunday. As you know, there was little chance of us winning that title. Celtic were leading 1-0 at Fir Park and the helicopter set off for Lanarkshire to deliver the trophy. We were winning 1-0 at Easter Road, but we needed Celtic to at least draw, as we had a slightly better goal difference.

'I was in the Easter Road directors' box with Sandy Jardine, and you could've heard a pin drop. All of a sudden there is this mighty roar, and our fans started celebrating, so Sandy and I started jumping up and down. After the game we were invited into the directors' room and the Hibs chairman, Ken Lewandowski, comes over to Andy Bain and myself and hands us a glass of champagne. Ken and I were pals, but he said to me, "Andy, just so you know, this champagne isn't for Rangers winning the league, it's to celebrate Hibs getting into Europe!" "Right you are," I said, and we all supped up and had a good laugh.

'I couldn't believe we'd won the league in such incredible circumstances. It was the most amazing feeling. My son Spencer and I popped into Ibrox on the way home and what a time we had. Barry Ferguson, big Dado Pršo, Peter Løvenkrands, Allan McGregor, etc. formed a big circle and put me in the middle, and drenched me in Budweiser. I was soaked to the skin, but what a happy soaking!

'And then the door burst open, in walked Marvin Andrews and every single player and coach stood up and applauded. Barry explained how big Marv had been keeping everyone's spirits up all week. And he was late because as soon as the match had finished he had gone straight to his church in Kirkcaldy to preach! What a man.'

But back to the 'present', and Cameron rewinds to the day Steven Gerrard was appointed manager. 'It took me about an hour to know he was the right choice. I was watching his arrival on TV, and enjoying the welcome he got from a packed enclosure. He was waving to supporters, giving them fist-bumps and he looked really happy to be here.

'I wouldn't say I was confident he was going to be a success, but he was a football man, and to me he looked every inch a Rangers manager. I look back at 1920, when tragedy hit Rangers and the great William Wilton lost his life in a boating accident. Bill Struth was our trainer and he got the manager's job. He hadn't done it before, but he had learned off a great man, and he is still the most successful manager in our history.'

With the league trophy secure, Cameron is hoping Gerrard will hang around for a while longer to oversee further success. He said, 'It's a difficult one. Liverpool are obviously his team, and we know that, like every other manager, he is only here for a spell. He has a contract at Ibrox until 2024, and I would love him to see that out, and perhaps even extend it for a couple more years. We are on a solid financial footing at the moment and it would be good to see what he could achieve.

'He has a great way about him and he has done a terrific job. I also like the way he operates in the transfer market. He has made some really good buys. The likes of Balogun, Bassey and Aribo are all good players. I also like the look of Scott Wright, and believe he can be a big player for us.

'I've watched every single game this season, and even when I was visiting my sons in Dubai and Singapore, I still managed to see the Rangers. Of course it's not the same watching your team on TV but it's the rules and we have to abide by them. On one hand you're gutted because you can't go to the game, but on the other it's made bearable as we've been so successful.

'Supporting Rangers has been a huge part of my life, and I've been very fortunate to get up close and personal with many of our players over the years. I remember doing a gig in Jim Baxter's pub one night. We were "pushing over the pennies" he had collected for charity, and at the end of the night I was sitting chatting to the great man over a coffee. Baxter was an outstanding footballer, one of our very best, but he said he couldn't believe the players didn't catch sight of a ball until the day of a game. They trained at Ibrox every day and would emerge from the tunnel and on to the running track, where trainer Davie Kinnear would be standing, and say, "Go right."

'One day, Baxter asked if they could mix up training to make it a bit more interesting, as it was the same every day. The following day, when the players were coming out of the tunnel, Kinnear was standing at his usual spot, and as Baxter approached, he said, "Go left." I was in stitches.

'My football team is everything to me, but I don't go in for a lot of the extracurricular stuff. Over the years I've worked everywhere and anywhere. I've hosted auctions at Celtic charity dinners, and I still crack jokes at Celtic's expense. I get a lot of good-natured banter, but that's what life is all about for me. They know I'm a dyed-in-the-wool Bluenose; I've never hidden it. But it's football first and foremost. My job is to entertain and if I get a booking to work at Celtic Park I take it.'

Cameron insists one of the greatest games he ever saw was the 1964 Scottish Cup Final win over Dundee, which clinched the treble for Scot Symon. He recalled the team, 'It was Ritchie, Shearer, Provan, Greig, McKinnon, Baxter, Henderson, McLean, Millar, Brand and Wilson. The Dundee keeper, Bert Slater, had a fantastic game and stopped us scoring at least six. It was 1-1 almost the entire game, but we scored two late goals. There was 120,000 inside Hampden, and two goals from Millar and one by Brand gave us the cup. We were superb and really turned on the style. One thing that sticks in my mind is the strip we wore that day. The famous blue and white vertical stripes, and I've often thought that in these days of three different tops, one of them should be that top as it was such an iconic jersey.

'I recall making a speech at a dinner one night, and mentioning that Jimmy Millar was my favourite Ranger of that era. After the speech, a clearly-annoyed Ralphie Brand pulled me up, and said, "What's this Jimmy is your favourite Ranger? He's not a better Ranger than me, in fact, he's a Hearts supporter, but I'm a Ranger through and through. We're both from Edinburgh but my uncle used to take me through to Ibrox when I was a boy."

'Ralphie Brand was a machine, but Millar was as tough as old boots. He was the best I've ever seen at holding the ball up and bringing others into the game. He used to take a lot of punishment but boy did he give it back. If you put

Jimmy and Mike Tyson in a boxing ring, I'm not sure who would win!

'I have been so fortunate, because there isn't a ground in Scotland I can't phone up and get a directors' box ticket. Even in the lower leagues, I'd be sitting in the directors' box at Stenhousemuir with Ian Durrant and Sandy Jardine listening to their words of wisdom. Durranty would say to me, "Don't fall into the same trap as a lot of people by watching the ball all the time. Look where the ball might go, see who's in the space, etc." I found it fascinating. But it shows how us punters see things differently from ex-players. I watched the Europa League home tie against NK Osijek with John Greig. I enjoyed the match, and the chat, but at one point Greigy said, "I'd take their left-back in a heartbeat." I'll be honest and say I didn't see anything special about him. I do now, and Borna Barišić has been one of our most consistent performers in the last couple of years.

'Seventy-five years I've watched Rangers. It's an absolute lifetime and you never forget the bad times, because that's what makes you able to enjoy the good times when they come along.

'When John Greig got the manager's job, I was close to him. I would pop into his office on a Monday morning for a cup of tea and a chat. We'd talk about anything other than football. Maybe golf, what was on the TV the previous night, etc., anything but football. He was going through a hard time but Greigy had a heart of gold and treated his players with respect and dignity.

'When we were in the Championship, I used to nip along to the players' lounge after every home game and take a player along to the suites to interview for the punters. On one occasion I grabbed Darren McGregor and he said to me, "Where are we going, Andy?" I said, "To the Chairman's Club for an interview. You'll enjoy it; it's good fun, and the punters love it. Oh, and what song are you going to sing?" He stopped dead in his tracks; beads of sweat forming. "Oh, but a dinnae sing," he replied, nervously. I told him it was a tradition, and that everyone sang a wee song after their first interview. So we finished the interview, and Darren had been good value, chatting away and interacting with the supporters. He started to walk away, and I said, "Darren, the song," and then gave him a big smile. The relief was written all over his face. That night, I got a text from Ally McCoist telling me I'd stitched the big man up a belter!

'I go over to Tipperary every year to play golf with a crowd of mostly Celtic fans. We have some great banter, but all I was getting recently was how they were going to celebrate ten in a row. I think the majority of Celtic supporters thought all they had to do was turn up and claim the ten. Well, they were wrong. Their complacency came back to bite them on the bum! They made some bad signings, while Steven Gerrard was working away quietly in the background to make the team better and prepare for the new season.

'That said, I couldn't believe we were 21 points clear at one point. I'd believed all the hype and thought the ten was a foregone conclusion. But we were terrific, and our performances in Europe were a bonus, because we weren't up against teams who were sitting in with two banks of four. Most teams had a go and that suited us down to the ground. To play so well against teams like Benfica showed how far we'd come under Gerrard.

'And when that culminated in winning the league title, I was euphoric. The 2020/21 championship is one I will never forget.'

Stephen Purdon

Glasgow, Scotland

Rangers 1 Hibs 0
Scorer: Hagi 33
26 December 2020

For the first time in more than a decade, the Purdon family was together on Christmas Day. Normally Stephen would have been treading the boards in Scotland's favourite pantomime at the Pavilion Theatre in Glasgow, but on this occasion Nicola and the kids had him all to themselves.

The coronavirus pandemic forced the closure of all public venues; the entertainment industry, of which Stephen has been a big part for the last 20 years, had ground to a depressing halt.

But after the Christmas Day festivities were over in the Purdon household, Stephen still had the football to look forward to the next day.

Rangers v Hibs at Ibrox Park. As normal there would be no supporters in for the game, but Stephen was able to retreat to his Rangers-themed man cave, and as he ran through his usual matchday routine of checking the TV was working, that the fridge was well stocked and making sure the blinds were tilted to the right angle, the nerves started to kick in. A wee bit more than usual, as Stephen recalled: 'Hibs have become almost like Aberdeen in the last couple of years. They seem to think they have a big rivalry with us and are always up for the battle.

'For us, it's just another game, but a tough one nevertheless because of the way they approach it.

'The game itself was a good one. Would I say I enjoyed it? Probably "enjoyed" would be pushing it. If you didn't see the game but read the papers the next morning, you could be forgiven for thinking we were hanging on at the end, but that's nonsense. Hibs had a decent early chance, they battled well, and never really went away, but that's about it. We were never losing that match.'

There was only one goal in the game – but it was a thing of beauty. Kemar Roofe took up an intelligent position to receive a pass before playing a low cross along the six-yard line, which Ianis Hagi anticipated superbly and got in front of his marker to stroke the ball past Marciano.

Stephen agreed: 'Roofe does really well, initially, but Hagi's off and running before the ball leaves Roofe's foot and the defender isn't on the same wavelength. It wasn't the most sensational goal in terms of distance or speed, but it was still a great goal – and it won the game for us.

'Hagi has come in for a wee bit of criticism from certain quarters during the season, but he's young and intelligent, and he never hides. He always shows for the ball and I love that in a player. I was delighted when we signed him on a permanent transfer because he was so highly rated on the Continent. He was the face of Pepsi and such a high-profile player.

'Hagi has contributed a lot to our league success. His numbers are excellent. Just look at the amount of assists he had, and passes completed successfully. He has a great football brain and it's probably no exaggeration to say that he and Roofe are on the same wavelength on the park. He's always buzzing about and trying to find space to receive the ball. I really like him.

'Our recruitment has been first class under Steven Gerrard. When we signed Glen Kamara for £50,000 from Dundee, a lot of people, including myself, were saying "Glen who?" but he has proved a fantastic capture.

164

'Kamara is a joy to watch. The way he changes speed and direction to ghost past players reminds me so much of Michael Mols in his prime for Rangers, and I loved watching Mols. Remember the Old Firm game at Ibrox the season before last when Kamara went past Scott Brown as if he wasn't there and set up the goal for Scott Arfield. Genius.

'If Kamara has a good Euros [the delayed Euro 2020 championship, taking place in the summer of 2021] his value will soar, and then there is the Champions League, which is another huge stage. He looks as if he can perform at any level, anywhere in the world, so it could end up being one of the best bits of business Rangers have conducted in many years. Borna Barišić should also be added to the list.

'There are a few players who fall into the same category. Most clubs are now selling clubs, and to remain competitive it's vital that our recruitment policy is good, and at the moment it looks perfect.

'The win over Hibs put us 19 points clear, and it was our 12th in a row (the last time we'd failed to win a league game was Hibs at Easter Road), so we were in a good place. The way I looked at it, though, was that we had bigger games on the horizon so the Hibs game was a must-win. Our next one was at St Mirren, and we'd lost at their place just a couple of weeks previous in the cup, so that was a big one, as was Celtic at Ibrox and Aberdeen away.

'When your defence is playing as well as ours is then you know that one goal will probably win the game, and that's the way I felt throughout this game. We also have a new-found resilience about us and are able to see games out much better than before. It's what champions do.

'So I was delighted to get the Hibs one ticked off, and even though it's a well-used phrase, it might have been the kind of game we would've drawn or lost two years ago. You know the type, a Connor Goldson drag-back, we lose possession and bang! Thankfully the big man has cut that type of thing out and was immense for us throughout the season. An absolute rock!

'With the grounds now empty, you hear which players are the shouters and who are the quiet ones. I know Tav's the captain, and I love him to bits, but big Connor is always talking to the players around him and barking out instructions. He is a real leader of men.'

Seven days before the Hibs match, Rangers showed fantastic resilience to come through a tough encounter with Motherwell, and three late goals meant the points remained at Ibrox. 'That was a massive test. I'm sitting in my man cave, virtual season ticket in my hand, and kicking every ball and getting extremely frustrated, not just with Motherwell's two banks of five but with my own players for not being able to break them down. Then it hit me. Does my frustration, along with the frustration of 49,999 other Bears, make it easier or tougher for the players in a situation like this?

'Regardless, it now seems drilled into the players, no doubt due to endless hours on the training field, that Steven Gerrard wants the players to keep prompting and probing until the final whistle. He doesn't want to see high balls lumped into the box for giant Scottish defenders to clear.

'Hibs didn't play such a low block, but we got there in the end and it was an important win, regardless of how it was achieved. Ibrox is a hard place for players if things aren't going well, but the likes of Tav, Goldson, Arfield and McGregor have all been there and endured it.

'From the start of the season, the players have looked so hungry, possessed almost. Is this the best Rangers team I've seen in my years supporting the team? Probably not, but they don't half work for one another, and they have so many other great qualities.

'It's Gerrard's footballing philosophy. But does that mean re-educating us supporters? And does it make it slightly easier for us to be re-educated because we're all sitting watching at home? It's a tough one, because maybe in the "Motherwell" situation, us getting on their backs isn't helping, but the flipside is it might be easier for them to down tools in that situation as they aren't getting anywhere against a parked bus and there is no one in to shout at them.

'But there is still Steven Gerrard, and he's probably their main worry. Gerrard has made progress every season, although it's difficult to remember another Rangers manager lasting two seasons without winning a trophy.

'Of course, he was clearing up the mess left by the likes of Warburton, Caixinha and Murty, so it was never going to be a quick fix. Probably the Scottish Cup defeat at Tynecastle in February of last year was as low as it got under Gerrard, and I think he came quite close to walking, but he has obviously gone away, did a fair bit of soul-searching and came back a stronger man and started to really implement the way he wanted to play. That might just have been a big turning point for the gaffer.

'I remember watching Rangers TV, when Walter Smith was a guest, and the great man was talking about Gerrard and saying how he had brought a certain amount of dignity and respect back to the club and position. His stature is something else. He looks and acts every inch a Rangers manager; exactly what you would expect our gaffer to be.

'Gerrard has been a winner from the day he was born. He has a winner's aura around him and you just know that with this first success, more is sure to follow because he doesn't look the type that will settle for anything less.'

This season has been one of the most incredible on record. It has been about Rangers getting back to what many view as their rightful place in Scottish football; about winning that elusive 55th league title; about stopping Celtic's quest for a tenth successive league championship. It has been all these things and more.

So, what number was most important for Stephen – 55 or ten?

He answered, 'For me it was about winning the league, and getting 55. I didn't want them to get to ten either, as no one wants their rivals to get one up on them. But more than anything it was about looking back to where we'd been during that shambolic period from 2012 onwards, and something that took us such a long time to recover from.

'From watching us play East Fife or Brechin City away on BBC Alba, and not knowing whether we were winning or losing because we couldn't understand a word the commentator was saying!

'It was about Pedro Caixinha hiding in bushes, Graeme Murty, Kevin Kyle, etc. The list is endless and we've taken a battering on social media, so this is for all that. We've been Rangers fans for many, many years, and we've witnessed our fair share of success, but the period from 2012 in the lower leagues seemed to last an eternity. So, it's about all that.'

Stephen remembered getting his hopes up in 2019/20 when Rangers went to Parkhead between Christmas and New Year and won 2-1, thanks to goals from Ryan Kent and Nicola Katić. 'I thought that was it; our time, but we imploded after coming back from Dubai and terrible results against Hearts, Kilmarnock, St Johnstone and Hamilton meant it was game over for another season.

'So this time round I was more cautious. That said, we'd been so many points ahead for so long that it was difficult not to get a wee bit carried away. We had always played a few games more than Celtic, but anybody will tell you that points in the bag are better than games in hand. Especially when you look at Celtic's form in January, winning just one of their first four games, so games in hand don't always automatically equate to maximum points.

'We'd been putting pressure on them virtually the entire season and it was nice to see how they would react to that for a change, and they didn't react too well, did they?'

Stephen has no idea who he would vote as his player of the year. 'Can I vote for them all? Seriously, it has been a real team performance. It's that togetherness that got us over the line. You watch the game at Easter Road at the end of January and there are 80-odd minutes on the clock and Steven Davis is sprinting from the middle of the park to cut out a Hibs attack.

'Before Arfield got injured he was a pivotal player for us, as has been Tav, Goldson, McGregor and others. But I look at Tav, and I see a player who was there when we were in the Championship. He has been through some dark times with us, and it was emotional to see him lift the trophy.

'In Tav's first season he was the Blue Cafu, bombing up and down the flank and looking a real threat. Then, when we went up to the Premiership, he seemed to lose his way a bit. I was thinking, "Oh, he's getting found out," but I was wrong. He's a completely different player under Gerrard, and that free kick he scored at Tannadice was one of the best I've ever seen.

'Away from the park, too, you never hear any negativity about him. He's a proper Ranger. Turns up and does his job. Steven Gerrard has instilled proper standards again at the club and that's fantastic.

'Ryan Jack is also morphing into a leader, and in a team with lots of big personalities that's quite an achievement. When he returned from injury against Ross County at Ibrox, you could see the hunger in his eyes. I try not to take the way we play these days for granted, and I struggle to think of a better team goal than the one he scored that day, but if that had been Manchester City or Bayern Munich it would have been on a Sky Sports loop!

'If I can go back to the start of the season; pre-season, in fact, and the tournament in France. We played superbly against both Lyon and Nice and I remember thinking that if we could take that into the season we would be okay. It was only pre-season but we looked good. So, the signs were there very early on.'

As the season wore on and Rangers looked in their rear-view mirror and saw Celtic morphing into a little dot, supporters such as Stephen started to breathe a sigh of relief. He said, 'I was pleased to see them become that dot. I wasn't interested in a close, two-team fight for the title. I'd suffered years of agony at the hands of my Celtic-supporting mates, so this was payback – and on a grand scale.'

Like many Rangers supporters, Stephen was delighted to see Ibrox become something of a fortress again, as it had been a long time coming. 'You always want your ground to be an intimidating place for visiting teams. It's something we've enjoyed a lot while I've been going to Ibrox, and to get that back is so important. I hark back to the Ross County game. We won 5-0 against a side who had just thumped Aberdeen 4-1, so it was a cracking result. After the game, their manager John Hughes praised Rangers for their great football and said, "That's the way you play the game."'

As a lifelong Rangers fan, Stephen has witnessed plenty of great times, talented players and trophies galore. But it's the simple things he misses the most; the bits we all used to take for granted, as he explained, 'I miss the whole Saturday afternoon ritual. Meeting my mates. Driving to the game and parking the car. Walking up to the stadium and drinking in the whole matchday atmosphere. Standing on Edmiston Drive chatting to folk and waiting to go into our seats in the Main Stand.

'From the moment my dad took me to my first game at Ibrox – against Beitar Jerusalem in the Champions League – I was hooked. The atmosphere was incredible; I'd never known anything like it.

'One of my favourite games was the Parma European match at Ibrox. What a game and what a night. For atmosphere, the Old Firm game that ended with Mo Edu scoring the winner is right up there. I had a ticket for Bar 72 in those days and that game sticks out like a sore thumb. Most recently, the Legia Warsaw Europa League game at Ibrox was unbeatable for atmosphere.'

When Stephen got the gig as Shellsuit Bob on the BBC Scotland drama *River City*, he was able to buy his first season ticket. That was a nice bonus. It was almost 20 years ago, and the character who didn't even have a surname in the early days is now the only original cast member left in Shieldinch.

'I feel so blessed to still be part of such a great show. To go from the last actor to be cast in a part to number one on the daily call sheet is a dream come true. I'm very proud of it, and often have to pinch myself – or maybe I just haven't been found out yet!

'In all seriousness, it has given me some incredible times. But I'm only a small part of a big team down at the studios in Dumbarton and I've been surrounded by an incredible crew since the day I started in 2002. I love my job and I just try to be as professional as possible when I'm working.

'During the coronavirus lockdown we were lucky to still be working. Sure, it was like a ghost town at times, as we couldn't work with more than two people, which meant no big scenes in the Tall Ship, but the need to stay safe was greater than anything else, and we were luckier than a hell of a lot of other actors who couldn't work because live venues were closed.'

And that meant no repeat performances of a live show that grabbed Stephen by the scruff of the neck – and had him shaking with fear in the wings. He explained, 'When I was asked if I would like to be a part of a live theatre show called *Rally Roon the Rangers* I didn't have to be asked twice. Celtic have had a few shows in the past, so why not us?

'Script readings and rehearsals went really well and we were all ready for opening night, or so we thought. I've worked live theatre for about 17 years, doing panto every year at the Pavilion, as well as other shows. I'm a veteran! But Grado and I were standing behind the curtain, waiting for it to go up, and "Four Lads Had a Dream" was playing in the theatre. The place erupted; it was bedlam. I had never heard an audience like it, and I looked at Grado, he looked at me, and the two of us were shaking. It was unbelievable.

'The theatre was rammed every night and we had the best time ever. Obviously the boss was delighted! Sadly it had to be cancelled last year, and it was supposed to be moved to this summer. How good would it have been going on stage every night for three weeks knowing we'd won the league?'

There is perhaps just one thing that can top that. A month or two before Gerrard was announced as the gaffer, Stephen was invited to take part in a Rangers Legends game at Ibrox. He said, 'It was just the most amazing experience; like watching a nine-in-a-row video, but playing in it. Imagine saying Ally McCoist had passed to you at Ibrox. Ally McCoist!'

Alan Denniston

Eaglesham, Scotland

St Mirren 0 Rangers 2
Scorers: Roofe 27, Morelos 33
30 December 2020

When Celtic arrived at Ibrox on league duty in November 2004, fans of both clubs were expecting big things. Rangers had just chalked up four successive league wins, including a 5-0 drubbing of Aberdeen, while the visitors were on a three-game Premier League winning run, with a Champions League victory over Shakhtar Donetsk thrown in for good measure. Something had to give.

With just 15 minutes on the clock, Nacho Novo stepped up to take a penalty for Rangers, awarded after he himself had been fouled by Joos Valgaeren. The diminutive Spaniard – with a heart of a lion – had just signed from Dundee for £450,000, but approached the ball with supreme confidence before burying it behind Magnus Hedman; 1-0 Rangers.

Ibrox erupted as though constructed on top of an active volcano. Alan Denniston was working as a camera operator that afternoon for Setanta Sports, and was stationed in the Main Stand. He recalled, 'The main camera gantry at Ibrox is slung at the front of the club deck and sometimes when a goal is scored in a big match the deck has, as part of its structural design, a slight bounce caused by the thousands of fans above us. That particular afternoon, the match atmosphere completely gripped me and I have to admit I added a little extra bounce to the close-up on Nacho after he scored the penalty – but that was a one-off!'

In a 30-year career behind the lens, he has covered in excess of 2,000 games for a whole host of broadcasters. But in the 2020/21 season Alan and several other Gers supporters in the camera crew reckon they were amongst the luckiest Rangers fans alive. With supporters locked out of stadiums up and down the country, he was with the team almost every step of the way on route to lifting the league title.

And never was he happier than when the team eked out a fantastic win at St Mirren Park, on the afternoon of Wednesday, 30 December. The victory successfully completed a tough 2020 for Steven Gerrard's side.

Jim Goodwin's Buddies had inflicted a rare domestic defeat on Rangers just a fortnight beforehand in the quarter-finals of the Scottish League Cup on the same ground. On that occasion, Gerrard had rested key personnel such as Barišić, Kamara and Davis, perhaps underestimating Saints slightly. There would be nothing of the sort this time round as the disappointment of missing out on the first trophy of the season still hung in the air.

As he filed into the stadium, from one of the main entrances on Paisley's Greenhill Road, Alan sensed this game would be different; this afternoon, league points were up for grabs, and Rangers would fight until the last whistle to maintain their unbeaten league record. It was Rangers' 21st league match of the campaign, and it was already Alan's 43rd.

He said, 'I've been covering football in Scotland for over 30 years, resulting in well over 2,000 matches. In the season just finished, that number was somewhere around the 100 mark, and included Rangers' great Europa League run. Sadly it was 100 more than any fan, which was a great shame, as many of these supporters had shelled out for season tickets – and every Rangers supporter wanted to be there when the team achieved 55.'

But there was another reason why a campaign with no supporters was a strange experience for guys like Alan. He explained, 'Normally during the build-up to kick-off, shots of fans in the ground form a key part of creating the atmosphere. A lack of fans is always noticeable at Rangers games, especially home games.

'Then you have the big European nights at Ibrox, which simply isn't the same when the stadium is empty. Picking out the great fan shots is an enjoyable part of our job. Many times, after one of these shots, I've wanted to go back and see them on their phones reading the messages, "You've just been on the telly!"

'A few years ago I did manage it when I spotted a girl in the crowd looking sad. I was delighted when we used the shot, and it was quite obvious that the multitude of messages coming through on her phone had put a smile back on her face as she was beaming from ear to ear. It was a match at Tannadice and we had certainly made one young girl very happy indeed.'

Alan began his TV career at Scottish Television, working in the studios on shows such as *Cartoon Cavalcade* and *Scotsport*, but a real yearning to get behind the camera paid dividends after many hours dedicated to learning his new trade. He had thoroughly earned his first set of 'cans'.

After eight years as a cameraman at Scottish Television's Cowcaddens HQ, Alan decided to take the plunge and go freelance. It was 1998, and while perhaps a natural move, it was still a bold decision to leave behind a steady job and head out into the often dog-eat-dog freelance world of competing for jobs and all the associated uncertainty that brings.

It was the correct decision, though, as since making the move he has been fortunate to cover more than 100 Old Firm matches, two Champions League finals, three UEFA Cup and Europa League Cup finals and three World Cups.

Add to that list events such as the London 2012 Olympics and Paralympics, the Confederations Cup in Brazil, the Women's World Cup in Canada, the Glasgow 2014 Commonwealth Games, 22 Scottish Cup finals and in the golfing world, 13 Open Championships.

He said, 'I've been very fortunate to cover some of the events that I have. It has been a wonderful experience. Being in countries like Russia and Brazil to work at the World Cup, one of the biggest sporting events on the globe, has been hugely satisfying. And there have been so many others, too numerous to give individual mention to. But when I look at the list of major events I've attended, it's a sobering experience.

'Still, and this might sound terribly clichéd, but the Rangers match at St Mirren was equally as important as the World Cup in Germany, or the Gold Cup in the USA, for two reasons. The first is that Rangers were chasing vital league points as they homed in on their first title in ten years.

'The second was a bit more personal. My son Scott is also a cameraman and we were down for cameras one and two, so we would be working side by side. He's a natural and I was proud to have him alongside me on the TV gantry.

'In previous seasons, I've always felt privileged to do the job I do but this season reminded me of that every time I entered a ground. The only way fans can watch the action is on TV and, of course, without camera crews this wouldn't be possible. Wednesday, 30 December 2020 was no different, although on this occasion the St Mirren v Rangers fixture had not been chosen by Sky for live transmission. This meant a reduced camera spec, primarily for highlights across broadcasters, although in the season just passed club TV channels really came to the fore by allowing fans to watch any game live. The match would be covered by four cameras. I was on the main wide camera and Scott was right beside me doing tight coverage and close-ups.

'Arriving and setting up was no different to any other game but because this was a Rangers match, we knew the audience would be larger and therefore more responsibility on everyone's shoulders due to the lower number of cameras.

'The run Rangers were on and, equally, the run Celtic were on was always going to keep audience figures high. Even more so because the only blip in Rangers' season had come on the same ground just two weeks earlier.

'The call time was 10am, which was comfortable compared to a live Sky match. With lunchtime kick-offs being the norm for the satellite broadcaster a call time of 7.30am is what you would expect. Also the match was in Paisley so for Scott and I, it was only a 30-minute drive.

'First things first and as soon as we arrived at the ground we immediately got on with rigging up the cameras. It was cold but fortunately dry, so as with any outside work we were all grateful. QTV Sports were providing the facilities, as they do with most SPFL matches that aren't chosen by Sky. Their pictures are then shared to all contracted broadcasters and to the club channels for fans to watch the games live; something that was so important this season.

'As Scott and I were on the main cameras covering the match from the TV gantry, there was an extra buzz about us as we knew there would be a healthy number of Rangers fans watching on the club channel. Normally, Old Firm games are covered by 16 cameras, so it gives you an idea of the difference.

'Every time I'm asked to cover a Rangers game I'm delighted, as I've supported the club since I was a kid. I attended my first match in 1969, a home game against Dundee United, which was also Willie Waddell's first game in charge. Both Mr Waddell and I got off to a winning start as goals from Willie Henderson and Colin Stein gave us a 2-1 win. It was in the middle of Celtic's nine-in-a-row period, so it was a few years until we won the league.

'But I became a regular for the next 17 years, usually standing in the Rangers end around stairway 19. One of my favourite memories from that period was a 3-1 win over Celtic, when John Greig scored as all the Celtic players crowded the referee claiming for a penalty. Rangers didn't mess about. They took a quick goal kick and moments later there were three or four Rangers forwards up against one Celtic defender and the keeper. It was bound to end in a goal and thankfully Greig tapped it into the empty net. The scenes at the Rangers end were incredible. Great memories.'

And then in 1986, Graeme Souness arrived at Ibrox to revolutionise Scottish football. Alan said, 'It was time to buy my first season ticket. I was in the Govan Rear near exit GR3 and watched every home game from there until 1991.

'My favourite memory from that era is another Old Firm match, although we didn't win this one. It'll be no surprise to most that the game I'm referring to is the 2-2 match when Richard Gough scored a crazy equaliser in the last minute, as nine-man Rangers – with Graham Roberts in goal – came back from 2-0 down to snatch a glorious point. The noise that day was simply the best; it was bedlam.

'But in 1991 I gave up my seat as I was working most Saturdays for STV, and there was no point in renewing my ticket each year if I couldn't use it. While I was delighted to be starting a new and exciting career, it was still a sad moment giving up my seat.

'Back to the game at St Mirren Park, my 15th Rangers match of a strange season, and something I hadn't really got used to. When we arrive at a stadium it's always empty, but that trickle of supporters grows greater and greater as kick-off approaches and by the time the teams come out, the stadiums are usually packed.

'Europa League nights at Ibrox were the strangest of the lot. Big flags replacing fans is something I'll never get my head around. European nights at Ibrox have been completely iconic since I was a teenager. No matter how the team was doing, there was usually a big crowd in. As a youngster, my first big experience was Bayern Munich in the 1971 Fairs Cup. Gerd Müller scored a late winner for Bayern, but I was still hooked.

'I've worked on over 200 European matches, including the 2008 UEFA Cup Final in Manchester between Rangers and Zenit, but more than 60 of the others have been at Ibrox. From Parma in 1999 to Braga 20 years later the memories are still fresh. With the noise generated by the fans, any cheering or shouting from me whilst working would never be heard, and trust me that happened often. Of course, we live in strange times, so when Alfredo Morelos scored against Lech Poznań to equal Ally McCoist's European record I let out a huge yell of delight, forgetting the stadium was near empty. Thankfully, several others did the same; coaching and backroom staff for example, but it shows that even without fans the European experience still gets to you.'

There were few people who believed St Mirren could beat Rangers for a second time, despite the home team being on form. Rangers were on a 12-game winning run in the league, stretching way back to September, during which time they had scored 37 goals and conceded just three, so Steven Gerrard's team were definitely favourites.

Alan said, 'As part of our pre-match routine, we have to know the squads for each side; the key players and what has happened with either club over the last few days. Scott Arfield was injured in the previous match against Hibs and looked likely to be out for some time. Ryan Jack had also picked up an injury, which meant two certain starting midfielders would be missing, although the depth of Rangers' squad would provide adequate cover.

'But with the game against Celtic just a few days away, how would Rangers line up? We watched that one with interest. As it transpired, Morelos played and he didn't let anyone down, so a solid starting 11 once again with Allan McGregor clocking up his 400th appearance for the club; an unbelievable servant.

'Before kick-off there was a one-minute silence for Jim McLean, the former Dundee United manager, and I wondered how history might have changed had he accepted the offer to manage Rangers in the 1980s after John Greig vacated the hot seat.'

With three big league points up for grabs, there was the usual tension in the air as the match kicked off and the camera crew focussed on following the action. After the game, Alan reflected, 'St Mirren started on the front foot and had a couple of early chances, but in six first-half minutes

Rangers took complete control with goals from Roofe and Morelos. Alfredo ended his goal drought by latching on to a mistimed back pass by Shaughnessy and scoring in his usual composed finishing style. So it was all but game over by half-time. There were chances to score more in the second half but as we witnessed many times during the season, Rangers did enough to take the points. There was another clean sheet, courtesy of a rock-solid defence, and it was time to put this one to bed and move on. With Celtic up next, a 2-0 victory in Paisley was all that was needed to secure the points and take the next step to 55.

'So the match ended and we had our scoring close-ups and manager handshakes and it was job done. It was time to pack up and go home. Of course, once again there were no celebrating shots of supporters, no singing, no flags saying 55 and sadly no atmosphere as the players disappeared down the tunnel and into the sanctuary of the dressing rooms.

'I have never forgotten how privileged I am as a Rangers fan to have worked at so many of their matches over the last 30 years. I will also never forget this season when I couldn't share that experience.'

Only thing left was for Alan to pick the top six matches he has covered:

Rangers 1 Celtic 0 – Scottish Cup semi-final, March 1992

An Ally McCoist goal just before half-time. He decided to celebrate in front of my camera in the pouring rain. This effectively became my first scoring close-up!

Liverpool 4 Arsenal 2 – Champions League quarter-final, April 2008

What a game. Gerrard was captain; scored one and an assist. There were three goals in the final six minutes. I was on the high camera in the Kop and I've never been hugged so much by strangers. Wonderful memories.

Rangers 3 Aberdeen 1 – Scottish Premier League decider, April 1996

Paul Gascoigne hat-trick. Need I say more?

Rangers 3 Celtic 2 – Scottish Cup Final, May 2002

Every Rangers fan will remember this match; that Peter Løvenkrands last-minute winner. I was on a camera in the corner between the Rangers end and main stand, so was surrounded by Rangers fans. As I followed the action, I had one decision to make as the ball hit the net – follow the celebration or offer a crowd shot. As Løvenkrands ran away from me the crowd shot was offered within seconds. I locked off and threw my arms up in the air. Needless to say I found lots of new friends that day!

Motherwell 2 Celtic 1 – Helicopter Sunday, May 2005

Okay, so I wasn't covering the Rangers game at Easter Road, but this was every bit as good. After the final whistle, we were asked for shots of sad Celtic fans. Easiest job ever!

Portugal 3 Spain 3 – World Cup Russia 2018

Slightly away from the main theme here but this is simply the best match I have ever worked on, and it should be noted that it was covered entirely by a Scottish camera crew! Arguably Ronaldo's finest match for his country, and one of the World Cup's greatest ever matches.

The Road to Redemption

John Gilligan, former Rangers director

Ayr, Scotland

THE 17TH-CENTURY English poet John Milton once wrote, 'Long is the way and hard, that out of Hell leads up to the light.'

Let's rewind to February 2012, and maybe even prior to that, when Rangers were in a state of peril. The vultures were circling and the gloom junkies, perhaps with much justification, were preparing their epitaphs.

In a desperate search for light amid all the darkness, John Gilligan had a string of great memories to dredge up. They might help blank out the awful things going on at the club he had supported for almost 50 years, and he could rely on them to put a smile back on his face. Thing is, he didn't want to blank out what was going on. He wanted it sorted. He wanted Rangers men in charge of Rangers. Good guys with the club's best interests at heart. Only then would he be able to rest easy and recall the highs of Barcelona 1972, Helicopter Sunday and more.

Sadly, there would be no quick fix for Rangers.

He said, 'Even before our well-documented problems of 2012, I didn't grasp just how bad the situation was. As time went on, pre-Craig Whyte era, I thought we would get good people in and it would quickly be sorted out. Once Craig Whyte got in the door, though, it looked as though he wanted to put the club into administration. That was a major worry to me, and I thought about how we could control it.

'When administration happened, more strangers got involved, and the questions I was asking were "Who are they?" "Why are they at Rangers?" Very few Rangers-minded people knew anything about them. It was a dreadful situation, and it was one crisis after another. These people had no affinity to our club whatsoever.

'I have never wanted Rangers owned by non-Scotsmen. We are a Scottish club and should be in the hands of Scotsmen. We have also had a long association with Northern Ireland, but Rangers is about Rangers supporters, us, and no one else.

'Before Dave King became personally involved we were scraping our way through the lower divisions, losing to teams like Alloa Athletic and Stirling Albion. I don't believe we were investing in the right players to ensure we were ready for an assault on the Premiership when we eventually got back up. We weren't improving the squad the way we needed for the challenges that inevitably lay ahead.

'We had been promoted from the Third Division and League One at the first time of asking, but there was the extra year in the Championship, and when we went into the Premiership we weren't ready, so looking back that was probably a couple of years wasted.

'Don't get me wrong, I still feel Mark Warburton and Davie Weir did a good job. We asked them to come in and get us out of the Championship, which they did, against a very good Hibs side. They also got us to a cup final so, although history might be unkind to them, I reckon they're due a bit of credit.

'There were hiccups after that, and with Pedro Caixinha and several caretaker managers, I felt we lost even more time; probably around three seasons in total for various reasons.'

Friday, 6 March 2015 will forever be an important date in the club's history. Tomorrow's history, today, and the moment Rangers were finally free of those who arguably didn't have the club's best interests at heart. It was the day of the Extraordinary General Meeting at Ibrox; the day Dave King, John Gilligan and Paul Murray were voted on to the Rangers board of directors, and Derek Llambias and Barry Leach voted off. One of the first decisions taken by the new board was to appoint Douglas Park as a director.

Prior to the short meeting, our football club was broken. That day, the board promised to fix it, and they were true to their word.

Gilligan said, 'We prepared for that EGM for months. The Blue Knights had tried to get control but lost out to Charles Green. They just lacked a bit of muscle. Meanwhile, Dave King was working away quietly in the background, planning with Douglas Park, George Letham and George Taylor for the moment the opportunity would arise to get our club back, so it was certainly no overnight success. A hell of a lot of work went on to ensure we would have sufficient votes to take control of the club.

'We were as prepared as we could have been, but when you're relying on people to vote a certain way, there is always the chance things might not turn out the way you want them to, even though Dave had been meticulous in doing his homework. But when it was announced that we had received 85 per cent of the vote it was an incredible feeling. We were always confident we could win, but you can never be 100 per cent sure.

'Prior to the takeover, Dave had asked me if I would step up and become a director, and I had no hesitation in doing that. I have only ever wanted what was best for the club.

'When the result was announced, I was so emotional; as emotional as I have ever been in my life. Once the deal was done and we had won the majority, we were elated. There was still some paperwork to be taken care of so we went across to the offices at Argyle House to sort things out. We were aware of Rangers supporters outside the building waiting to greet us, but we didn't know just how many. Fans had been there for ages waiting on us making an appearance, but when we opened the door and walked out I was an absolute wreck. We had just won arguably one of the greatest victories in the club's long and illustrious history, and it showed on the face of every single supporter. We were gobsmacked. I stood there taking it all in. I have seen my team win some great matches, but this was far more emotional than any of them. I am a Rangers fan first and foremost, and we had just got our club back. It's that simple.

'There were folk I was brought up with in Bishopbriggs; guys like Douglas Yuille, who I have remained friends with. We hugged each other because it meant so much to both of us. My cousin Gordon McEwan was also there, and he insisted on driving me around after that EGM because he was so happy with the outcome. There was such an outpouring of emotion.

'But here's the thing, and I mean absolutely no disrespect to Dave King, or any of the others involved in the takeover, but we only won because of the supporters. It was their stoicism in standing tall and supporting their club through the dark days that made our victory possible. Buying season tickets, turning up for games, standing tall and supporting their club. They never wavered; they remained the one constant throughout the whole debacle. The supporters stayed with the club, and the club survived. That should never, ever be forgotten.'

The first thing the new board had to do was take stock, think carefully about the present, and plan prudently for the future. Gilligan said, 'I'm quite fortunate in the way I look at life. I'm a one-problem-at-a-time kind of guy, so I wasn't worried about it. No, it wasn't great, but it wouldn't have mattered to me how bad it was – because we had already won the most important battle.

'But one day in particular stands out. It was early on, and we all just looked at one another with that type of stare which says, "This is a hell of a lot worse than we expected it to be!" But we were undaunted, because the adrenaline was still pumping from the takeover victory.

'My first issue, though, was that being a director and a fan, I couldn't tell anyone just how bad it was, because we had just come out the other side of the most turbulent times at the club and we didn't want to burst the bubble. It would have destroyed the feelgood factor, so we carried that burden on our shoulders and we got on with it. We couldn't start saying "this is murder, there is no money and X, Y and Z needs doing". That achieves nothing, but X, Y and Z did need doneto be so you just have to find a way to do it.

'That was the moment we rolled the sleeves up and got stuck in. Guys like George Taylor, George Letham, John Bennett, Douglas Park and the rest of us started the process of rebuilding our great club.

'The first thing we had to do was stop the rot and try to rebuild staff morale. We made some mistakes along the way; we're only human, but every single thing we did was for the good of the football club.

'On a personal level it took its toll on me, more so because I wasn't able to share that burden with friends. That was probably the biggest thing for me. God knows I wanted to tell folk how bad it actually was, but we had to stay positive and get on with the job we had signed up for.'

Two years after joining the board, and what was a seemingly never-ending struggle to get the club back on an even keel – while still trying to get results on the pitch – Gilligan stepped down from the board. He had made a huge difference. Now, he could watch games as a supporter again, but a supporter who had played a vital role in the road to redemption. But how did he become a Rangers fan in the first place?

He said, 'I wanted to get fed – it was that simple. If you weren't a Rangers supporter in my house there was a real chance you could end up malnourished! My whole family were Rangers-daft. My dad, my uncle, it was a no-brainer. I was born into it.

'I loved it from day one. I wasn't a great player. I played a bit of amateur football and five-a-sides, so I was better off watching and I loved watching Rangers. My dad would take me to Ibrox, and like a lot of others in the same boat, we would go to see Partick Thistle if Rangers were playing away.

'I can't actually remember my first game. I wish I could, but the first one I remember attending is the Scottish Reserve Cup Final, at Ibrox, against Celtic, which we won 2-1. We had guys like Jim Forrest, Alex Willoughby, Willie Henderson, Bobby Hume and Bobby Watson in our team. It was really exciting seeing Rangers lift the cup in front of a healthy crowd.

'We were into season 1964/65 before I started taking an interest in the players and remembering games, but I recall seeing the great Jimmy Millar, Ralphie Brand and Davie Wilson; three fantastic players.

'The first time I set eyes on Ibrox I thought it was Buckingham Palace! At that time it held about 100,000, and there were 90,000 for the first big game I attended. Rangers v the great Real Madrid; Ferenc Puskás, Gento, Alfredo Di Stéfano et al. It was 1963 and I was 11 years old. My dad put me on the wall down at the front of the terracing so I had a great view of these genuine superstars. All the kids used to be on the wall at that time, and the dads would come and get us at half-time and full time. I was vaguely aware of these top players and I loved watching them. Di Stéfano is the only player, to my knowledge, to represent three countries – Argentina, Colombia and Spain. He was an incredible player, and I'm delighted I got to see him play in the flesh.

'I was once asked the biggest sacrifice I'd made to watch Rangers play, but the truth is I don't view going to see my team as a sacrifice. What I will say, with some trepidation, is that I got engaged to Maggie in 1972, and we saved long and hard to buy an engagement ring. And then Rangers qualified for the European Cup Winners' Cup Final in Barcelona. Well, something had to give!

'I hurried down to the travel agent and booked up for Spain. What a time I had. It was incredible. To see Rangers win a European trophy was unbelievable, and to share that moment with 25,000 other Rangers fans was mind-blowing. At that time Spain was under a dictatorship. Franco ruled with an iron fist and it wasn't easy to get into the country, but 25,000 managed it okay. To this day I still talk to people who wish they had made the "sacrifice", because there is an awful lot of regret there.

'And how did my relationship with Maggie work out? Well, we're married 48 years now, and she eventually forgave me! We were married the year after Barcelona. At the time, my priority was to get to the final and I would worry about it later. Thankfully it all worked out in the end.

'Being a football fan is all about highs and lows. I have a mate who favours the Rangers but doesn't go to games. When I asked him why, he said, "I couldn't handle the highs and lows. I look at you. One week you're bouncing, next you're miserable." He's absolutely right. It doesn't matter what age you are. If Rangers lose, I won't watch any other football on TV that weekend. I'm just not in the mood, but that's how it gets you.'

Thankfully, then, since Steven Gerrard took over, there haven't been too many disappointments. 'I liken the appointment of Steven to bringing in Graeme Souness, with some notable differences. Aberdeen and Dundee United were doing well when Graeme arrived, although Celtic weren't as strong. Graeme had a lot more money to spend – and he wasn't trying to stop ten in a row!

'One of the big advantages Graeme had was that English clubs were banned from European competition and so attracting the top talent to Ibrox was a little easier. Once we got Terry Butcher and Chris Woods in the floodgates opened.

'Steven Gerrard is a global iconic brand, and just oozes quality. He speaks well and gives the impression he is everything a Rangers manager should be. In short, he looks like a Rangers manager.

'When he was appointed and endorsed by the board, he was probably given around 18 months to two years to build a squad, and he has made a fantastic job of it.

'Now, we are riding on the crest of a wave, and like most supporters I simply didn't see this coming. To have lost just one goal at home in 14 league games was something else. At the beginning of February our goal difference of +60 was better than the goal difference of the entire league. We were miles ahead of the competition.

'Some of our players, like Tavernier, Goldson and Barišić, are into their second and third seasons as Rangers players under Steven Gerrard, and there is a steel in them, and they play with great style. They look like Rangers players. Guys like Glen Kamara have also come to the fore and showed their true ability.

'We are now at the stage where you look at the bench and you're almost seeing an alternative first team. It's a great position to be in. And then we're introducing lads like Scott Wright into the team as part of our future.

'We have also been fantastic in Europe. To top a section including Benfica shows just how far we have come in the last three years. We will also be simultaneously planning for an assault on the Champions League, which was unthinkable a couple of years ago.'

Gilligan insists this title has given him levels of satisfaction never before experienced in all his years as a Rangers supporter. He said, 'It's the best ever as far as I'm concerned. People my age have lived through a lot of success at Rangers; our European Cup Winners' Cup triumph in Barcelona, Colin Stein's title-clinching goal at Easter Road in March 1975, Terry Butcher's header at Pittodrie when we won the league up at their place in 1987. The Løvenkrands Scottish Cup Final and Brian Laudrup clinching the title at Tannadice in 1997. We've been spoiled, but this takes some beating.

'I've also lived through two separate decades when we didn't win a title, but the nine years prior to this one was completely different – and all because of social media. We got slaughtered as Celtic were winning everything. This is payback time, and we're enjoying it.

'I grew up with supporters of smaller teams calling me a glory-hunter as I chose to support Rangers. But after following Rangers through the four years in the lower leagues, I haven't heard anyone call me a glory-hunter since. Nothing glorious about watching your team play East Stirling at Ibrox or standing on a grass verge at Borough Briggs for a game against Elgin City.

'So this title has been fantastic on so many levels. One thing I didn't envisage was our margin of victory. I mean, who saw that coming? But I don't want to make this about their failings. This is about how good we have been. Whether or not they could or couldn't handle the pressure we've put them under, and whether or not they've cracked, this is ALL about how good we have been. We have been relentless.

'I've watched every single game in the house. Just before the last lockdown I was invited over to Ibrox, but for me our title-winning season has been all about sitting in front of the TV watching the games on either Rangers TV or Sky.

'I've been very impressed with the way we've played. It would appear the manager has changed the entire mindset at the club. The 1-0 win on day one at Aberdeen set the tone. Good teams win games 1-0. Don't get me wrong, it isn't good for supporters but if we can grind out a 1-0 win while not at our best then that's the stuff of champions.

'As a team we were outstanding; it was all about our togetherness. Any bother and the players stood shoulder-to-shoulder with one another. The likes of Goldson, Barišić, Katić, when he was playing, Ryan Jack, they get in about it and stick up for their mates. They don't get bullied. We are a proper team. We score a goal, there is a reaction from every player on the field and everyone on the bench. They are in it together.

'There were so many contenders for player of the year. Take Allan McGregor, for example; he was outstanding throughout the season, but I wouldn't give it to him, because that would be like saying we were under the cosh for large parts of the season, which isn't true. But just about every time he was called on to make an important save, he did so. He is fully entitled to be our player of the year, but I would probably have gone for Tav or Davis.

'I've missed not being able to get to games more than I could've imagined. I've missed the guys I would stand and talk to outside Ibrox, or at away games. Just having a chat about life and the football. It's the small things. But I managed to take that on the chin as we were winning just about every week.'

Tam Young

Maryhill, Glasgow

Rangers 1 Celtic 0
Scorer: McGregor 70 (own goal)
2 January 2021

Rangers supporters attending the Old Firm game on 2 January 1971 were surprised to see Gerry Neef in goal. It was his first appearance of the season, and with 85,000 in the ground – and in party mood – Neef knew there was little room for error. Dave Smith had also been recalled by manager Willie Waddell after a lengthy absence.

Celtic were without Bobby Murdoch, Billy McNeill and John 'Yogi' Hughes, but with six league titles in a row, and a recent second European Cup Final appearance behind them, the Parkhead club were favourites to win.

Mind you, anyone trying to predict the outcome of an Old Firm game – even in the midst of Celtic's first nine-in-a-row sequence – would be accused of gross folly.

Captains John Greig and Tommy Gemmell shook hands in the centre circle after referee Mr Anderson had tossed the coin, and the game got under way.

Up in the Main Stand – very close to the thin blue line segregating supporters of Rangers and Celtic – sat half a dozen young guys from Maryhill, all cheering on the boys in blue. Among them was Tam Young, a joiner from Fernie Street, who had travelled over to the game on the supporters' bus from McLeod's pub with his brother, Robert, and four mates.

They felt like toffs. It was the first time any of them had been in the Main Stand. They normally stood in the Rangers end, and entered and exited the ground via Stairway 13, which took them down the steps to Copland Road, via Harrison Drive, where they would either get the bus or subway back to St George's Cross, in Maryhill. But earlier that week, they had been offered six gold-dust stand tickets, as the mother of one of the lads worked at Ibrox. They were snapped up without a moment's hesitation, as Tam explained, 'We never missed a game, home or away, but it was always really difficult to get a ticket for an Old Firm game as they were as rare as hen's teeth.

'In those days, no one really had a season ticket. I don't think you could buy one for the terracing, just the Main Stand, and we didn't have enough money for that. We loved standing in the Rangers end so we wouldn't have been interested in sitting in the stand every week anyway.

'Apart from the home match against Celtic, there was never an issue getting into Ibrox. The stadium held more than 80,000 then, and with run-of-the-mill home games attracting an average crowd of around 25,000, you just rolled up to the turnstile, paid your admission money, and in you went. We only played Celtic once a season at Ibrox in the league so the tickets were hard to come by, so you took whatever you could get, and that day we were delighted to get our hands on the tickets for the Main Stand. It was like a wee day out!

'We were right next to the Celtic supporters, and there was a fair bit of needle going on. I wouldn't even call it banter; it went beyond that. The club had organised an athletics meeting before the match to try and keep everyone entertained, but it only worked to a certain extent.'

When Greig and Gemmell walked on to the park side by side, another contemporary rarity, the noise levels inside Ibrox were cranked up a notch or two. It was game time.

Celtic kicked off and went straight for the jugular. Fans were packed on to the terraces like sardines; the tension inside the ground was palpable, and several early mistakes were attributed to nerves.

Possession was mostly with the away team and the vast majority of the crowd were getting restless, and trying to urge their team to put their foot on the ball and calm things down.

In clearing one such attack, Jimmy Johnstone took a Willie Mathieson howitzer straight to the face. It almost knocked him over but he regained his balance and remained, stoically, on his feet.

Celtic had the first real opportunity when Harry Hood played in wee Jinky Johnstone, and the tiny terror had a yard start on Rangers centre-half Ronnie McKinnon, but the former sprint champion of Govan High School put his extra-curricular talents to good use and got back to rob the Celtic forward of the ball.

Loud and hearty songs were emanating from both ends of the ground, and like a seasoned pro, Derek Johnstone – who was just 17 years old – started to spray some neat passes around. This helped Rangers grow into the game. Willie Henderson followed his lead by trying to get a foothold while Alfie Conn and John Greig were teaming up to good effect. It was morphing into an excellent game of football.

With 21 minutes gone, Colin Stein beat George Connelly to the ball but looked on frustratingly as Evan Williams saved his shot.

Up in the Main Stand, Tam and his pals were completely focussed on the game. They were willing the ball into the net. The action was keen and tough, but clean, and when Derek Johnstone went close with an overhead kick you could hear the collective sighs of the huge Rangers support.

Henderson then took a full-blooded Gemmell clearance in the chops and laughed it off. This was a game for tough guys!

Before the break, Celtic turned the screw. Jimmy Johnstone and Jim Brogan had great efforts saved, Sandy Jardine cleared a Hood effort off the line, and Neef saved brilliantly, again from Johnstone.

Midway through the second half, a thick fog began to fall on the playing surface and for a short while it looked like the game might be abandoned. As it lifted, Rangers entered a purple patch. Derek Johnstone headed for goal but Brogan popped up on the line to nod clear.

It was anyone's game now, and the impression given was that one goal would win it. The surface had remained slippy from the first moment to the last, and it might have been the case that a mistake would lead to something tangible.

And then, with time running out – just 60 seconds were left on the clock – Bobby Lennox took a pot shot at goal. The ball thundered off the crossbar and doing what he did best, Jimmy Johnstone followed up and dived to head the ball past Neef. That was that.

Many Rangers supporters headed for the exits. It was game over, or so they thought, but Colin Stein had other ideas. Unlike Lennox, who had been quiet up to that point, Rangers' midfield ace Davie Smith had been one of the better players on the park and he sent a cross into the box. With three Rangers players waiting to pounce, Stein got there first to prod the ball home.

The scenes inside the ground – or at least three-quarters of it – were unbelievable. Up in the Main Stand, it was bedlam. Tam Young and his pals never left an Old Firm game early and their mantra of 'anything can happen late on' was backed up by Stein's dramatic late equaliser.

Tam said, 'We were that elated, and celebrated so hard, that a couple of us ended up a few rows in front of where we had been sitting. It was incredible. We had suffered so much in terms of Celtic dominating the domestic scene that we were just so delighted to salvage something from what, in all fairness, was a really good game. The players had put so much into it, but we got what we deserved.

'The final whistle had sounded and we were delighted, but the only thing now on our minds was getting out of the ground and back to the supporters' bus. The rule was the bus would leave no more than half an hour after the full-time whistle. It was parked way along Edmiston Drive, near Paisley Road West, so it wasn't that far away, but getting out of a packed Ibrox was quite a challenge so we clapped the players off the field and made our way – slowly – to the exits.'

As the Maryhill contingent headed back to the bus, the Celtic fans headed in the opposite direction. When they eventually reached the conga line of supporters' buses – which stretched as far as the eye could see – they located the McLeod's bus and climbed aboard.

'The mood was fantastic. Even the few supporters who had left the ground when Jimmy Johnstone had scored were by now well aware that Stein had equalised, so everyone was on a bit of a high.

'Exactly half an hour after the match had finished, the driver started the engine, flicked a switch to close the front door of his bus and indicated to pull out. As we headed east along Paisley Road West the place was heaving with jubilant supporters. Okay, we didn't win, but we had come from behind to grab a draw with a very good Celtic side. That was enough for a celebration.

'The bus was only about half full as we headed back to Maryhill. It wasn't a massive surprise, because folk often missed the bus back, and we had done it ourselves, deciding to stay in the Ibrox area for a couple of pints before catching the subway back to Maryhill. We were lucky that the subway got us back to Maryhill in ten minutes.'

With no radio on board, the occupants of the bus headed back to their base completely unaware of the tragic events unfolding at Ibrox, on Stairway 13. Hundreds of supporters had been caught up in the worst kind of accident and, by the end of the night, 66 fans – including many kids and one woman – would have lost their lives.

'We had no idea,' said Tam. 'We were just happy that we had made it back to the bus on time, and as we travelled up Maryhill Road, the six of us asked to get dropped off near

Queen's Cross, at a wee pub on the corner of Dalmally Street called Mason's. It was run by a lovely guy called Andy Mason who had been a boxer. It was a great wee pub.

'We filed into the bar and ordered up pints of lager. As we started to knock them back, our view was diverted to the black-and-white television on top of a cabinet. The news was on, and reports were starting to come through from Ibrox. At first we didn't recognise it as Ibrox, or any football ground for that matter, as it was dark and all you could see were folk hurrying between piles of bodies.

'As soon as we realised what it was, everyone in the pub was huddled round the TV. It was surreal. We hadn't long returned from that very place, but now it was a disaster zone, with police and ambulance men working so hard to try and deal with a very serious situation.'

It wasn't long before the telephone in the pub started ringing. And then it became constant. 'Is so-and-so there, is this guy or that guy in the pub.' Folk watching the news at home were desperately ringing round the pubs to see if their loved ones were there. This was one occasion when they desperately hoped their menfolk WERE in the pub.

Tam said, 'We all just stood there, totally helpless and sad beyond belief. Nothing we could do bar watch the news for updates on everything that was going on in a desperate attempt to save the lives of those Rangers fans who had only left the house that day to attend a football match.'

Reports were soon coming through of Willie Waddell, Jock Stein, Jock Wallace and players and officials from both sides helping to attend to the injured. It was all hands to the pumps.

'Later on that night,' Tam said, 'the phone rang, and it was for me. I took the receiver and the voice on the other end said, "Congratulations, you're a daddy!" My wife Cathie had been taken in to Stobhill Hospital and our son Bobby was born. It was an unbelievable feeling. Here was hope amongst all the tragedy.

'The following day I discovered that one of my pals, Les Clark, who was a wee bit younger than me, and travelled on the John Greig Loyal supporters' bus, also from Maryhill, had been caught up in the awful events. He was only 18 at the time and it turned out he had come down Stairway 13 at the exact moment the disaster was occurring, and was completely lifted off his feet. Thankfully, he was lifted up by fellow supporters and physically thrown through the air and landed on the embankment which ran on the outside of the staircase and steel handrails. He lost a shoe, but other than being completely shaken, he was physically unhurt. It was a dramatic escape for him.

'I also spoke to my brother-in-law, James Tran, who, along with his brother-in-law, Jimmy Eccles, who hailed from Northern Ireland, had been caught up in it. They travelled over on our supporters' bus that day, but missed the bus home. We wrongly thought they had gone off somewhere local for a drink but it transpired that James, believing that Jimmy had been a victim of the disaster, had spent ages looking at all the dead bodies in an effort to find his relative. It was only when he couldn't see him that he headed home, and found Jimmy safe and well.'

Every 2 January, Tam watches the match with his son, Bobby, either at Ibrox, or like this season, on TV at home. It's a poignant reminder for both of the frailty of human life. This season, though, most fixtures have been viewed without the need to look through the cracks in your fingers, and Tam normally takes the time to remind Bobby of a question he asked his dad at the age of just five.

Tam explained, 'I started taking Bobby to the games when he was about four. It was the season we stopped Celtic winning ten in a row. We would stand in the Rangers end, and quite often I put Bobby up on my shoulders. On one occasion, though, one of my mates, Campbell Pears, took Bobby down to the front, so he could lean on the wall and watch the match.

'We lost to Hibs, and when Campbell brought him back up, he turned to me and said, "Dad, will Rangers ever win anything?" That's the way it seemed in those days, but, of course, we won the league that season and we were all delighted.'

Moving forward to this season's Ne'erday game at Ibrox, Rangers were overwhelming favourites to beat Celtic, and open up an even bigger gap at the top of the table. But what is that they say about the best-laid plans?

Tam takes up the story: 'I always try to keep an open mind for these games, but we couldn't help but be confident ahead of this one. Being the 50th anniversary of the Ibrox disaster meant it was an incredibly poignant occasion. Watching the captains lay wreaths in the centre circle brought all the memories of that terrible day flooding back.

'When the match started, though, I couldn't believe what I was seeing. Maybe Celtic saw it as something of a last-chance saloon, but they pinned us back early on and Allan McGregor had a few saves to make.

'Bobby and I kept thinking the tide would turn, and we would dominate possession, but it didn't really happen and once again McGregor was called into action to save a shot from Griffiths. The game seemed to turn when Nir Bitton was sent off for hauling down Alfredo and they lost a wee bit of belief then, which was great. Not long after that, James Tavernier whipped in a corner and the ball came off Calum McGregor's shoulder and flew into the back of the net. That was the cue for some wild celebrations.

'After that, we were on the back foot for periods, but I don't think Allan McGregor had another save to make so, like many of their supporters say, they didn't pound us the entire game.

'I'm not exactly one for statistics, but they made for great reading after that game. The win put us 19 points clear – NINETEEN – and it was our 14th win in a row, which was some going. It was also another clean sheet, and that was something we made a habit of this season.

'Late on, that big Shane Duffy gave the ball straight to Ryan Kent, and he should have made it a wee bit more comfortable for us all sitting at home biting our nails, but Duffy got back to block his shot. I turned to Bobby and said, "It would have been karma for Kent to score after Duffy's mistake, as five minutes earlier Duffy was lucky to stay on the park after chopping the wee man down!"

'It was a fantastic win, and that old cliché, "It doesn't matter how you win, as long as you win," had never been truer. I still believe that was one of our most important wins of the season, and went a long way to helping our players believe they could finally do it. Equally, it took the sting out of Celtic and they failed to win any of their next three games. Maybe that was the day their dream of achieving ten in a row finally ended.

'For me, though, once the house was quiet again, I had a thought for all those who had perished in the disaster. It was awful, and not something I've spoken about until now; 50 years on.'

Tim Webb

Portadown, Northern Ireland

Aberdeen 1 Rangers 2
Scorers: Morelos 32, 50
10 January 2021

If lockdown and the absence of supporters at Ibrox had any positive side to it all, it's that Tim Webb managed to get a bit of a lie-in on matchdays. Normally, when Ibrox-bound, he's up around 4.15am as there's a ferry to catch from Belfast.

God knows what time his alarm would've been set for had he been going to Aberdeen v Rangers at Pittodrie on 10 January, for that's when Tim – from the comfort of his home in Portadown – first started to allow himself the luxury of believing that this might be the club's year.

We all have our own private thoughts of when title number 55 nudged closer to reality, but that gloomy day at Pittodrie did it for Tim – although he insists it wasn't the day the title was won. He explained, 'It was a massive win for us at a traditionally tough venue. And given that our next match was an Old Firm encounter against Celtic, we really couldn't afford to lose. The game at Pittodrie could have gone either way and was always one I was a little nervous about. To get the win against any rival is always important but with the way the league table was looking beforehand, it was definitely a key game.

'Having this particular fixture the day before Celtic were due to play Hibs was also a factor as the three points would heap even more pressure on them.

'Watching any game on the run-in to 55 was always going to be nerve-wracking, simply because of what was at stake, but this game had more than a few edge-of-the-seat moments, like the debatable yellow card that could so easily have been a second red for Aberdeen when Curtis Main went in high on Borna Barišić. It was dangerous and Borna could have been seriously injured.

'We also had some "nearly moments" that could have provided a few more goals, while Aberdeen had a couple of chances, but thankfully we had the very capable hands of Allan McGregor in our corner. Allan is a phenomenal keeper and has never once let the gaffer or us supporters down.'

At the other end of the park, Alfredo Morelos had remembered his shooting boots, and his two goals ensured all three points were Ibrox-bound. Tim was delighted to see Alfredo make his mark again, and said, 'He's a cracking player and a great goalscorer, and has delivered on numerous occasions when we've needed him most. He hadn't been in great form going into this game, but he came up trumps once again. We have witnessed a different Alfredo this season as he was asked to come a bit deeper and link up play, rather than playing as an out-and-out penalty box striker.

'It was also good to see the goals shared around more, as it meant we had a threat from all over the park. That's a manager's dream. Equally, I know how important it is for a centre-forward to score regularly. But as we strive to continually improve and be constantly in the hunt for major trophies, we will take goals from any quarter.

'But it was a little frustrating to see us relax a bit more than we should've at 2-0. There was still half an hour remaining, and when Aberdeen reduced the leeway to 2-1, it heaped unnecessary pressure on us. The closing stages were far more nervy than they needed to be.

'I should admit, though, that I get nervous before all Rangers games. It doesn't matter who we're playing; it just means that much to me. But I think it's healthy and a good thing for the players to be nervous as it gives them a bit more determination to go and get the win.'

Two visits to Pittodrie brought two victories, and while both were secured by a single goal the six points accrued not only helped cement our place at the top of the table, but also sent out a message to those teams who might have believed, more in hope than anything else, that the Rangers challenge might falter again after the turn of the year.

'Up until the match at Pittodrie, the season had been almost perfect. I had this very comforting sense of unity within the squad and what was going on behind the scenes. It was also clear as daylight that the management and players had far more hunger to see the season out with a league title win, and resolve past slip-ups with regards to past title challenges.

'Every single Rangers supporter wanted the players to remain focussed until the last match of the season. That was key. But we needn't have worried, as you could see the determination in the players and coaching staff week in, week out. That was one of the beauties of watching on television: you got the chance to see close-ups of the players and the gaffer at various stages of the games. And the message remained the same. From start to finish it was "one game at a time".'

In a season which produced a collective like no other, and many great individual performances, Tim finds it difficult to choose one player who stood out from the crowd. 'Our captain, James Tavernier was a model of consistency. He became a great leader of the squad and is someone I think the younger lads look up to with pride and respect. He always comes across as very professional, and I would be more than happy for him to see out the rest of his career at Ibrox. I was delighted when he signed a new contract.

'But for me, the gaffer was number one. I couldn't be happier with the job he's doing. I always admired Stevie as a player and as a man who never shirked a challenge in his life. He is professional in everything he does for the club, and I love it that he takes no nonsense from our detractors and critics. I firmly believe in him and what he wants to achieve as manager of the world's most successful club.'

But while Rangers have gone about their business in a ruthless and efficient manner, Tim was sat at home wondering what might have been had supporters been allowed into the games. As a regular at Ibrox since he was a kid, he has missed his fortnightly pilgrimages to Govan – and their increasing significance – greatly.

He said, 'It's the whole Saturday thing, isn't it? Of course you miss being inside Ibrox, savouring that unique atmosphere, and watching the team in action, but it's much more than that to me. It's about travelling over to Scotland with my dad and my friends; guys I see regularly on the journey over. And also the many great relationships I've built up over the years with friends in Scotland. People I meet up with on matchday, whether inside or outside the stadium. I can't underestimate how big a part Rangers plays in my life, and has done for so many years now.

'As a wheelchair user I sit in the designated area of the East Enclosure and my seat/space is roughly five yards from the home dugout. Yes, that close! I can hear the management team barking out instructions to the players, and it gives me a great insight into how management and players interact with one another.'

A few years ago, Tim was fundraising to buy a wheelchair which would give him greater freedom. Members of the Rangers family came together to help him reach the target he had set. He was overwhelmed. As a way of giving something back, he hit on the idea of producing a metal lapel badge to raise funds for the Rangers Charity Foundation – and what better design than 'The Wheelchair Loyal'. He said, 'You have no idea how thankful I was when my fellow Rangers supporters came to my aid and helped me secure a new chair. I was really moved. I decided to produce a badge and to my astonishment it became so popular not just by people from the UK but right around the world.

'Initially I thought it might be a good idea to get a couple of hundred made but that was soon blown out of the water, and I have now sold more than 1,000. I have just been like, "Wow!"'

Mind you, it helps when the main man – Stevie G – can be seen proudly wearing a Wheelchair Loyal badge in the Rangers dugout, which helped Tim realise he has extra special powers of persuasion. He said, 'I had a strong urge to at least try to get a Wheelchair Loyal badge to the gaffer but I knew it was a long shot. I have contact with ex-players who have become good friends over the years and I asked Ally Dawson if he could find a way of getting a badge to Steven.

'Ally kindly agreed, so I arranged to meet up with him to hand over the badge at the next home game. It was then into the stadium to get to my place, just as the gaffer emerged from the tunnel and walked over to the technical area. He was alone, so with me being so close, and having a few spare badges in my pocket, I headed over to the dugout, and called out to him in the hope that he might hear me. Luckily, Steven heard my shout and came over. I took a badge from my pocket and offered it to him, but he produced one from his own pocket and said he had been given it by Ally Dawson. He then placed the badge on his coat. Next thing, all these photographers were taking pics of him putting the badge on, which was incredible. As I headed back to my space, Stevie gave me a big smile and there was a burst of applause from the supporters around me. It was fantastic.

'To see a legend like Steven Gerrard proudly wearing one of my badges was a great moment, not just for me but for my dad, who is a huge Rangers AND Liverpool fan.'

Which begs the question, why did Tim become a Rangers fan, and not just support Liverpool? 'You are born a Rangers fan; you don't just become one. The first season I remember is 1993/94, the one after the great treble-winning season, and the European run. I was five years old. Not that I knew of the significance at the time, but although everyone talks in hallowed terms of the great riches 1992/93 brought, we were only one goal away from another treble in my first season as a supporter. Not too bad, huh!'

Since Tim and his dad, Ivan, have been travelling over to Ibrox for games, they have fallen into something of a well-oiled routine. Up at the crack of dawn – 4.15am – with the help of his parents, and then Ivan drives to Ibrox from Portadown, 170 miles as the crow flies.

Tim said, 'The journey consists of a few pick-ups along the way towards the boat terminal for the 7.30am Larne-Cairnryan sailing. We routinely arrive at the stadium just before 12noon. The return sailing leaves Cairnryan at 8pm, and we get home at roughly 11pm. It's a long day, but I love it.

'We pick up some great friends from the Shankill, Newtownards, and around the surrounding areas, as well as more local to where I live. We also sit at the same seating area on the boat every week and enjoy the banter during the crossing with one another. The crew on the boats know us so well now and they give us a bit of craic about the Gers.

'When we are heading down towards the boat for home, we have a half-hour stop in Girvan for fish and chips and maybe even an ice cream. It really is a great day out.'

But when one has to rely on a ferry to get you from A to B, and back to A again, it isn't always plain sailing. 'At the end of December 2018, we were all really buzzing for the Old Firm game at Ibrox. We couldn't wait to get across, but the boat was delayed that morning. We could see the ferry out at sea, so close to docking. The weather wasn't great and we were a bit unsure of whether or not the boat would actually sail, so we had our reservations about getting to the game. We eventually did get going, but we were really late, and even though my dad did his usual great job of getting us to Ibrox, we narrowly missed Ryan Jack scoring the only goal of the game – 15 minutes before half-time!

'The boats have also been cancelled due to bad weather on occasions. I can recall one morning in particular that we were literally heading out the door when the phone rang to say it was off due to very high winds. But that doesn't happen too often, thankfully.

'I've been very fortunate to meet so many players, ex-players, managers, etc. while over at Ibrox. Guys like Marvin Andrews, the late Sandy Jardine, Willie Johnston, Colin Stein, Mark Hateley, Richard Gough, Ian Durrant, Paul "Gazza" Gascoigne. And so the list goes on.

'I have also had the honour of getting to know Ally Dawson, Derek Parlane and club historian David Mason in recent years, and again they have become good pals.

'And I'll never forget when we were down in the lower leagues and I was invited on to the field to be a flag-bearer before a League Cup tie against Falkirk. My dad was alongside me. On that particular day I had the pleasure of speaking to Kenny McDowell, who at that time was assistant to Ally McCoist, and goalkeeping coach Jim Stewart. After meeting Jim Stewart, he started to look out for me and got to recognise me about the stadium on matchdays. At Hampden Park just before kick-off on cup final day, he handed me his match programme. It was a lovely gesture.

'Another amazing experience was getting to meet the genius that is Paul Gascoigne. The day I met Gazza he slipped his training top off and handed it to me. As he did so, he called over a photographer to take some pics, which a fortnight later appeared in the Rangers programme.

'These are all unforgettable experiences, but they were perhaps eclipsed the day three famous Rangers players came to Northern Ireland for a family fun day. My dad was driving them around, and Dad being Dad, decided he would make a quick stop-off at my school. Imagine my complete surprise when Sandy Jardine, Mark Hateley and Willie Johnston walked towards me at my school to say "hullo, hullo"! Gobsmacked doesn't even cover it. Mr Jardine said, "Hi Timothy, how's things with you, pal?" I'm not going to lie, my jaw dropped.

'After school, I arrived home to a massive blue bag sitting in the living room. I opened it immediately to find a Broxi Bear suit! I just had to try the head on, and when I looked in the mirror, I was Broxi Bear. What a moment for a Rangers-daft schoolboy!

'You know something, I can't wait to get back to Ibrox. My love for Rangers has never waned, but this season has made me realise just how much I love the club. During lockdown, Rangers and my Wheelchair Loyal badges have been such a welcome distraction, for a number of reasons. I'll be honest and say with the pandemic and lockdown in place, all things Rangers helped me remain positive and helped keep my mindset in a decent place. Without the Rangers family and the wonderful friends I have made, it would have been much more difficult for me. It has been amazing to know that everyone has stood by me in those difficult days.

'The other interests I have include archery, which I have been taking part in for around nine years, and another area where I have made wonderful friends. I also have a keen interest in the band scene and marching season. I have been in a few flute bands, one of which has a massive family connection, as my dad and uncle were founder members of the Portadown Defenders Auld Boys Flute Band.

'In 2011 the band celebrated its 40th anniversary but sadly we lost my Uncle Denver, one of the men who influenced me to support Rangers. It was difficult for us as a family and, ten years on, it's still difficult, although great memories live forever. With it being the 40th anniversary of the band, I was asked to represent my late uncle in the ranks. It was a real honour and to march the streets with the band, alongside my dad and brother, Matthew, who pushed me while I played the cymbals on parade, was a very emotional experience. Memories of Uncle Denver, Dad's brother, came flooding back.

'Just before lockdown, I had organised a fundraising event to help with my new chair. It was an evening with a total of 15 bands, and a nine-year-old lad called Alfie, who played a Lambeg. To see the room filled that evening was truly humbling for my family and I, but to top it all off, in walked two of the security staff from Ibrox with my new chair. That was so emotional. It was a coming together of two of my greatest passions, and summed up the love and respect that so many people have for me. I was speechless.'

Andy Scott

Kilcreggan, Argyll and Bute

Rangers 5 Ross County 0
Scorers: Kent 6, Helander 28, Aribo 37, Jack 66,
Goldson 81
23 January 2021

Perhaps January will go down as the most important month of the season. It was the month we cemented our position at the summit with a series of gritty, determined performances. The 5-0 win over Ross County provided a one-off display of style and flair, movement on and off the ball, and a lesson in the art of finishing.

Sandwiched in between a draw with Motherwell and a hard-fought single-goal win at Easter Road, this was the elegance as opposed to the dowdy. Even hard-to-please visiting manager John Hughes demanded an encore.

Andy Scott watched the match at home, and was in raptures with what he witnessed on Rangers TV. Watching on the box during lockdown became a necessity, and it seemed an acceptable alternative to climbing aboard the Moses McNeil supporters' bus; destination Ibrox. The bus leaves from the Rosneath Peninsula and picks up between there and Cardross. Andy has been the bus steward for the last 16 years, and his fortnightly pilgrimage offers an opportunity to enjoy some banter with his like-minded mates, grab a few pints in Brechin's Bar in Govan, and watch the team he has supported all his life, before heading back home to Kilcreggan – population 1,270.

He said, 'We had a healthy lead over Celtic heading into December, and it looked like a case of win our games between December and January and we would be well on our way to 55. It wouldn't be easy as we had Celtic, Aberdeen, Hibs twice, Motherwell twice, Ross County twice as well as Dundee United, St Johnstone and St Mirren. We had gone into the game with County dropping only two points from 27, and that was against Motherwell in the previous game, though it could be argued we'd rode our luck a bit in that one.

'We needed a reaction from the previous weekend and the foot was to the floor from the start. We worked hard throughout, and Ryan Kent had one of his better games of recent weeks, while Ryan Jack was back in the starting line-up after injury. It was also good to see Nathan Patterson get the last 20 minutes to show us what he had to offer.

'But while it was pleasing to see us up our game considerably, and a great way to respond to some pretty flat performances, we would win our next few games by the odd goal – although I wasn't complaining.'

Andy was delighted to see five different scorers on target against County – although there was one glaring omission from the most important of after-match stats. 'It's always good to see the goals spread throughout the team, although I would have liked to see Alfie score. This season though, he has been much more than a goalscorer.

'We were three up at the break and the game was as good as over, and we even had the luxury of Tav missing a first-half penalty. I was pleased to see us keep up a good tempo in the second half.'

The man who put the gloss on the scoreline with a real touch of class was Joe Aribo, and Andy admitted he loves watching the Londoner when he is playing at full pelt. 'His goal was the best of the bunch, no doubt about it. There is no end to what this boy can do when he puts his mind to it, and he's another player we stole for a mere £300,000.'

The match against County was Steven Gerrard's 150th in charge, and the landmark didn't go unnoticed by the media, who reported that he was the fastest of all Rangers managers to reach this figure.

'I can't believe how quickly it has gone. Taking into account his only previous managerial experience was at under-18 level, and his first game with Rangers was a Europa League qualifier, he has done extremely well. More than 25 per cent of his games have been in the European arena, and he has won over 60 per cent of his games overall, so he has undoubtedly been a success.

'It's hard to compare him to previous managers, though, as he was forced into a complete rebuild at a time when we were still rising from the ashes. One could point at his lack of silverware but 55 has been massive. Once again we achieved good things in the Europa League, so I think he can hold his head up among the rest, which is no mean feat.

'After what we had been through in the previous six years I couldn't have been happier with his appointment. The day the news broke, we were on holiday in Fuerteventura and I listened to his presser in a bar with my headphones on. I remember it distinctly as my wife Pam didn't speak to me for a few days as she was severely pissed off. In fact, she still reminds me of it!'

It was the dawning of a new era for Rangers, and after 7,000 supporters left cheers ringing in his ears, Gerrard settled down to work. The long road to 55 began. How to overturn so many years of domination from the other side of the city was top of the agenda.

Andy said, 'First and foremost I was hoping he would bring stability. Then I was looking for success. After the mess with Pedro, and then Graeme Murty, we were plummeting towards the depths again. We were getting pumped from Celtic and beaten by teams who should've been nowhere near us.

'I didn't have a problem that Gerrard hadn't managed a senior club before. His name was good enough for me, and he surrounded himself with a great backroom team; guys he knew could do a job for him, and so it is has been proven.

'We all knew this was no overnight project. We had a serious rebuild on our hands, and that takes time. And it seemed Dave King with his "house of cards" statement was prepared to give him that time. Much as we all want overnight success, the players we had at that time would have to be moved on to make way for the guys Gerrard wanted. This wasn't another [Dick] Advocaat project, because the manager didn't have £30m-odd to throw at the team.'

Great patience was required. But it was a Catch-22 situation, because the more you sacrifice the present for the future the further into the distance it allows your main rival to travel. Gerrard couldn't allow Celtic to head off into the horizon, although some might argue they were already there.

'We did see progress over the first two seasons,' said Andy, 'but I didn't realistically think 2020/21 would be our season until we headed to Parkhead in September and took them apart in their own back yard, and without them having a shot on goal. That was the moment right there. It was time to start dreaming a little. Sure, it was early in the season, but we had laid down a marker. So, I'm not massively surprised by the way Celtic collapsed. It was always going to happen, eventually. They had taken their eye off the ball and believed success was their right. They have supporters who have never known anything other than league glory, just as we have some that had never seen us win it. I have watched the team at the top work hard to get there, but it is so hard to stay there. These things work in cycles and they started to believe their own press: e.g. Terry Munro [a mock obituary placed by Rangers fans in a Scottish newspaper in March 2021 to goad Celtic supporters over the impending failure to win a tenth successive title]!

'Celtic seemed more concerned about the shit team we had than what they had themselves. It's like they thought they were still playing against Harry Forester, Rob Kiernan and Ian Black and only had to show up to take five off us. Slowly, Gerrard started to improve the team, not by purchasing stars, but players who could do a job and fit into his plan. This was also down to a good director of football and a great backroom team. Michael Beale is a God, by the way!'

When it comes to the question about what was most important, stopping the ten, or winning 55, there seems to be no debate. 'Fifty-five always. Fuck their ten. Stopping that just became part of us achieving our 55th league title.'

And a big part of achieving a 55th title was a superb defensive record, with Andy having his own theories on how we managed to become so frugal at the back. 'Connor Goldson didn't miss one minute of a match, so for that reason he is the one the gaffer put his ultimate trust in. For a man with an alleged heart problem he was outstanding, and even found the time to chip in with some pretty important goals. Tav was also a rock, but with the system we play the midfield has to be prepared to help out at the rear, which they did admirably. The defence play as a unit and as such should be praised as a unit.

'I love playmakers and so I can't see past Steven Davis. He can split a defence with one pass. Kamara has also been outstanding and after the Euros we will be able to name our price as he sticks out like a sore thumb in the Finland team. And then there's Allan MacGregor, who, for a 39-year-old has been outstanding all season and is as good now as he was ten years ago. Kent and Aribo need to be a bit more consistent for me but the roles they are asked to play may make that difficult.'

Being forced to watch the games at home, after having paid for a season ticket, is a big ask for supporters, and shows just how committed the fanbase is. So, it has been Rangers TV through a virtual season ticket for most. 'Same for me,' said Andy, 'or occasionally Sky Sports or Premier's less-than-perfect coverage!

'I'm missing getting to the games loads; the atmosphere, having a crack with the support around me, who have sat in the same seats for years, and going with the guys I have gone with for years. Oh, and Brechin's for a drink or two before the games.

'Very rarely do I miss a home game. Only if work or holidays get in the way, which is maybe once or twice a season. I also get to around half a dozen or so away games a season. I was on the continuous credit card scheme for away games but I don't know how it will go now with the My Gers scheme.

'I had a season ticket when I was younger but let it go when my priorities changed, but I've had this one for 18 years, and I sit in the Sandy Jardine front, about eight seats from the halfway line. It's the best seat in the house!'

'What does being a Rangers supporter mean to me? That's a tough one. Like all Rangers supporters, it consumes a huge part of my life. Podcasts, radio shows, Twitter, Every other Saturday, as the song goes, away games, European games, etc. Where do you finish?

'I've been going since I was about 15. My dad was a Third Lanark supporter and after they folded football died to him, so he never took me to a game. I went with my school pals and guys I got to know when I was a teenager.

'My first Rangers top was probably the round neck, long sleeves of the mid-70s. I've never really been one for tops, but I've got drawers full of Rangers polo shirts! Bearing in mind in those days we only changed our kit every three or four seasons, so there weren't that many around. The last ones I remember having were the Adidas three rings (not hoops) on the sleeves and the Nike V-neck in 2000.

'I started going to see Rangers during the last old-style First Division championship in season 1974/75. I loved it from the word go, and my favourite player was Derek Johnstone, though the greatest player I have ever seen in a Rangers strip is Brian Laudrup. That's not even up for debate.

'In 35-plus years of supporting my team I have witnessed many incredible matches, great comebacks, amazing victories, etc., but surprisingly enough, probably my favourite game is a relatively recent one, and it's Braga at home. After going 2-0 down we looked dead in the water, but the gaffer introduces Ianis Hagi and we walk away with an incredible 3-2 win. What an atmosphere inside the stadium that night. The closest I can remember is the 3-2 win over Porto in 2005. Again, Ibrox was bouncing.'

Like many Bears, Andy loved the last-day drama of Helicopter Sunday, but acknowledges it didn't come with the emotional baggage of title number 55 because while Rangers had won the league in 2002/03 – just two seasons before Helicopter Sunday – it had been so long since we had last witnessed the flag flying over Ibrox before this one.

He said, 'Fifty-five was a huge get-it-right-fucking-up-you to every other shitty club in this country. It proved to all that we were back in our rightful position as the principal team in Scotland. Back in 2012 the rest of the clubs had their foot on our neck and tried as hard as they could to destroy us. They tried their "Sold-out Saturday" initiative and failed, Celtic had to shut half their ground because they couldn't sell their tickets. I can remember TV companies from all over the world turning up at Stirling, Cowdenbeath, Stenhousemuir, etc., to cover how the mighty had fallen – but how their support had continued to follow. I'll be surprised if there isn't a documentary series falls out of this which will really put a smile on my face as it'll piss the other clubs off even more.

'I had just got off a plane when I heard we had gone into admin and it was like the bottom had fallen out of my world. We all knew the financial situation had been bad for a few years and the quality of players we were buying had diminished since Dick [Advocaat] had gone. International-class players replaced with, in many cases, poorer quality individuals. How did I feel? Shattered.

'We'd known about the big tax case but not to the extent that it would affect us, and we also knew we were in debt to the banks but that the debt was being serviced on an annual basis. To this day I still feel there was a conspiracy to create this perfect storm to bring down the biggest club in the country. Clubs like Arsenal and Man United were using EBTs yet none of them were brought to book the way we were. We were used as a test case, yet nobody was tried after us. The whole thing stinks.'

Andy continued to support his team in the lower leagues. It wasn't even up for discussion. 'Yes, I continued to go every week. I wish I could say that I gave up my season ticket when the spivs were there but I didn't. Right or wrong, I couldn't take the responsibility of starving my team of cash. I enjoyed the journey and visiting grounds that we should never have had to go to.

'There wasn't a time when I contemplated not going back. No matter how bad the spivs, SFA, SPFL and the other clubs treated us, I couldn't contemplate not supporting my team. The closest I came was when the spivs treated us like second-class citizens at the AGM, when they used a tent at the Broomloan end, and when people complained, that prick of a supposed chairman, David Somers came out with the line, "When you're the chairman you can run the AGM how you want." That was as close as I got to not going back. Livid doesn't do it justice!

'The lower-league journey was just something that had to be done. I do think we could've taken the opportunity to build from the ground up via the youth. Did we have to go through the Second Division unbeaten? Why we were spending thousands a week on the like of Kevin Kyle is beyond me. Ally McCoist did a great job as a player and as a defender of the club but unfortunately he wasn't a manager.

'We all knew that when we got back up to the SPL we wouldn't conquer it overnight. Teams have to be built, style of play, getting the right players, etc. all takes time. There was no quick fix. Remember Sir Furious [Alex Ferguson] nearly lost his job at Manchester United before he turned the corner and look at what he achieved at Old Trafford.

'Don't get me wrong, it was tough at times. When we were getting hammered by Celtic, going to work or to the pub suddenly became difficult to stomach. Watching the 5-1 gubbing at the piggery with Joey Barton thinking he was a player, [Philippe] Senderos getting sent off, losing nine goals to them in two games over two weeks was awful. For the semi-final against them in 2018 at Hampden I was right next to their support in the North Stand. With 20 minutes to go I realised I was the only one left in my row – so it's good to see them suffer now!

'I think after Ally and Kenny McDowall we all thought Warburton might be the man. He started off fairly well and had credit in the bank, but after the 5-1 drubbing at Parkhead the doubts kicked in. When you watch the same tactics every week, and are told that Plan B is to do Plan A better, or we go again next week, then it isn't really going to end in anything other than disaster. Rinse and repeat.

'But if it took those years of failure to get to where we are today, then it was worth it. Had we not endured the bad years, we would probably have a mediocre manager (Derek McInnes?) in charge and be struggling to beat mediocre teams, as well as getting our arses felt in Europe. At the moment I don't think there is a team in Europe who sees us as an easy option, so we can hold our heads up proudly.

'As much as I would like to dominate the Scottish game for a long time I am enough of a realist to know that all things operate on cycles. They only got to eight and three quarters because they had a free run at it while we were out of the league for four years, and then there was the ten-point deduction in 2012.

'I'd be happy to get to 60 before dropping one to Livi, or a club of that stature. Enough titles to keep a large gap between us and them that they never forget their place and get ideas above their station.'

And finally, a big thank you to those who made it all possible. 'We need to salute guys like Dave King and Douglas Park. Dave and the others put their money in because they are Rangers men, unlike the charlatans before them. They have built from the bottom up but also with their eye on the main prize – 55.

'I also admire Dave King because he was prepared to sell his shares to Club 1872 at cost, and to do so on the drop and not on the open market, giving the fans the chance to be a major shareholder in the club. If the fans have a holding of over 25 per cent it would prevent the shambles we had under Murray ever happening again.

'I also love to see Celtic travelling to their games on Park's coaches. Gives me a tickle to know that when Douglas Park buys shares, or loans money to the club, he could be doing so with money received from Celtic!'

A Season to Remember

Murdo Fraser, MSP

Perthshire, Scotland

ON THE wall of Murdo Fraser's Holyrood office hangs a photograph of Brian Laudrup – signed, of course – which served as a timely reminder of better days during a predominately dark period for the Dane's old club.

In 2012, Rangers had been jettisoned down the divisions as a result of financial impropriety and as one catastrophe followed another, supporters needed something tangible to cling to. What better memory to have than of this elegant and creative winger who was blessed with the pace of a gazelle and a heaven-sent artistry.

Both Rangers and Fraser have now reached the magical number of 55, and the Member of the Scottish Parliament for Mid Scotland and Fife can sleep easier knowing the balance of footballing power in Scotland has once again shifted towards the blue half of Glasgow.

He said, 'When we first entered administration, my first thought was just how incredulous the whole situation was. Several questions needed answering, like how could this great institution find itself in such a desperate position? How could we be in such financial difficulty that we had lost our place at the top of Scottish football and had to go down to the bottom division and work our way back up again? It was almost unbelievable. And clearly there was this terrible resentment amongst our supporters towards the other clubs in the league who had decided that Rangers should be relegated to the Third Division.

'But enormous credit to Ally McCoist and his players as they quickly picked themselves up and got on with the job in hand, which was to get through the leagues and return Rangers to the top flight; something we eventually earned the right to do.

'This included away matches to grounds that the majority of our supporters had never been to; all these far-flung parts of Scotland, which were normally out of bounds for Rangers fans. But we took our medicine and now we're back. It was a really dark time for the club, and a dark time to be a Rangers supporter as inevitably there was a huge amount of stick coming our way from rival fans.

'I knew we'd be back as there was always going to be such a large base of support for Rangers, both from within Scotland and outside the country too. Initially there are doubts, but you soon realise there is no way our club could disappear for ever. We had to return to our rightful place, and return we did.'

It took several years for the right people to gain control of Rangers; those with the club's best interests at heart, a commodity which had been in short supply since David Murray had sold Rangers to Craig Whyte for £1. A successful takeover bid was launched during the EGM of March 2015, and the back-breaking task of repairing and rebuilding a 143-year-old institution began in earnest.

It was so far removed from the Rangers that Fraser had started supporting in the 1970s. Growing up in Inverness, 170 miles north of Ibrox Stadium, the future lawyer described how his love affair with the club began: 'In those days, everyone in Inverness supported their local Highland League team, which in our case was Inverness Thistle. But you also "required" a "big team", and for no particular reason other than my brother was a Rangers fan, and in order to avoid any further conflict within our house, I followed suit. So I was a Rangers supporter all through school, and like everyone else I knew all the players and would boast when we won trophies.'

Fraser was born in September 1965, a few days after Rangers opened their league campaign with a 3-2 win over St Johnstone at Ibrox. A couple of weeks later they edged Celtic 2-1 at Ibrox in a feisty league encounter watched by 76,000. Sadly it wasn't enough to prevent Celtic winning the Scottish First Division, the first of their then-record of nine titles in a row.

It was the late 1970s before the Inverness teenager was old enough to start travelling down to Ibrox to watch his favourites. 'I really enjoyed going to the games. Obviously being from Inverness meant it was a bit of a hike, but it was also great fun; a bit of an adventure. There was something special about leaving the town to go down and see Rangers at Ibrox.

'My favourite player was Derek Johnstone. He was a fantastic centre-forward, great in the air, and he could also play in defence. He was my first Ibrox idol, as he was for a lot of people, but he was just such a fantastic all-round player for the club.

'I didn't become a season ticket holder until much later, but I had my seat in the Club Deck pretty much all through the '90s. I witnessed some great games at Ibrox and I loved going there. And that continued for around a decade until the usual things, you know, family, work, took over and I simply couldn't commit to it any longer. I wasn't getting to the games as much as I would've liked, so I stopped taking a season ticket, although I still tried to get to as many games as I could.

'I still occasionally go to see Rangers nowadays, but life is very busy and I have so many other commitments. I still obviously follow the club avidly and it has been great to see such a revival over the last couple of years.'

First impressions of Ibrox are usually lasting, and for the future Conservative politician it was no different. Going to Ibrox was a day out; a special occasion, and more than 30 years on, that feeling of anticipation has never changed. He said, 'There were two things about Ibrox that gripped me. First of all, the sheer scale of the place when you visit for the first time. When Ibrox comes into view you see this vast, impressive stadium with its incredible red-brick facade. And then when you get inside, it's full of people; 50,000 there to support the team. Such an impressive spectacle.

'But there is another aspect to it and that's simply the entire matchday atmosphere in and around the stadium. Every time I go to Ibrox it begins when you're walking along Paisley Road West. It's that sense of the adrenaline starting as you get closer, and the crowds start to come together, and the noise begins to build. It's the sense of excitement, and the quickening of the pulse as you get nearer the stadium. There is always such a special atmosphere around home games at Ibrox, and I love it.

'I would especially enjoy the big European nights, when we were involved in the Champions League, and playing against teams like Marseille, and all the others who visited our place. Those were great nights.

'But the best for me was the evening we played Leeds United in the inaugural Champions League competition. If memory serves me right, the earlier rounds were the last of the old European Cup, and we were fighting for the right to get into the Champions League proper. It was billed as the Battle of Britain, and it certainly lived up to the hype. We won the home leg 2-1 after going behind early on to an incredible strike by our current assistant manager Gary McAllister, and then produced an unbelievable performance down at Elland Road to win by the same score.

'The media had a field day and as soon as the draw was made they were billing it as the champions of England against the champions of Scotland, which of course it was, but they then suggested Rangers had no chance because the top league in England was so much better than our Premier League, and Rangers would be rolled over by Leeds. Of course, the complete opposite happened.

'I remember when Ally McCoist scored the winner at Ibrox the place erupted, and that remains to this day my best memory of a game at our ground, because it meant so much to us all. It was Rangers arriving on the big stage, and showing we were a force not only in Scottish football, but in European competition too. We could take on and beat the champions of England over two legs, so that was such a big moment for us.'

And while Rangers were taking care of Leeds, a certain Danish international was making waves in Serie A with Fiorentina. Two years later, following a stint on loan at AC Milan (after La Viola were unexpectedly relegated), he would arrive at Ibrox to be unveiled as Walter Smith's latest big-money signing. It was an ambitious move by Rangers, and the beginning of something special. We are, of course, talking about the 82-times capped Danish international Brian Laudrup.

Fraser enthused, 'When I had my season ticket and was going regularly in the '90s, Brian Laudrup was my favourite player by some distance. He was an absolute god! That signed photograph of our Great Dane hangs proudly on my office wall in the Scottish Parliament, and it was a rather ingenious birthday present which offers a timely reminder of the way we were. How would I describe Brian Laudrup as a player? He was just absolute class. Is there another way to describe him?

'He ghosted past players like they were non-existent. His wing play was terrific, and every time the ball arrived at his feet there was this enormous sense of anticipation and excitement because you just knew he would do something amazing with it. He was such a great player for us.'

After watching players like Laudrup and Gascoigne cast a magical spell over Scottish football in the mid-1990s, it was almost unbelievable to think that just over a decade later, the club would find itself in the Third Division.

Admiring his hero: Stephen and Barry Ferguson. Pic by Willie Vass

Alan Denniston with his fellow camera op son Scott

How's that for a cup final backdrop?
Alan Denniston sitting comfortably

Tam Young talks about the tragic events
of 2 January 1971

Tim Webb enjoying another visit to Ibrox

Chairman Dave King poses with Portadown man Tim Webb

Ally Dawson passed on a wheelchair loyal badge to gaffer Steven Gerrard for Tim

Andy Scott, centre, with son, Danny, and friend Baz Aitken, left

Murdo Fraser with retro Rangers top on

The splendid Lewis and Harris Rangers Supporters Club

John Macinnes with Rangers legend Ronnie McKinnon

The Lewis and Harris RSC members enjoy a day out at Ibrox

Flying the flag!

Former Rangers captain Ally Dawson

Satty Singh with his son, Mark Walters Singh, and ex-Ranger Mark Walters (centre)

Ally Dawson with Graeme Souness

Satty and brother Bobby, right, with Walter Smith

Satty's grandson Juggie is a massive Rangers fan

Alex Totten with manager Jock Wallace on the day he joined Rangers

Champions: Alex Totten with the late, great Davie Cooper

*Nancy Honeyball gives gaffer
Steven Gerrard a big smacker!*

*Family fortune: Nancy with her dad
and son*

*I'll be your hero:
Nancy Honeyball
with Ally McCoist*

On the wall: Former Rangers manager Alex McLeish, left, in the Ibrox Blue Room

Rangers through and through: Sir Brian Donohoe

It was so tough for Rangers fans everywhere to comprehend, and Fraser was no different. He recalled, 'There was a lot of anti-Rangers sentiment around, but that's what comes with being at the top of the tree for so long. People are simply jealous of success. Rangers had been so dominant over such a long period of time that there was this huge outpouring of *schadenfreude* amongst supporters of other clubs, who seemed happy to see the giants of Scottish football being brought to their knees.

'But it didn't surprise me one bit the way our magnificent supporters rallied round. Even though we were in the Third Division people were still supporting the club, spending hundreds of pounds a year on season tickets, and when we were playing lower league matches at Ibrox the "Sold Out" signs were a permanent fixture. So these were not fair-weather fans by any stretch of the imagination. These were people who were sticking by their club through thick and thin. True supporters.'

And then we went through a succession of managers after Ally McCoist left the club. We had permanent managers, caretaker managers and interim managers. All guys who wanted to do their best for Rangers, but who ultimately came up short. Thankfully, the board eventually identified the man they wanted to take the club forward, and the day Steven Gerrard was appointed, there was both hope and expectation.

Fraser said, 'Mark Warburton was a decent enough manager, while Pedro [Caixinha] never really made much of an impact, so when Steven Gerrard was announced, it was such a massive statement. The appointment definitely excited me, and I'm sure I wasn't the only one who felt that way. Here was such a big-name player with a huge international reputation, and he was heading for Ibrox. It was the sort of announcement any Rangers supporter would have been delighted with, and it really lifted our spirits. It was a statement of intent from the board, and showed they were prepared to invest in the future of the club.

'One moment I won't forget is when my pal Humza Yousaf, the Justice Secretary, put out a tweet around the time it broke that we were in talks with Gerrard. He tweeted, 'Spoiler alert: Steven Gerrard will never be Rangers manager!' He [Humza] is a big Celtic fan, so don't think for a moment I've let him forget that particular faux pas!'

There were bona fide challenges for the title in Gerrard's first two seasons at the club, and while both ultimately amounted to little, it was the perfect rehearsal for the moment we finally got it over the line. The joy and relief was palpable as the wait had been a lengthy one. The news that Celtic had failed to win at Tannadice, coupled with Rangers' excellent 3-0 home win over St Mirren 24 hours previous, was the cue for celebrations to move into overdrive.

Fraser said, 'Our 55th league title was sweet; just incredible, and there were two reasons for this. First of all, because it has been such a long road back, and ten years is quite a wait between league titles. But let's not forget this is part of a two, as it stopped our great rivals getting a tenth successive title, and there's no doubt that was a sweet part of the equation.

'But let's leave ten in a row aside for a moment, because this was always about Rangers. It was taking all the issues which had occurred during our spell in the lower leagues, as well as the problems we were faced with when we got back up to the Premiership. There was a lot of adversity there; a lot of hurdles to overcome. Building the club back up from its very foundations presented different challenges, but we overcame them.

'We went through a period where we had the dual challenge of trying to find the right manager and also find our feet in the Premiership, while not really presenting a serious challenge to Celtic. And then the board make such a big, bold signing. Steven Gerrard. Someone without a lot of managerial experience, of course, and we took a bit of a gamble on him, but it was absolutely the right thing to do, and everyone is just delighted that it has paid off for him and the club.

'I suppose the only real worry now is that he doesn't disappear off to Liverpool any time soon. We all know that one day he would love to manage his hometown club, but the hope is that he we can hang on to his talents for a few years more.

'I think for him to go to Liverpool right now would be a mistake. He's probably got another couple of seasons at Ibrox where he can build on this success. The great unknown factor is how well the club can progress at the top table in Europe, and that has to be the manager's next big target.

'Our title-winning season brought lots of the usual worries and nervy moments, but by and large it was all incredibly enjoyable. Not just in the winning of matches but in the way we won most of them. The difference was in the consistency of our performances. We hardly played a bad game all season and even when we didn't play as well as we could, we were still getting results, still scoring goals, and, crucially – the big difference during the season – keeping the back door closed. Allan McGregor and his back four were simply outstanding, and a massive improvement in terms of the way we defended our own area.

'At the other end of the park, we weren't reliant upon any single player, unlike the season previous when we depended heavily on Alfredo Morelos to score our goals. This season they were shared around more, and that meant the pressure on individuals was more evenly distributed. It was a positive in many ways, not least because we weren't so concerned about Alfredo getting injured or sent off! I still think we should've sold him last summer when there was supposedly a bid somewhere in the region of £20m on the table. Equally, he made such a valuable contribution on the park and was a big part of our league-winning team. I suppose you can't have it all ways!

'The hope now is that we can go on and enjoy a sustained period of success, as the heads are definitely down at Celtic. There are many changes on the horizon at their place so you would kind of expect it to be a year or two while they sort themselves out and get back to what they were. All the momentum is now with Rangers and it looks like there are more good days on the horizon.

'It has been a long time coming so I think we're due it, and after what we've been through the past nine or ten years, it's a very welcome change of circumstances. The only thing missing at Ibrox was the supporters, but once we are allowed back in I'll definitely be getting back along to Ibrox when I can. It will be great to soak up that atmosphere again. It's so special.'

John Macinnes

Stornoway, Isle of Lewis

Hibs 0 Rangers 1
Scorer: Morelos 51
27 January 2021

Record-breaking Rangers reached another impressive landmark with a 55th top-flight league title. It was a significant notch on the bedpost of the world's most successful club – and 280 miles north of Ibrox, in Stornoway, the main town of the Western Isles, another record is close to being secured. The Lewis and Harris Rangers Supporters' Club – already the largest RSC in the world – is within touching distance of welcoming its 1,000th member. It's a phenomenal achievement given that the population of Stornoway itself is just 5,000.

The supporters' club was inaugurated 46 years ago, just as Colin Stein was scoring that famous goal for Rangers at Easter Road to clinch the 1974/75 title. Simultaneously, plans were afoot to start the club in the faraway Western Isles, and who knew back then just how popular it would become, or if there would even be sufficient interest to sustain a supporters' club so far from Ibrox.

This is a club which hasn't just survived, but positively thrived.

John Macinnes is the manager of the supporters' club, and a lifelong Rangers fan. He said, 'We were formed in 1975 and built our own premises on Inaclete Road in Stornoway. The building was opened by the great Jock Wallace in 1984, a day which still holds great memories for those who were present, and we count ourselves very fortunate to have had such a great man do the honours.

'We witness steady growth year on year, and with almost 1,000 members we are officially recognised by Rangers FC as the world's biggest Rangers supporters' club, which is a fantastic honour. I would say the majority of football fans in Lewis and Harris support Rangers.

'For us to get to Ibrox for a match it is at least a two-day, 600-mile round trip involving a couple of flights or a long ferry and bus journey. Despite this we have groups of members who travel to every match, home and away, pre-COVID, obviously!

'Not everyone can make the trip to Ibrox regularly though, so that's why it's great for us to have our own place in Stornoway where we can get together and watch the games. Our members get the whole experience, from the family atmosphere the club provides, to watching Rangers win on our TVs. It's always a special occasion.

'I must give credit to the bar team, committee and members for creating such a great atmosphere and environment at the club, as apart from Ibrox, there is nowhere I would rather be on matchday. We are honoured and fortunate to have Rangers legend Ronnie McKinnon as an ambassador of our club. Ronnie made over 500 appearances for Rangers in the 1960s and '70s and retired to Lewis in 2000. He now attends all our events and big trips, and he does so because he loves being involved. He turned 80 in 2020 but is still very passionate about his team. He follows all the games and results and like us all, he was delighted when we won the league this season. Ronnie spent his entire Scottish career with Rangers, winning ten major honours, and still loves the club dearly.'

Like many families, who pass down heirlooms to be cherished and nurtured from generation to generation, John revealed how his inheritance was also something money can't buy. He explained, 'My father was a big Rangers man, and my grandfather before him, so it was passed down to me. My first memories of watching Rangers are from the 1995/96, eight-in-a-row season. We had some amazing, world-class players back then, such as Goram, Gough, Ian Ferguson, McCall, McCoist and Laudrup to name a few, but for me Gascoigne was the best, a genius, and I often watch old games featuring Gazza. I still can't figure out how he scored some of the goals he did – like the two solo efforts against Aberdeen to win the league in '96.

'I feel privileged to have met and spent time with many of the Rangers legends I grew up idolising, as they have visited Stornoway as guests of our supporters' club. I also appreciate how lucky I am to have the job up here, although it certainly doesn't feel like work most of the time!'

The 2020/21 season has been special, and John watched every single minute of the action. He insists it's right up there with anything he has witnessed in his 25 years following Rangers. But we asked him to home in on Rangers' second visit of the season to Easter Road, to see if we could better the 2-2 draw in September 2020.

He said, 'What a season! Hopefully we've closed the book on what has been the toughest period in our history, at least the part I've lived through. I grew up during the nine-in-a-row days and have followed the club through the Advocaat and McLeish eras and into Walter's return, and in my time I don't recall us ever going more than one season without winning silverware – until Craig Whyte took control in 2011 and the ensuing chaos that set us back years.

'But there were many key fixtures this season and a few important periods on our way to the title. In the opening months we had a lot of tricky away matches, and the December schedule wasn't much easier as it was packed with nine games in just four weeks. Every game became more important than the last and at the end of a very tough January we travelled to Easter Road on a Wednesday night to take on Hibs. As well as a key match, it was a potential banana skin as Hibs had already given us two of our toughest matches of the season.

'We needed to keep the momentum going, but also to deny our main rivals any hope of getting back into the race as they had dropped an unusual number of points after the new year. I watched the match with one of my friends and both of us were really nervous. Probably because it was starting to sink in that we could really win the league. After the heartbreak around the same stage in recent seasons, we didn't want to take anything for granted and both knew the match at Easter Road was a must-win.

'As expected, Hibs competed well. The first half was an even affair with neither team creating many clear-cut chances and I felt we would have to raise our game a bit after the break if we were to get the win. As it transpired, the second half was a close affair too but thanks to a great goal from our maverick centre-forward we dug out three vital points.

'Once again Alfredo was the star of the show, and he seemed to be at the centre of everything that night. From his moment of madness in the first half, when he got involved with Hibs defender Ryan Porteous, to his goal – a fantastic finish to a typical Rangers 2020/21 move. Alfredo started it off when he picked up the ball out wide and made an easy pass to Tav. The skipper moved it on to Ryan Jack, and both Steven Davis and Joe Aribo had touches while Alfie made his way into the box. He got on the end of Aribo's clever little flick to beat the Hibs defender to the ball and fire home from ten yards. Alfie took a bit of a whack in the process, but that has never bothered him before, and the smile on his face spoke volumes.

'He had a great chance later on when Glen Kamara played a low ball across the face of goal and Alfie missed a "certainty" from inside the six-yard box! It looked an easier finish than the one he scored, but we got the three points, and that was the main thing.

'Alfie was on his toes the entire match and that's why I love him. Even when he's not scoring he's working his socks off for the team and making things happen for others. He has played like this since he joined us four years ago, and always gives 100 per cent for the shirt. Even when things aren't going his way, as he showed again a few weeks later in the away match at Livingston, he refuses to hide. Once again, he'd missed a few chances, but scored the only goal of the game to prove his worth to this Rangers side. Good strikers don't hide, and he never gives the opposition defence a moment's peace. He has been one of our best players this season and I think he will be up for the player of the year award along with McGregor, Davis, Goldson, Tav, Kent and probably a few others. It's a difficult one to call.'

At the end of the Hibs game that night, the first emotion John experienced was one of relief. 'The joy came after the relief, as I knew how important it was. It was also our 20th clean sheet of the season, which was remarkable. Steven Gerrard has put together a great defence, which is the foundation of any successful team. Our defensive record this season is impressive, and I think that's down mostly to McGregor, Tav, Goldson and Barišić being almost ever-presents in the last couple of seasons. It has given them a great opportunity to build relationships. Gerrard has kept faith in them, even when the latter three were prone to a few gaffes, but they are paying him back now – and with interest.

'Around the period of February/March we won a lot of games by the only goal, which again illustrated just how important a good defence is. But it was after the match at Easter Road that I genuinely felt for the first time we were going to win the league.'

Of course, when the title was indeed confirmed – as Celtic failed to beat Dundee United at Tannadice – John was in bits, although still very much in the mood to celebrate. He said, 'It's difficult to put into words the feelings and emotions I've had as a supporter since the title was won. There were setbacks and there were times when I wondered if we would ever do it, even during Gerrard's time. I'm so happy the board gave him the time to build a team. That was crucial.

'From the standards Gerrard brought back to the club, the coaching team and backroom staff he put in place, along with the signings he has made over the past three years, they have all come together this season to make us champions of Scotland and a force in Europe again. Gerrard was the perfect guy to lead us back to the top. He is a born winner, a strong character with integrity and class, and someone who demands 100 per cent from everyone, every single day. All the things required to be a great Rangers manager.

'A lot of credit must also go to Dave King and the board. Sure, they have made mistakes since taking over the club, but they never once gave up, and they backed the manager until he proved a success. Now that we are over the line with 55 I hope we can get back to how it was when I was growing up, and that was challenging for and winning trophies regularly along with our annual forays into Europe. European football has always been important for Rangers, but even more so now with the financial benefits, which all clubs need to remain competitive, especially as COVID has seen to it that stadiums were empty.'

On that subject, this season has been especially tough for supporters the world over. For many, the weekend fix of going to see their favourite team is their one escape from the routine of work and family. It's a chance to relax, enjoy watching your team or grab a few beers in your local pub or club. John admitted the loss of the social side this season has had a big effect on many. He said, 'As well as missing out on getting to Ibrox to enjoy this incredible season we have also missed getting together for games at the club. We have been closed for the best part of 12 months due to the pandemic and I have no doubt it would have been rocking for all the live games this season. There is also the effect it has on individuals who rely on the club for social contact. That shouldn't be forgotten.

'I remember the day we won the league against Kilmarnock in 2011. The atmosphere was incredible. In recent years under Steven Gerrard these types of days and nights have come back with a bang – especially for the Old Firm and Europa League games. The years in between, when we were down in the lower leagues and struggling, our members continued to support their team. Never once did they waver.

'The events of 2012 galvanised our support and the Lewis & Harris RSC continued to thrive despite the turmoil at Ibrox. Our members are a real credit to our supporters' club and to Rangers Football Club and it's such a pity we weren't able to properly celebrate clinching such an historic title, as I have no doubt it would have topped all the great days I have witnessed at the club. But let me assure you, we will make up for it as soon as we can open up again!

'Rangers supporters far and wide deserve this title more than anyone. Let's not forget it was the fans who were punished for the wrongdoings of individuals like Craig Whyte, Charles Green, Mike Ashley, etc. and yet we stuck by the club and fought long and hard for it while others might have floundered. Without our supporters, we would not be back at the top of Scottish football.'

Damn you coronavirus! That might very well be the words of the L&HRSC as they missed out on their annual pilgrimage to Ibrox. It is a sight to behold, as John explained, 'Once a season, we hire out the Ibrox Suite and take in a game with full hospitality. Our last trip was Rangers v Kilmarnock in March 2019, when 150 of us travelled down together and despite the 1-1 scoreline we had a fantastic day.

'We were visited in the suite by several past and present players and some of the Rangers directors. They told us they really appreciate the effort the island supporters make to get down to support their team, which were welcome words. Allan McGregor came over after the match to collect his player of the year award and took the time to chat to our members and have his photo taken with everyone.

'Coronavirus meant we couldn't get down to Ibrox this season, but the hospitality trip is a special day on our calendar and we look forward excitedly to the next one.'

John admits he is a Ranger for life, and equally, he will never forget the thrill he gets each time he sees Ibrox Stadium in all its glory. Like some sort of magical Groundhog Day, the first time he stepped inside the stadium will live with him forever. Oh, and Rangers won that night.

He recalled, 'Rangers 3 Porto 2. It was a Champions League match in 2005 and that was the first time I had been to Ibrox. What a game for starters. Peter Løvenkrands scored the only goal of the first half, and the big crowd was buzzing with anticipation as the teams emerged for the second half. Sadly, Pepe equalised just after the restart, and although Dado Pršo showed great strength to force Rangers ahead, Pepe equalised again.

'That set up a grandstand finish, and it was an unbelievable feeling when [Sotirios] Kyrgiakos headed home a Barry Ferguson cross. Ibrox erupted; the energy levels were off the scale. I remember leaving the stadium that night on a real high, but being brought down to earth a little when told, "It isn't always like this, John!"

'I was 19 at the time and had started going to the matches regularly. I remember walking round the stadium before kick-off and witnessing a sea of blue in the streets. There is nothing quite like it. It was an amazing game and Champions League nights at Ibrox under the floodlights are always special. I look forward to their return next season!'

And let's close with the club's Gaelic motto, 'Sinne na daoine', which translates to 'We are the people'. And who would argue?

Ally Dawson
Glasgow, Scotland

Hamilton Accies 1 Rangers 1
Scorer: Easton 80 (own goal)
7 February 2021

You're at a dinner party and are asked to name your greatest achievement. To be able to say you'd played for Rangers would be quite the boast. To mention you'd captained the team would be another step up, but to say you'd lifted a trophy at Hampden Park as captain of Rangers would be on another level altogether. Ally Dawson will never forget the unrestrained joy he felt walking up the steps at the national stadium in May 1981, moments after Rangers had thumped Dundee United 4-1 in the Scottish Cup Final replay, to receive the cup from Her Majesty the Queen's cousin, Princess Alexandra.

He had just endured an injury-hit year, but the moment he lifted the cup the pain disappeared. He said, 'The manager John Greig had asked me if I wanted to be captain, to succeed Derek Johnstone, and to say I was thrilled would be an understatement. How quickly can you say yes? I had many great moments at Rangers but these were two of the best.

'We had drawn 0-0 with Dundee United on the Saturday and I had picked up an injury, but there was no way I was missing the replay. It was a fantastic night. John MacDonald scored a couple, and Davie Cooper and Bobby Russell were also on the scoresheet. That's the game where Coop slipped that incredible pass through to John for one of his goals.

'After the game, we took the applause of the vast army of Rangers supporters inside Hampden before walking up the steps to collect the trophy. What a thrill that was. It's moments like that you dream of as a kid. It was an incredible way to end what had been a terrible 12 months. If ever I see clips of that game it still gives me goosebumps – and it was 40 years ago.'

Dawson was skipper for three and a half years of his 12-year playing career at Ibrox, but has been involved with Rangers in many different capacities for just over 25 years – and was presented in the spring of 2021 with a memento to mark the occasion.

He played more than 300 first-team games for Rangers, from 1975 to 1987, and while most were at left-back he also performed admirably at right-back and in the centre of defence. He said, 'I was a left-back to begin with at Rangers, but that only came about after I was taking part in a youth tournament in France, and was playing centre-back. When our left-back got injured I stepped in, and I felt quite comfortable there. I was naturally right-footed but I worked really hard on my left side until I became quite adept.

'I had such a hard act to follow as I took over from John Greig at left-back when he retired. My first goal for Rangers was a left-foot volley up at Tannadice against Dundee United. Hamish McAlpine, the United keeper, had no chance, but to this day some folk still insist it was meant as a cross!

'I like to think I could play anywhere across the back line, and Graeme Souness put that to the test in the 1986 League Cup competition when he partnered me with Terry Butcher in the middle of the defence in our semi-final win against Dundee United at Hampden, and then again in the final when I lined up alongside Dave McPherson when Butcher was injured. We beat Celtic 2-1, which was fantastic. Stuart Munro came in that season and did really well at left-back, so I was used in other areas.

'Rangers have been a huge part of my life. I signed as a schoolboy and made my debut under Jock Wallace as a precocious 16-year-old on a pre-season tour of North America, and when Graeme Souness told me my time was up, there was absolutely no bad feeling. It was my time. I signed for Blackburn Rovers, had three great years down there at a club with a lot of tradition and a family-type atmosphere, not dissimilar to Rangers, and then moved back up to Scotland with Airdrie, before a stint in Malta as player-manager of St Andrews.

'I then had around 11 years as a coach at Murray Park, which was almost as enjoyable as playing, as it gave me a chance to work with a lot of highly promising kids. We had Greg Taylor for a couple of years, and he did reasonably well, but it says a lot for the lad that after being let go he really knuckled down at Kilmarnock and is now at Celtic.'

It was while working with the Rangers academy that he noticed Steven Gerrard taking his first tentative steps into coaching. At that time, Gerrard was still playing for Liverpool, but along with Jamie Carragher they would turn up at Liverpool's academy complex to pass on their knowledge to the young players coming through the Anfield ranks.

Dawson explained, 'It was probably five or six years ago that we took our under-14s and 15s down to Liverpool to play their youth teams. It was the done thing then. There weren't many teams who could compete on an equal footing with the Rangers and Celtic youth teams at that time, apart from maybe Aberdeen, so we were playing the top teams from England and abroad. It was good for the kids and challenged them to become better players. From ruling the roost up here they would be up against players their equal, or perhaps slightly better teams, with different styles, so it was good.

'That was the first time I saw Gerrard working with the kids, and the fact he was still playing speaks volumes as he was already putting the building blocks into place for the next stage of his career.

'Around that time, I had also started working in hospitality at Ibrox, doing the pre-match rounds with other former players, which was another good way for me to remain involved at the club. I would be in and around the suites and on one occasion I spotted Gerrard chatting to a couple our directors in the Blue Room. I saw him a couple of times when the Liverpool academy side came up to Murray Park, and realised that something might be on the cards. It was maybe 18 months before he was appointed, but it showed the way the board was thinking, and they went about it the right way, in my opinion, by keeping it all under wraps. They knew who they wanted but waited their time, and nothing came out in the press.

'Bearing in mind the board were under enormous pressure to get the next appointment right, it's to their great credit that they pulled it off – and wanted to keep it quiet. It has been a wonderful appointment. You look at what he has achieved in the game, and that's just the start, as he is now building an excellent reputation as a bright young manager.

'The longer he stays at Ibrox the better, but whether that's another two years or five years, he is building something really exciting, and which will last. We have also fared much better in Europe than I had imagined, while domestically, supporters have had to show a lot of patience, which they have done, and are now reaping the rewards.

'You only have to look at Steven Gerrard; the way he carries himself, the respect and dignity he has, to know that he's a perfect fit as Rangers manager. He is confident but not arrogant. He reminds me a little of the great Jock Wallace, but perhaps without the brashness. When Jock asked a player to do something, he did it. Jock had the respect of the players, and that's something I think Gerrard also has. The players look as though they trust him, and that's huge for a manager.

'Being a manager is a tough gig. I was in charge at Hamilton for a couple of years and one of the jobs I found difficult was releasing players that didn't figure in my plans. Maybe it was just my character. Since Gerrard came in, he has cleared out quite a few. It's never an easy part of the job but he looks as though he has a steely determination about him, and if you aren't performing, there's no doubt he will move you out; all successful managers need that characteristic.

'Graeme Souness told me I wasn't his type of player, and that I'd need to move on. I'd had a year under Graeme and he'd made his mind up, which was fine. I'm quite pragmatic, so we didn't fall out over it. He had a job to do. I was 29, and had been fortunate to have 12 great years at Rangers, so off I went with no hard feelings.

'Steven Gerrard will make mistakes, as all managers do, but he looks the type of guy who will learn from them pretty quickly, and that's a great attribute. The basic thing he has got right is to make the team better, harder to beat, and one that plays great football. I thought it might take a bit longer to get to the stage we're at just now, but that's down to the hard work and dedication of the manager and his backroom team.'

Dawson has been around long enough to know that a 38-game season is never going to end without a few blips along the way, such as when Rangers travelled through to New Douglas Park at the beginning of February. Having thumped Accies 8-0 earlier in the season at Ibrox, and with the home side languishing at the foot of the table, Rangers were overwhelming favourites to win.

Dawson said, 'There were a couple of regulars missing, but the manager picked a team which should still have been capable of winning. The fringe players who come in need to be ready, though, and that's up to them. It's tough, but you never know the moment you'll get the call, and you have to be prepared to take your opportunity.

'Rangers got the breakthrough pretty late on, but the lack of a killer second proved fatal. Our game management could have been better. It has been excellent this season but maybe the full-backs didn't need to be so high up the pitch so late in the game. Maybe 20 or so yards further back might have helped, but that said, there were still enough bodies in the box to deal with the cross when it comes in. I know it comes from James Tavernier's side but he can't take all the blame.

'Tavernier has definitely defended better this year, as well as shouldering his attacking responsibilities. He has contributed so much, while Barišić is another who is great going forward and a perfectly capable defender, although sometimes his body shape could be better.

'But that's me being picky, because Rangers have been terrific; an absolute joy to watch and such a different side from last season. That said, we can trace the origins of the change in Rangers' mentality back to the League Cup Final of December 2019. We lost 1-0 to a hotly disputed goal, but that game gave Steven Gerrard and his players the belief that they could compete with Celtic on an even footing. Rangers played very well that day and fully deserved to win. For me, that was the day the pendulum swung in favour of Rangers.

'Later that month, Rangers went to Celtic Park in the league and won there for the first time since 2010, so that was another part of our rehabilitation. Now there is no inferiority complex when the two meet. We are more consistent, we have better players in and can deal with these matches far better. There is no reason why the players shouldn't continue to have that belief, because they are capable, and if, for some reason, they drop these standards, they will soon know all about it.

'The manager has a core group of nine or ten he can trust implicitly, and that again is a huge asset. You need that core group, but not every manager has it. The majority will be experienced players, like Steven Davis, who was fantastic throughout the campaign. His level of consistency is a manager's dream. You never see him running about all over the place but he still has the knack of being in the right place at the right time. He is a fantastic outlet for those around him and I'd imagine he would be a dream to play alongside.

'But to get back to Hamilton, I think it showed that Rangers quite clearly don't like playing on artificial surfaces, and they aren't alone in that. It was the same at Livingston and, to a certain extent, Kilmarnock. That surface is the biggest leveller in the game, and the pitch at Hamilton isn't even the best of that type of surface going around.

'Suddenly a manager has to think differently, and will take things like age and the chance of injury into account, and make the appropriate changes. It's no coincidence that almost every big league in the world doesn't allow them. As a player, it can get inside your head. It's a totally different mindset from preparing for a game on a nice grass pitch.

'It still shouldn't stop you from defending properly, though, and that is how we lost the equalising goal. We had four or five players in or around the six-yard area and they didn't take responsibility. Walter Smith was the master of game management, but as I said there are definite signs that Gerrard has that in his locker.

'Allan McGregor was terrific at Hamilton and you could sense his frustration at the two dropped points. He had very little chance of saving their goal but that didn't stop him being livid. He had some really good saves throughout the game, which meant Hamilton created a number of good chances, but Allan was always there to thwart them.'

Dawson watched almost every game in 2020/21, whether live or the highlights, and was hugely impressed with the defensive unit. He said, 'It helps if you can play the same guys week in, week out. It's not always possible, but guys like McGregor, Tavernier, Barišić and Goldson have been almost ever-presents all season. Thanks to this, and the quality of these individuals, we had a great consistency throughout the campaign.

'Goldson is a good organiser. He takes charge of that central defensive area and makes sure everyone is doing their job. He goes and wins headers and tackles, which gives those around him confidence. He also reads the game fairly well, but it's the 60- and 70-yard crossfield passes he clips across the park that really impress me. It's a big factor in starting attacking moves.

'Mind you, when Allan McGregor is taking a goal kick and he plays it short to Goldson inside the six-yard box, and he plays it out to Tavernier, sometimes your heart is in your mouth. But even though it's a fairly new thing, lots of teams in England are doing it, and it's a good alternative to just thumping the ball up the park. If you have the players who can pull it off then great, although it's just something we need to get used to.

'When Rangers work the ball into the midfield, they have good players who are always one step ahead; they know what their next pass is, and I see this in guys like Joe Aribo, who is fantastic with the ball at his feet.

'There are many reasons why Rangers won the title. Consistency is one, but it seems to have been a culmination of three years' hard work by Gerrard and his coaches. And almost everything that Rangers did was better than their main rivals. Very seldom did we become complacent, and at Ibrox it was usually a case of trying to get the job done inside an hour so the manager could give others game time.

'The talk now is of whether or not the balance of power in the city has shifted to Ibrox, but it might be a bit too soon to be talking that way. Celtic have dominated for so long that getting the league back was always going to be a big ask, but we've done it and that's the first step.

'I don't see where another sustained challenge is coming from, so it'll probably be Rangers and Celtic for the foreseeable future and it's down to how Celtic react to losing the title, and how they come back from that.

'Gerrard is constantly adding to his squad, and building from a position of strength is always a good sign, but we will have to wait and see what Celtic do about it.

'This title was special. Right up there, and arguably the most important in our history. From where we've been in recent years, we now seem to have a solid structure in place again, so it was sweet and things are moving in the right direction both on and off the pitch.

'There will always be speculation on how long Gerrard will remain manager. After winning the title, probably as long as he wants. Part of the battle is knowing when the time is right

– for both parties – to move on. But the board will now realise exactly what type of manager suits the club.

'I'm overjoyed that Gerrard was given time to build a team. We really have reaped the benefits of that. If there hadn't been any light at the end of the tunnel then the best thing for both parties would have been to go their separate ways, but there has been noticeable progress from the first season, especially in Europe, and the style of football Rangers quickly started to play.

'Something else I like about the manager is that he didn't come in and make any big promises. He just worked away quietly and got on with the job of improving the team.

'When we were down in the lower leagues, I always envisaged us being back in the Premiership and winning it. Only thing I didn't see was it happening so quickly. From where we've been to where we are now, in terms of the level we're playing at, takes a lot of work, and to be holding our own against teams like Benfica in European competition really is remarkable.

'It's now up to everyone at the club to keep working hard and keep improving and there can definitely be many more good times ahead. I don't think Gerrard will allow the players – or anyone at the club – to rest on their laurels. He's a born winner and will want to continue winning things with Rangers – and that's great news for every single one of us.'

Satty Singh

Glasgow, Scotland

Rangers 1 Kilmarnock 0
Scorer: Jack 38
13 February 2021

Satty Singh won't forget the first time he served Walter Smith in his Glasgow restaurant. Rangers' most decorated manager of the modern era was seated just five yards from the kitchen door, but the short walk was proving more difficult than normal for the seasoned restaurateur.

He was worried that his knocking knees would upset the pile of plates on his arm and cause a kitchen disaster of Gordon Ramsay-size proportions. And that was before he noticed that the papadums were chipped around the edges!

Satty insists that feeling of dread returned during the title-winning season as Rangers edged ever closer to their first championship in ten years.

He recalled, 'The first time Walter (sorry, Sir Walter!) came into the restaurant I was terrified. He is a man of great stature and was an incredible manager. I have never been so nervous in my whole life. My knees were literally knocking together. Anyway, he had ordered papadums with his meal, and when I went into the kitchen to collect it I just looked at them. I said to the chef, "These papadums are chipped at the edges. I can't give Walter Smith chipped papadums!" He said to me, "How long have you had this restaurant? All papadums are a wee bit chipped; they're so brittle." "Aye, but these are for Walter

Smith!" Walter and I had a good laugh about it the next time he visited, and thankfully I had calmed down a bit by then!

'When we were four or five wins away from the title, instead of loosening up a bit I became really nervous. We were so close. I try to remain as calm as possible before games, but this title was so important that it was often impossible. I have meditational prayers I do and that helps. I try to keep the energy positive and stay focussed.'

Kilmarnock's visit to Ibrox should've been 'just another routine home win' but with new boss Tommy Wright at the helm, they gave Rangers a tough time of it and it took a Ryan Jack thunderbolt to separate the teams.

Satty said, 'It wasn't the prettiest of games but we ground out an important win. We were easily the better team, although it reminded me a bit of the nine-in-a-row days; we knew we could win and we did, but it wasn't always pretty. It was good to see Ryan Jack and Steven Davis back in midfield after missing out at Hamilton, and both guys made a big difference.

'I enjoyed the season immensely, particularly some of the great goals we scored, like Kemar Roofe's against Standard Liège. The ones that got closest were Jermain Defoe's volley against Livingston at Ibrox, which was his 300th career goal, and Tav's stunning free kick at Tannadice.

'But how about Ryan Jack's winner against Killie! He had about a dozen bodies in front of him and yet still had the ability and composure to control it with a great first touch before smashing it into the top corner. What a strike.

'Jack is really stepping up to the mark and showing his quality, and after he gets his calf issues sorted he will be such an important player for us in the next three or four years. He has come on leaps and bounds under Gerrard, and will also be learning from being a part of the national team.

'Steven Davis can't go on forever, but I'm glad he got a year's extension. He looks after himself very well, and I reckon he has another year after this, although we may have to use him sparingly – a bit like Defoe – but he is such an important player for us. That said, the best person to know when it's time will be Steven himself. He uses his head just as much as his legs and reads the game so well.

'Overall, we have the nucleus of a good side for the next few years and the manager seems to constantly have one eye on the future.'

Satty is long enough in the tooth to know that the business end of the season is all about getting the points, with pretty performances a bonus. He said, 'It's up to us to do enough to win football matches and the rest takes care of itself. Against Killie we should have been out of sight in the second half. Ryan Kent is through on goal and if he scores, then perhaps the floodgates open and we're comfortable, but it was still a very mature performance to see the game out.

'As Steven Gerrard said, the way Rangers now play has been three years in the making. There isn't a team on the planet that has introduced a winning formula overnight. And you can have the greatest coaches in the world but if you don't have the players who can take on board their methods then you don't have a lot. Every time we identify a prospective player, he has to be the type who can fit into the manager's system and way of thinking. It's not enough anymore just to be a good player.'

It's perhaps easy to criticise Rangers for 'only' winning 1-0 against Killie, but to do so without three recognised strikers – Morelos, Roofe and Defoe – puts the victory into perspective, says Satty: 'It shows the value of having a good squad. I like Cedric Itten. He has great potential, but I prefer him in a two up front as he seemed isolated when playing the lone striker role. The Rangers jersey is a heavy one, but I believe Cedric will grow into it.

'The defence was incredible, and to secure so many shut-outs was the real cornerstone of our success. Allan McGregor reminds me so much of The Goalie [Andy Goram], the mainstay of that great nine-in-a-row team. Another aspect of that wonderful side was the organisation and chat of Richard Gough and [John] "Bomber" Brown, and Connor Goldson is from a similar mould. He and the others have a great midfield in front of them, with Davis, Jack and Arfield pulling the strings, and the others all chipping in.'

The game against Killie was as one-sided as they come, as McGregor didn't have a single save to make – but he was always there directing the traffic, and Satty said, 'It's testimony to the way we set up these days that we are so difficult to break down. To achieve what Gerrard has in just under three years is incredible. They hit the ground running at the start of the season and won games with flair or by grinding out results. It was the mark of true champions.

'When it was all done and dusted, and it was time to celebrate, I headed to the temple. My faith is important to me so I wanted to thank the good Lord. It would have been lovely to see Rangers clinch the title in the flesh but it wasn't to be, so I celebrated with the Holy Spirit – and then another kind of spirit! It was a sentimental moment.

'This title was well deserved. It's up there with our other great achievements. When Brian Laudrup headed in the only goal at Tannadice in May 1997 to clinch nine in a row, I didn't think that feeling would be bettered, but this is close. We now have good people in the boardroom. The commitment of Dave King, travelling back and forth from South Africa, which must have been a real bind, is commendable, as is the major contribution from guys such as Douglas Park, George Letham, John Bennett and George Taylor, and the present board, who are all Rangers-minded people.

'In March 2015, Rangers director John Gilligan asked if he could have a private room at Mr Singh's to meet with Dave King and Paul Murray. It was the night before the big takeover bid and I was honoured to provide the guys with somewhere quiet and private – and then a couple of years later we're welcoming Steven Gerrard to the club.

'The new manager had a bit of a job on his hands as the finances of Rangers and Celtic were worlds apart, so we needed Gerrard to get the team playing better, winning matches and slowly making inroads into the chasm that existed between the clubs. That was never going to be easy, but he kept chipping away to see where it would take us.'

And it led us straight to the promised land of 55. That magical number which has been on the lips of every Rangers supporter since 2012. That time was now.

Satty said, 'When Dick Advocaat was in charge he had a heavy cheque book to assist him, and was able to bring in players of the class of Arthur Numan, Michael Mols and Gio van Bronckhorst; players who don't need much coaching. They were good to go. It was much the same with Graeme Souness. When he signed Trevor Steven from Everton he was buying a ready-made, class player, which makes the manager's job much easier.

'As a massive Scotland supporter, Souness was one of my favourite players so I was delighted when we brought him to Ibrox. I'd say Souness and Kenny Dalglish are my all-time favourite Scotland players, Davie Cooper my all-time favourite Rangers player, and Brian Laudrup my favourite overseas Ranger. Well, you can't just have one!

'A string of fantastic European performances gave us hope that our domestic fortunes would take a turn for the better, and thankfully that happened. The appointment of Gary McAllister was a masterstroke. I've played golf with Gary Mac and he's a big Bluenose. Both Gary and Steven knew that the management team would need to show signs of progress and getting the first Old Firm win was one of those things that bought time. Getting in guys like Michael Beale, Tom Culshaw and Jordan Milsom was also crucial.

'Liverpool have always been my English team because of Souness and Dalglish, so I'll be delighted if Jürgen Klopp stays at Anfield for many years as that means we get to keep Steven longer.'

Satty was born in Aberdeen in 1968, but the family moved south to Glasgow four years later. Rangers might not have been on the young man's radar at that time but another member of his family was already well tuned in to the Light Blues. Satty explained, 'We lived in Pollokshields, but I went to Bellahouston Academy. I was the youngest of five kids and my big sister Jaswant was Rangers-daft, so I followed suit. She would send me out for her *Rangers News* and I started to read it on the way home from the shop, which helped me get to know the players. The *News* was 5p at the time, and it was a brilliant read.

'Ibrox was near my school, and at lunchtime my brother Bobby and I would walk along to the Copper Pot in Paisley Road West for a roll and chips before going to the Albion to watch the players train. One day we were standing at the side watching the drills when this ball came my way. I dropped my roll and chips and caught the ball. It was a magical moment for me.

'I was watching guys like Derek Johnstone, Tom Forsyth and Colin Jackson, and after that training session I remember walking alongside the players as they headed back over to Ibrox and big DJ taking my hand as we crossed busy Edmiston Drive. I told DJ the story many years later and I said to him, "You won't remember it, but I've never forgotten it!"

'Bobby was pals with Tam Marshall, and his dad was Mr Marshall, the Rangers groundsman, so he used to get Bobby in to some games. My sister Bembla was in the same class as Tam and Billy's brother Ian Marshall, and our two families are still friends to this day.

'My first game was against Clyde at Ibrox, and my mate Rizza, whose parents owned a newsagents in Paisley Road West, managed to get us tickets for the Govan Stand. I was made up. It was an evening match and we won convincingly. Ibrox under the lights was magical and I remember Iain Ferguson scored a couple. I was about 12, and it was my first experience of a game at Ibrox.

'Our stadium is just incredible. In 1990, while work was going on to construct the Club Deck, I was invited to have a look at how it was progressing. My business partner Tariq was pals with Franny, a scaffolder on the job. I really don't like heights, but I had a peek and it was awesome.

'It wasn't until I was invited into hospitality that I actually saw behind the scenes at the stadium, and that's the real Ibrox. You see everything close up, and it's even more impressive than from a distance. I discovered then that anywhere you go inside Ibrox gives you goosepimples.

'I was on the committee of the Rangers Charity Action Group, and even going to meetings was a great experience; 6pm on a Monday evening and you're walking up the wonderful marble staircase. It was something I could never take for granted. It makes you feel so proud that you're doing something for your club; you're a tiny part of this huge institution.

'When Rangers and Indian Super League champions Bengaluru FC announced a partnership in 2019 I was asked to come on board. The deal was seen as something that could benefit both clubs, so I was delighted to accept the invitation from Stewart Robertson. It was also a great opportunity for Rangers to grow their worldwide audience and to have a look at some of the top talent in India. The prospect of the two clubs working together excited me.

'We hosted a dinner for both parties at Mr Singh's, and there was another reception in the Blue Room at Ibrox. The Indian representatives loved their visit, and former Rangers player Alan Gow, who had played in India, was also present. Rangers were represented by people like John Bennett, Alasdair Morrison, James Bisgrove and Gary Gibson.

'I have been privileged to watch so many great Rangers players, but when I was growing up I idolised Davie Cooper. I have a 5ft by 3ft painting of him in my hallway which I bought at a charity dinner. I was fortunate enough to meet him a couple of times. I loved many other players, including Ally McCoist, but who doesn't love Ally?'

Satty and his wife Kulwinder married in 1987, and were overjoyed to learn that Kulwinder was expecting a baby at the start of 1989 – 2 January, to be exact. Satty takes up the story:

'We were out for dinner on New Year's Day, and the following morning, Kulwinder started to get some pains, so we went straight to hospital. Our son was born that day.

'While Kulwinder was pregnant we decided that if it was a boy I would name him, and my wife if it was a girl. I was a waiter in a restaurant at the time and I got chatting to a Celtic-supporting customer and told him I was going to call the baby after the Rangers player who scored the winner the next day. He said, "What if Rangers don't score and Anton Rogan gets the winner, are you going to call him Rogan Josh?"

'The following day was the big game, and I was in my seat in the Govan Stand nice and early. We won 4-1 with Mark Walters running on to a great through ball by Derek Ferguson to score and clinch victory. Mark Walters Singh it was!

'Young Mark had started school by the time baby number two was on the way and due in, yes, you guessed it, January 1994, although not until later in the month. I was in the Colonial India restaurant in High Street at the time and I used to deliver to Baird's Bar, which was a massive Celtic pub, and the Mermaid, in Bridgeton, which was the opposite.

'Anyway, it was the Old Firm game again, and I went with a similar strategy. It was New Year's Day and we travelled to Celtic Park full of trepidation, but won 4-2. Mark Hateley and Alexei Mykhaylychenko (who scored twice) gave us a 3-0 lead at half-time. Celtic pulled one back before Oleg Kuznetsov clinched the win with 15 minutes remaining. Yip, Oleg Kuznetsov, so you can imagine how popular I was when I went home to Kulwinder after the game! "You can't call him that," I think were her words. When my second son was born on the 19th, we compromised a little and settled for Oleg Gurpreet Singh!

'When we were ready to try for baby number three, my wife had by this time tippled about January births and I was sleeping in the spare room during April. No more January babies!

'Baby number three was due in July 1995, and I decided that if it was a boy I was going to call him John Viola Singh, after my good mate, who was also my financial advisor. But then in July 1995, Rangers signed Gazza. I'm in the restaurant talking about babies' names, and John is warning me that I better not change it. I said, "How does John Viola Gazza Singh sound?"

'But my daughter was born on the day Rangers played Steaua Bucharest at Ibrox in a pre-season friendly, and Gazza played really well. I had a few pints after the game and had bought a nice wee dress to take up to the hospital. My wife was in hospital for a couple of days and had been mildly sedated, but when I suggested we call our daughter Paula, she was on to me in a flash. "No!" So, Kiran it was – and my family was complete!

'I've heard John Brown speak at events and he tells the story about asking me why I didn't name one of my kids after him, as he'd scored an Old Firm winner. He would say, "How about Oleg Bomber Singh! On second thoughts, 'Bomber' Singh might not look too good on the kid's passport!" He's hilarious.'

Satty opened his first restaurant in 1990 – the Colonial India, in High Street. He was a partner in the business with Tariq Iqbal and Taqir Malik. Sadly, Taqir – a world-class chef – passed away. 'Taqir was one of the best, and that's not an exaggeration. He was outstanding. I loved the location of the restaurant – until they opened a Celtic shop next door! I was there two and a half years, and then took a year out before opening Mr Singh's in Elderslie Street in 1994.

'People ask if I've always had an interest in cooking, but the truth is I could probably get away with boiling an egg. That's about my limit. Front of house has always been my forte. I once tried to make naan bread, but burnt my hand!'

Mr Singh's is now recognised as one of Glasgow's top restaurants and is a favourite haunt of many well-known faces, including footballers from both halves of the Old Firm. Satty said, 'A mate of mine, Dougie Donnell, brought Ian Armstrong into the restaurant one day. Ian was the ticket office manager at Ibrox. Word got about that Mr Singh's was a good restaurant and so Neil Murray and Davie Dodds came in for a meal one night. They were the first Rangers players I had in.

'Alex Cleland and Gary Bolland were next, and before long we had Craig Moore, Barry Ferguson, The Goalie, Charlie Miller and then Walter Smith himself. We have a room in the corner where players can have a wee bit of privacy. It's partitioned off with a curtain, but I'll tell you this, if the walls in Mr Singh's could talk!

'When I played football I was a defender, so I've always loved centre-halves. One of my favourites was Gordon McQueen. A couple of years ago, Gordon's daughter Hayley came in with the Sky Sports team, and I was saying how her dad was a hero of mine. Gordon came in not long after that.

'Odsonne Édouard was in before an Old Firm match and I had a customer asking if I could put a little something in his meal. When I winked and told him the chef was on it, he burst out laughing. Nobody loves a bit of banter more than me.

'I've always maintained that the restaurant is for everyone. If you see a pic of Brian Laudrup on the wall, you can be sure Henrik Larsson will be right next to it. Alex McLeish has been a regular, and as a former manager of Hibs, Rangers and Scotland, I'm in my element when he comes in. Of course, the golden rule is to let customers enjoy their meal in peace, but there's always an opportunity to chat.

'Neil Lennon, Martin O'Neill, Gordon Strachan and Andy Gray have all been customers over the years, so we've been blessed with the cream of football talent in our restaurant. And then you have the likes of Ally McCoist and Gazza; it doesn't get any better.

'I had great banter with Pierre van Hooijdonk a couple of days before an Old Firm cup tie at Hampden. As he was leaving, he signed a £5 note, handed it to me and said, "I'll wave to you when I score the third goal." I replied, "Aye, but it'll be 2-0 to Rangers at the time!" And sure enough it was, although I can't remember the big man waving to me.' I reminded Pierre when I was invited over to Feyenoord for a game by Michael Mols and Arthur Numan. Gio van Bronckhorst was the Feyenoord manager at the time, and we met Pierre in the stadium. That was a brilliant trip, and full of great memories.'

Satty has become friends with many of his customers – from all walks of life – since he opened Mr Singh's 27 years ago. He is good friends with Walter Smith, who brought the family in for his 60th birthday. He was with wife Ethel and sons Neil and Stephen. Satty said, 'It would have been a privilege to serve them, but Walter had other ideas. He said to me, "Sit down, Satty, and have a pint." That's the kind of man he is. He has this aura about him, but he's a fantastic man. He called me when I was in hospital, and that meant a lot to me.

'I've also become close friends with Brian Laudrup, his wife Mette, and the kids. We keep in touch regularly by text, and whenever he's in Glasgow he doesn't leave without visiting the restaurant or getting in touch. He is a lovely guy and a gentleman.

'When Mark Walters signed I was delighted, as not only had we signed a great footballer but he was also the first high-profile black player to join Rangers. Every time he had the ball at his feet it was just so exciting. Such a terrific talent and he broke down many barriers.

'Which leads me to the Rangers campaign Everyone Anyone, which is a fantastic initiative. I've been to a few meetings and it's much more than a photo shoot; it's the real deal. Rangers really is a club for all.'

Satty admits he missed getting to Ibrox this season, like a lot of supporters. 'My brother Bobby lives next door so at least we have been able to enjoy the journey together. Our houses are a 15-minute walk from Ibrox, that's from my front door to my seat! Bobby and I are in the Main Stand near the press box. We have four season tickets and its Bobby and I and two grandkids Dylan and Harpreep. I love having the grandkids at the game. They're the next generation of Rangers fans. When I was invited to the opening of the new Rangers shop, I had to buy nine tops for the grandkids!

'I'm glad our grandkids follow Rangers, because it has been in our family so long now. Don't get me wrong, there were times when I was picked on due to the colour of my skin. One incident I remember clearly was the Davie Cooper testimonial match against Bordeaux in 1988. Coop led Rangers out on to the park while the great Jean Tigana was alongside him with the visitors. This guy next to me screamed at Tigana, "Away you go ya black bastard!" I was a bit older and wasn't prepared to accept that rubbish so I pulled him up. He looked at me and said, "I wasn't talking to you pal, you're no' black, you're brown!"

'I've also had my turban knocked off a few times by morons, but I soon learned that for every one idiot there were thousands of decent Rangers supporters who accepted me for who I was. It was annoying, but it didn't stop me going, because I loved Rangers and they were my team as much as anyone else's.'

It has been quite a journey for Satty, but the triumphs and celebrations have more than made up for the disappointments and up until Rangers won the league this season, Helicopter Sunday topped the list. He said, 'We woke up that morning knowing it was out of our hands; all we had was hope. I had been in Cardiff for the FA Cup Final the day before, and I went to Easter Road with Alistair Forsyth. We could've won 10-0 and still lost the league because all they required was a scrappy 1-0. But what a day it turned out.

'That night, Alex McLeish came into the restaurant with some of the players. Maurice Ross still had his Rangers top on, while Barry Ferguson gave me his medal. That was such an emotional moment.

'The restaurant has provided so many great memories. We've all worked so hard to make it a success. We want folk to come in for a meal and go away having enjoyed a relaxing night and a good meal. I enjoy what I do, which makes a big difference.

'Sadly the pandemic hit the hospitality industry hard; the worst I can remember. During the first lockdown we went from 90 covers to 55, 28 tables to 15, and 70 hours trading to 37. We installed screens, hand sanitiser, a digital temperature machine and all staff wore gloves. Once we had established these protocols we were safe to open, but the government implemented a blanket ban.

'Initially many businesses thought about closing, but we decided that to do so would make it so difficult to reopen after a few months of inactivity, so we decided to offer a weekend takeaway service, so that at least we could hit the ground running once the ban was lifted.

'And once things get back to normal, we can have customers in again, and make new memories.'

Alex Totten

Dunipace, Scotland

Rangers 4 Dundee United 1
Scorers: Hagi 35, Kent 38, Aribo 48, Morelos 64
21 February 2021

Alex Totten was an old-school right-back; a defender, first and foremost. It's backed up by his stats. In a 14-year playing career he made more than 200 first-team appearances for the likes of Dundee and Dunfermline, and his goals haul is measured in single figures. Defending was the name of his game.

His playing career began under the watchful eye of the great Bill Shankly at Anfield, just as The Beatles and Cilla Black were becoming a fixture in the 'hit parade' and playing regular gigs at the legendary Cavern Club in Liverpool.

He moved on from Anfield after four years as first-team opportunities were limited, but the apprenticeship he'd served was second to none and it helped him win a move to a very successful Dundee side, managed by Bob Shankly, brother of Bill. Later in his career, Totts enjoyed a two-year spell as assistant manager to Jock Wallace, and despite leaving Ibrox 35 years ago he very seldom misses a Rangers game on TV these days.

He admits the role of right-back has changed beyond recognition since he played the game between 1964 and 1978, and said, 'In my day, you won the ball from the opposition winger, fed your own number seven, and in turn he took the ball up the park and either passed it or tried to beat a player or two. That was my job done. Not anymore. It's all about wing-backs now, athleticism, and having the energy to get up and down the flank from minute one to the final whistle. Perhaps these guys aren't the greatest defenders in the world but they bring so much more to the team by creating opportunities for team-mates.

'We weren't encouraged to get up the park. Two of the leading full-backs of the day were Rangers pair Bobby Shearer and Eric Caldow, two great defenders. I remember reading a piece which said Alf Ramsay had done away with wingers when England won the World Cup in 1966, to which one wag answered, "Bobby Shearer was doing away with wingers long before that!" Shearer wasn't nicknamed "Captain Cutlass" for nothing!

'Nowadays, we have James Tavernier and Borna Barišić almost wearing out the right and left flanks. Tavernier has been fantastic this season and the number of goals and assists he has is impressive.'

Sadly Tav was missing from the Rangers v Dundee United match at Ibrox due to an injury picked up in a Europa League tie in Antwerp. Leon Balogun was given the nod for the visit of the Taysiders.

Totten was pleased with the overall performance, although not the opening portion of the match, and said, 'Rangers weren't great in the first 20 minutes or so, but I fully understand why. They'd had a tough game in the Europa League just a few days beforehand and that takes it out of players. The actual match in Antwerp, the travelling, etc. I had an idea they would start slowly.

'But every game is about what happens over 90 minutes, and not in the first period of the first half. Rangers have shown this season they are a true 90-minute team. They have their instructions and they don't deviate from them, and once again it worked out well.

'Dundee United had a couple of chances in the first half but they found out just how good a keeper Allan McGregor is. He has been fantastic this season and would probably be my player of the year. Time and again when Rangers needed him he stepped up to the mark. You could see how angry and frustrated he was when United got the late goal to spoil his clean sheet.

'After such a sluggish start, Rangers really came into their own and once they got their noses in front they were a completely different team. It was a typical Rangers performance. They passed the ball very well and their movement, both in and out of possession, was first class.

'So many players have enjoyed an excellent season, but the great strength with this Rangers side lies in their squad. Take, for instance, the substitution Steven Gerrard was forced to make just 25 minutes into the game. Ryan Jack, one of his most influential midfielders, limped off injured. Glen Kamara came on in his place. Later on, Jermain Defoe replaced Alfredo Morelos; Scotty Arfield on for Hagi. Three substitutions, which in my opinion didn't weaken the team. That's demoralising for the opposition.

'The manager has cleverly built a fantastic squad, and Rangers now have a couple of players for each position; players who can more than hold their own when they either start or come off the bench.

'When you can play a settled side it makes such a difference. When I was at Liverpool, and someone asked Bill Shankly what the team was, "Same as last year," he would say, quick as a flash. Continuity is everything. Look at Liverpool now. When Jürgen Klopp had his first-choice 11 available they were virtually unbeatable. This season was a different scenario altogether.'

Totten admits he was really impressed by the quality of Rangers' third goal, scored by the twinkle-toed midfield maestro, Joe Aribo. 'It was the pick of the bunch,' he said. 'It's that type of play and finish that gets people up out their seats; the type of goal players dream about scoring. Joe Aribo is an excellent player. He's an absolute natural; you don't coach players the type of skills that lad has.

'I was on a podcast a week or so after the match with Derek Ferguson and Ian Durrant, two players who were also naturally gifted and Aribo is another.

'Steven Gerrard has probably mulled over Aribo's best position, and come to the conclusion that he can play anywhere. He knows when to hold on to the ball, the best time to release it, etc. It's all natural instinct with him, but he certainly made a big impact in the game against Dundee United. He is clearly a talented individual, but isn't selfish, so he fits into the manager's team with ease.'

While Rangers took the plaudits thanks to a superb 4-1 victory, Totten had a few comforting words for the visitors, 'United deserve credit for the way they approached the game. Unlike some visitors to Ibrox, they didn't come and park the bus, they had a go and it made for an entertaining game, which is what football is in the first instance. They tried to win the game and they had a few chances. Rangers came good in the end and won quite comfortably, but it was tough going for a while.

'Rangers' fourth goal – scored by Alfredo Morelos – might have been a lucky one, but Morelos deserves so much credit because if he gives up the ghost he doesn't score. He chased it down and was in the right place for the ball to rebound off him and into the net. I love that quality in players.

'Scoring 13 goals in an eight-day period, at home to a good team like Dundee United and in the two Europa League ties against Antwerp, is a fantastic week's work by any team's standards.

'I was also impressed by how Leon Balogun stepped up to fill the right-back position in Tavernier's absence. It shows that the lad is willing to play anywhere for the team. He put in a really good cross in the first half against United from which Morelos should have burst the net.

'There is always pressure at a club like Rangers. Everyone has been desperate to win the league for years now and that pressure rests squarely on the shoulders of the players and management. There is more pressure at Rangers than any other club, because the fans demand success. And the players and coaching staff have handled it magnificently. The goals for and against columns speak volumes. There was a lot of pressure on the players to stop ten in a row but they did it – and with style.'

Totten was impressed with the way Rangers knocked the ball about against United, the urgency of their play once they'd scored the opening goal, and their relentless pressure thereafter.

He said, 'First and foremost football is a team game, and while Rangers have great individual stars they are also a first-class collective. I love playing golf, but in that game I only need to depend on me. When I was a manager I had to depend on the 11 players on the park, but every one of those Rangers players have played their part this season. You've got Tavernier and Barišić putting some great balls into the box for the forwards, and Kent terrorising defenders. He scored a great goal over in Antwerp to give us a flavour of what he is capable of.

'Since the start of the season, Rangers, as a unit, have shown unbelievable consistency. I'd like to think that supporters of all clubs, and not just Rangers, have been impressed by some of the great football they've played. They have been almost faultless in the league and are worthy champions.'

Despite the win over United, and Celtic's subsequent loss to Ross County later that night, leaving Rangers needing just seven points to secure a 55th title, Totten insisted the league was over long before Rangers hosted Dundee United. 'That has been down to consistency. Rangers play with a great confidence and are good to watch. Their movement off the ball is outstanding and it means the player on the ball always has an option, and that's invaluable. When punters are saying things like, "If Rangers lose three games," it doesn't make a lot of sense. They haven't lost all season, are playing magnificently, and yet some are suggesting they might lose three or four of their last eight games. I think it's down to wishful thinking on their part, and not based on any science.

'We all accept that no team can go through an entire season being brilliant in every game. Sure, it's an entertainment business, but when you win games while not at your best, that's the mark of true champions.

'When I was second in command at Rangers, big Jock would say to me, "Totts, we just have to win today. I don't care if it's a scrappy 1-0. A good performance is the icing on the cake. Football is all about winning," and he was 100 per cent right.'

When Totten turned on the news in May 2018 and saw that Rangers had appointed Steven Gerrard as manager, he was delighted – although a little surprised. On one hand Gerrard had the potential to be a success, but like many others, Totten worried about a lack of managerial experience.

He said, 'Rangers took a chance, but it was a calculated chance. It's difficult managing a club the size of Rangers with very little experience. Normally, the club would go for a manager with a bit of a reputation in the game. When Rangers appointed John Greig in 1978, sadly it didn't work out, likewise Aberdeen with Willie Miller in 1992. So, there's always an element of risk involved in appointments like this.

'But Gerrard had such a high profile and vast experience of playing for both Liverpool and England. He had learned from many great managers so he always had a chance. It takes time to build any team, let alone a highly successful one, but he has done so with great patience and skill and the end result is the league title. I was delighted for him when the moment arrived.

'First and foremost, Gerrard looks and acts every inch a Rangers manager. The way he carries and conducts himself on and off the park is impressive. He was so calm in the lead-up to Rangers winning the league and never once celebrated early or engaged in one-upmanship. He was well respected as a player, and now he has that same respect as a manager. He's an impressive character.

'No matter if Rangers have been poor or failed to win a match, he always comes out and speaks to the media, and he's a straight-talking guy, which I like. Rangers' supporters have been reared on success, so there is an expectation that has to be handled, and I think he handles it brilliantly.

'He has been learning as he goes along, and has made some great signings, notably off the park. Ross Wilson, the sporting director, is a fantastic guy. I worked with Ross at Falkirk and he impressed me no end. He is both professional and meticulous. He has worked at Huddersfield, Watford and Southampton, and when Ronald Koeman moved from Southampton to manage Everton, he wanted to take Ross with him, but Ross decided to stay.

'Rangers were in for Ross a few times but he had a job to do at Southampton and wanted to see it through. I know that Steven Gerrard has a lot of respect for him, and he has definitely played his part in this success. There is a big team behind the scenes at Rangers and they are very much like a family the way they work together.

'I've also been impressed with the way the manager has handled Alfredo Morelos. Morelos is a smashing player and really brings a lot to the team, but his indiscipline has come to the fore a few times. When I was a manager I would probably have handled him differently from Steven; I might have lost the head, but Steven has remained calm, and I'm sure the player appreciates this.

'Life is all about common sense and Steven seems to have a lot of it. You don't demand respect, you earn it. I demanded discipline from my players, and if respect came as a result of that then great.

'Pressure is a constant at Ibrox. When Rangers were winning, Jock Wallace didn't ever get too carried away, because he knew that if we lost a couple of games the tide would turn. He would say to me, "In football, you're either a king or a clown – there is no in between."

'Apart from being a very good manager, who has learned so much, Steven also seems to be a fair manager and that will stand him in good stead. It's a great quality to have, and you can't do anything but admire him.

'Managers can rant and rave and give players a hard time, but there is no greater deterrent to a player playing badly, or acting up, than to see a jacket hanging on his peg in the dressing room. Competition for places will always trump ranting and raving. It's Rangers, and you don't want to lose your place.'

Totten's lifelong affinity for Rangers takes in a few generations now, with his son and grandson currently season ticket holders at Ibrox. He said, 'My two grandsons were delighted when we clinched the league. Alexander is 20, and Jake four years his junior. It's really the first title they fully remember Rangers winning. Alexander and his dad have season tickets for the Main Stand and they never miss a game. My dad was a big Rangers man so it has always been in the family.

'I was managing Falkirk in 1984 when I got a call from Jock Wallace to ask me if I would like to be his assistant at Ibrox. Would I ever? When I told my dad you could see a tear welling up in his eye. It was one of the most emotional moments of my life.

'I arrived at Ibrox as proud as punch and when I walked through the front door and looked up at the rich wood panelling on the walls, and the marble staircase, I was in awe. I had walked through the front door numerous times as a player or manager of the opposition, but this time was different. I was a Ranger.

'I walked slowly up the marble staircase, stood at the top and stared down at the portrait of the great Alan Morton. The hairs on the back of my neck stood to attention. Ibrox is such a special place. There is no other place like it for provoking all these different emotions. Big Jock met me at the top of the stairs and gave me a warm – and forceful – handshake. "Welcome to Rangers, Totts," he growled. "Now let's go and meet the directors." I walked into the Blue Room and the likes of Willie Waddell and Rae Simpson were standing before me. It was a real "wow" moment.

'Years later I took my grandsons on a tour of Ibrox and when we got to the manager's office one of them said, "Did you ever sit in that chair, Grandpa?" But I hadn't. I hadn't earned that right.

'I remember my dad coming through to see me at Ibrox, and I took him up to the office. Jock was there to meet him, and the big man said, "One day, this will be Alex's office. He will be manager of the Rangers when I step upstairs to general manager." John Paton, one of the directors, said the same thing.

'Every day after training, Jock and I would go up to his office to talk about the team, how training had gone and which players were doing well, etc. I didn't dream of sitting in the big man's chair. It wasn't mine, and sadly it never would be, as events took a dramatic turn in 1986 when Graeme Souness was announced as the new manager after Jock had left.

'Jock visited me when I was manager of St Johnstone and it was great to see him. We were doing really well and had gone from near the bottom of the Second Division to the top six of the Premier League. As we walked out on to the pitch, he said to me, "I knew you would make a great manager Totts. What you've done here is nothing short of miraculous." It made me so proud to hear the big man say that. We had a great relationship but he didn't hand out praise like sweeties, you had to earn it.

'I was at a player of the year event once, and this guy stopped me and said, "I hope you don't mind me saying, but you should have been manager of Rangers." I was really pleased to hear that, but this voice from behind us says, "Aye, the guy's right, you should've!" We both looked round and there was the great Jim Baxter, echoing this chap's sentiments. What a fantastic moment!

'I look back on my time at Rangers with great fondness and a lot of pride. Also for my dad, because I know what it meant to him. We won a couple of League Cups – when Coisty scored the hat-trick against Celtic at Hampden – and when we beat Dundee United. Jock would say to me, "Totts, you've never lived until you've beat Celtic in a cup final!" The big man was magic that day and gave me his medal, as the assistant managers didn't get one then.

'Later on, we were sitting in his office and he said, "I want you to take the team for the Tennent's Sixes at the Coasters Arena in Falkirk." It was a six-a-side competition involving all the top league sides, and it was in my home town. I know it was only the Tennent's Sixes, but I was in charge of the Rangers team that included guys like Davie Cooper, Ian Durrant, Derek Ferguson, etc., and it was an absolute honour. And, of course, we won it.

'We also went on a world tour and that in itself was full of great memories, seeing places like the USA, Canada, Australia and New Zealand. And we would go to the likes of Germany and Switzerland for pre-season camps. It was such a great footballing education for me, especially playing in Europe against clubs like Inter Milan.

'I've now retired from Falkirk FC. Part of my duties on a Saturday afternoon was to mix with sponsors and punters, and it's something I loved. But I've been involved with football since the moment Bill Shankly signed me for Liverpool in 1960, and it was time to call it a day. I've had such an enjoyable career, but I certainly won't be a stranger to football.'

Nancy Honeyball

Dunoon, Argyll and Bute

Rangers 3 St Mirren 0
Scorers: Kent 14, Morelos 16, Hagi 46
6 March 2021

If Steven Gerrard didn't entirely grasp what winning a 55th league title might mean to Rangers supporters, he was made aware as he turned up for work before the home match against St Mirren.

It took his car fully 15 minutes to travel 50 yards from the roundabout at the junction of Broomloan Road and Edmiston Drive to the iconic stadium gates. With the team standing on the cusp of a first title in ten years, there were a 'few' well-wishers keen to pass on their best regards to players and management.

The scenes were busy and noisy, and reminiscent of the many demonstrations which had taken place during the dark years – only this time anger had been replaced by happiness. This was a club which had been transformed by many, but for the moment, jubilant supporters wanted to express their gratification to the manager and his players.

Victory over St Mirren would all but assure Rangers of the title. To make it mathematically certain, Dundee United would be required to hold Celtic to at least a draw the following day.

Truth is, it was in the bag and the final denouement was just a matter of time. Thirty-three miles away, on the 'island' of Dunoon, one supporter sat glued to her iPad watching videos of the pre-match celebrations being uploaded on to social media platforms, and there was a tear in her eye.

Nancy Honeyball loves Rangers, but like so many others she has suffered from afar while the players have ruthlessly gone about their business week on week. She has missed sitting in her seat in the Sandy Jardine Front, sharing banter with those around her and cheering on her team. It has been tough, so Nancy completely understood the outpouring of emotion before the St Mirren game.

She was also delighted with the way the encounter went, and three superb goals was the icing on the championship cake. She said, 'We definitely had our swagger on. That was as good and as polished a performance as I'd seen all season. We shouldn't forget that St Mirren are a good side and have enjoyed a terrific season.

'At times, though, it looked like a training session for our boys, but that was mainly down to the accuracy of our passing. We had Saints running around all over the park chasing shadows. It must be really difficult to play against us when we are in this mood.

'It genuinely was like watching some of the greatest Rangers teams in my lifetime the way we kept the ball and moved it on. Let's just say we haven't had a lot of days like this in the last ten years!'

Like most, Nancy has many favourites peppered throughout the Rangers team. And while she thought Ryan Kent deservedly won the man of the match award, she had nothing but good to say about the outstanding talent that is Joe Aribo. She enthused, 'He is like a ballet dancer. His feet are magical. He can have three or four defenders around him, but he always gets out of the tightest of situations and finds a team-mate with a pass. Even when he is at the corner flag, running down the clock, he does it so well.

'Kent was everywhere during the game. I liken him to a yo-yo because no one can get the ball from him. He moves it on and invariably it is never more than a couple of feet from his toes.

His close control is astonishing. Like the others, he has his own role to play but he pops up everywhere; he's so versatile. There was one moment where he was back defending and conceded a corner. Next thing he's in the box and clearing it away.

'But I have to give a special mention to Allan McGregor. He had one fantastic save in the second half, which shows just how switched on he is. And as a McGregor myself (before I ended up a Honeyball!) we need to stick together. But seriously, he has been a godsend for us and proved such a big player throughout the season. I get that it's hard to give a goalkeeper the player of the year award when the team has been so awesome offensively, but he definitely deserves recognition.'

All three goals were worthy of goal of the game, although Nancy reckoned Kent's opener, which he fizzed past Saints keeper Jak Alnwick, was one the best he's scored this season. She said, 'It was a great pass from Connor Goldson to find wee Kenty, but the touch he took to deceive the defender was unbelievable and the finish? Well, no keeper in the world would have stopped that one (apart from maybe Allan McGregor!). He scored one similar against Hibs in April.

'It was also fantastic to see Alfie get his name on the score sheet again, after his winner at Livi the previous midweek. I love when he scores because his celebrations are always straight from the heart. The way he kisses his tattoos, and makes the love heart sign, they make me smile – and isn't that what football is all about?

'He has been treated appallingly since he arrived in Scotland, and that embarrasses me. He's just a young guy playing his football in a foreign country and trying to get on in life. He is from a different culture and has an aggressive style of play – as have the defenders who rough him up – but he has been hammered all over the media for it, for reasons I simply don't understand.

'He does so much good for impoverished children back home in Colombia, but that goes largely unreported as certain folk prefer to accentuate the negative. But if you watched his interview after the Saints game – when he did his best to speak English, and did very well – I challenge you to say you weren't bubbling. I know I was! He might not always do everything right, but he has a heart of gold.

'And you could see how much the supporters love him by the reception he received when he arrived at Ibrox for the game. The Colombian flags were blowing in the wind and wee Alfie looked emotional.

'He gets frustrated when he misses chances, and I get that because he tries so hard for the team. But he has set a few records at the club and he is adored by everyone. I don't know if he is aware of just what he has achieved at Rangers but he should be very proud of himself.'

Victory at Ibrox was accompanied by a 24th clean sheet of the season, and just two goals conceded in 16 home league matches didn't augur well for St Mirren in their quest for the top six. The meanest defence in Britain didn't disappoint.

'That's all down to guys like Connor Goldson,' said Nancy. 'When he first joined Rangers I felt he was a bit ropey at times but he has been almost flawless this season. I feel safe with him at the heart of the defence, and I'm sure the midfield did too.

'Goldson's passes out of defence have been a big part of our success, while Borna and Tav getting up and down the wings also added to our goal threat. Our defenders have struck up this incredible understanding and it bodes well for the future. They read each other now, not just the ball.

'I was gutted for Tav when he was injured in Antwerp. He's our longest-serving player and I was relieved when he was back in time to lift the trophy. There was a time when Tav was getting criticised left, right and centre, but thankfully that's all in the past.'

The only regret from an amazing season has been the empty seats, which provide the backdrop to the TV pictures we see week in, week out, and Nancy moaned, 'Being there is so different from watching on TV. Ibrox can be electric, and when everyone is singing and getting behind the team there isn't an atmosphere like it. I've been to some amazing concerts, like The Who, Lady Gaga, Madonna, and while there's always a great buzz about the place, it's nothing like Ibrox when it's rocking! When we went through all the protests, and the Union Bears weren't singing, the atmosphere was just awful, so it shows you what these young supporters bring to the table. I had to sing to myself in those games!'

Nancy admits she was delighted when Steven Gerrard was appointed manager. He had little experience of life in the dugout but she is all for rookies being given an opportunity. 'It doesn't matter what the job is, folk just need a chance. I don't think Steven Gerrard would have been short of job offers but I'm sure it was important to him to start off in the right one. That said, they don't come much bigger than Rangers. My husband, William, was born in London and is a massive England fan, so we've watched just about every international game he played. His passion and commitment was undeniable. I thought that if he could bring that into the job at Ibrox then we would be okay.

'To appoint him in the first place was a great decision by Dave King and the board. They believed in him from the start and ensured he would get the time to rebuild the playing side from top to bottom. He did that, and what a job he has made of it.

'He is still so young, and it looks as though he can go on and have a long and successful career in management. I just hope he stays with us for a long time, because he is now ingrained within the fabric of our great club. He has bought into the Rangers ethos and we are delighted to have him.

'When he speaks, people listen. He is dignified and commands respect. He has transformed Rangers both on and off the pitch, and he knows exactly what he wants. One thing I love, though, is when the camera is on him in the dugout, and the ball comes to him and he gives a cool wee flick or pass. That gets me every time!

'I must admit, I think the world of him. After one game last season I waited outside the stadium to see the players, and when Steven came out I forgot myself for a moment. I gave him a big kiss on the lips and my sisters thought it was hilarious!

'But he is a great ambassador for the club, and even when he got into trouble for his verbal assault on the referee at Livingston, it was only because he was defending his player. He was in the stand for the second half but I'm sure his players will have appreciated his passion – I know I certainly did.

'He was a great player but that's never a guarantee someone will make a great manager. When I was at the Rangers v Liverpool legends match and Stevie came out with a Rangers top on that was me done. The effect it had on the fans was unbelievable – but my mascara started to run!

'The weekend we clinched the title, it was great listening to guys like Ally McCoist, Graeme Souness and Alex Rae talking about what it means to win a league with Rangers. Their reactions were incredible. Souness was on Sky Sports, and in the studio with Roy Keane. Graeme didn't mince his words, and when he finished with, "I wish I was in Glasgow right now," I was very emotional.

'All the players who have achieved 55 should now be immortalised in our Hall of Fame. They have done so well, been so consistent and so far ahead of the competition that if it was a boxing match it would have been stopped halfway through!

'Even Scott Wright has slotted straight in and looks as though he has been at Ibrox for years. All the new players that come in from now on will be desperate to fight for a shirt, because they all want to be part of a special team. It has been a long time since that was a feature at Ibrox.'

The day after the win over St Mirren, Nancy dipped in and out of the Dundee United v Celtic match, but when the final whistle blew, and Rangers were confirmed as Premiership champions, the emotions got the better of her.

She said, 'My first thought was for my dad, James. We lost him on 15 January. He was 91, and he was the inspiration behind my love of Rangers. When I was young, I loved watching all the matches on television with him. Then, we would all go to Ibrox together, and that was just magical.

'I remember him telling me about his first Old Firm match. It was before I was born. He hadn't planned to go to the game, but mum asked him to go out and get some sausage rolls for the kids' lunch, and so off he went. He met a pal on his way to the shops and he just happened to have a spare ticket for the big game, so off Dad went with him. Several hours later he arrives back at the house and Mum asks him where the sausage rolls are, and he replies, "We ate them at the game!" I always laughed when he told me that story as a kid.

'Dad was great friends with Jimmy Shand. He loved his Scottish music and once told me that Mr Shand turned down a request to play for the Queen as he had a prior date in a small club and didn't want to disappoint his regulars.

'My son Connor, who is also a big Rangers fan, has followed in Dad's footsteps. Connor loves Scottish music and plays the bagpipes. He works for Wallace Bagpipes, and Dad bought him his first set of pipes. He doesn't have a season ticket but still goes to a lot of the games. He was a big fan of Fernando Ricksen, and when Fernando passed, Connor was upset, so he asked if I thought it would be okay for him to take his pipes to Ibrox after work and pay his own tribute to Fernando. I told him it was a lovely thought, and so he did. Just him. No cameras, nothing. But someone filmed his tribute at the main gates, and must have uploaded it on to social media because it went viral. He was then asked to pipe at Ibrox on the day of Fernando's funeral, and he stood beside the John Greig statue to play his lament. It was beautiful and I was so proud of him. My dad was also very proud.

'Connor also played for the victims of the Clutha disaster in 2013 [ten people lost their lives as a result of a helicopter crashing into a Glasgow pub]. He is just such a caring lad.

'I got my love of Rangers from my dad and I'm sure he will be sitting up in heaven looking down and smiling as we have won the league after all those years. I don't normally drink, but I had a few to celebrate winning the title, and I raised a glass to my dad.

'Winning 55 means more to me than winning the lottery. It's almost indescribable. I'm supposed to keep my blood pressure down, and it didn't help! I'm the youngest of six and we are all big Rangers fans.'

It's anything but a straightforward run to Ibrox from Dunoon, but since 1999 – when Nancy and her family moved back to Scotland from Cornwall – it has been the way of it. She said, 'We've been in Dunoon 22 years now – and we won the league that year as well, when Dick Advocaat was manager.

'But even from Cornwall it was Rangers all the way. What was it The Proclaimers sang? "I would walk 500 miles," and if you'd added another 30 I could have been at Ibrox! You never stop loving your team.

'There are a lot of Rangers fans in Dunoon, so the ferry across to Gourock is always busy on matchday. We pick up the supporters' bus at Gourock, or sometimes get the train in from Greenock. It's more cost-effective that way. It can be fun and games if Celtic are playing somewhere local on the same day!

'I go to all home games and most of the away ones. I've been going to see Rangers for many years now, and hardly missed a game during the journey through the lower leagues. I was there when the ball landed on the hedge at Brechin, and went to just about all of the wee grounds.

'When I initially heard the news about admin on TV I was heartbroken. We were teased and tormented by lots of fans from the smaller clubs, with them singing, "You're not Rangers anymore," which really annoyed me. And when we returned to the Premiership, it was the turn of supporters from the clubs who had voted to demote us to sing the same songs, but we'd heard them all before. There was nothing original, despite them having had all those years to come up with something new!

'When Dave King insisted Celtic hadn't won nine in a row because we weren't in the top league, that resonated with me. And when he said their empire would tumble like a house of cards once we were back, I clung to that image. And it happened; toppled like a house of cards. It was wonderful!'

The Helicopter is Changing Direction

Alex McLeish, former Rangers manager

London, England

HIBS HAD enjoyed a tremendous start to the new millennium. A third-place finish secured a spot in Europe, while they reached the Scottish Cup Final and posted a 6-2 mauling of Edinburgh rivals Hearts. The stock of manager Alex McLeish was never higher. And then his phone rang. 'Hi Alex, David Murray here. I bet you didn't think you would be hearing from me.'

No, he didn't. There had been interest from England, West Ham in particular, but nothing concrete, and certainly nothing from Rangers. Dick Advocaat was in charge and had enjoyed success in his first two seasons. The third, however, hadn't gone to plan, while the fourth, well, half of it, had seen Celtic open up a healthy lead at the top of the table. In December 2001 Advocaat had decided to step upstairs, hence the reason Murray was on the blower.

McLeish recalled, 'Up until Sir David called, I hadn't heard anything from Rangers, nor had there been any speculation in the press, so it wasn't on my radar. West Ham were apparently showing an interest, but you just take it as it comes and don't get too hung up on what you're reading.

'All of a sudden I get this call from David and he says he's been given permission by Hibs to speak to me, and would I like to come to Rangers. I said, "I have to be honest and say I thought you'd be going down the Continental route now since you brought Dick Advocaat in."

'He said, "We've seen how well you've been doing, and we think you can step up." Hearing that gave me great confidence.

'It's funny, because there was a story doing the rounds that Dick had championed me for the job, and I know that David and Dick like to have a wee argument about this, but Dick has assured me, "He told you it was his idea? No, I told him about you." That was wee Dick's pigeon English version of events!

'Thinking back, I'd visited Holland when I was manager of Motherwell. Dick was in charge of PSV Eindhoven and I was after one of his players, Mitchell van der Gaag, a big centre-half. He'd suffered a bad knee injury and never quite made it there, but we got him in at Motherwell. I got on well with Dick and he invited me to watch their training, which I appreciated. Maybe he had my name in his head after that, and it sparked the conversation between Dick and David after the Wee General decided he was moving upstairs. I don't know for sure, though.

'I enjoyed my time at Hibs, and had built a good team. I'd also done much the same at Motherwell, so I'm sure David and Dick had noticed. At Hibs we had a strong third-place finish, while we went one better at Motherwell. To be more accurate, I inherited that Motherwell team from Tommy McLean, but I asked them to express themselves a bit more than they had been doing.

'I remember Tommy Burns paying me the ultimate compliment by saying he would like his Celtic team to play at the level of Motherwell. Tommy was coming in at a difficult time for Celtic, but we had a really good back-three formula and we were getting our defenders bombing up the flanks.

'Dick and David had probably acknowledged the half-decent introduction to management I'd had, but it must have been a shock to Rangers fans because the first question I was asked at the press conference was, "What did you make of the underwhelming welcome you got from Rangers supporters?" I thought, "Jesus Christ, are you trying to knock my confidence!"

'I tried to turn it into a positive by replying, "My goal is to change the Rangers fans' perception of me," and we got off to a flyer with the Bert Konterman goal against Celtic in the League Cup semi-final at Hampden. My cousin called that one the Berty-yarder!'

McLeish admits he was stunned when offered the Rangers job. He knew he'd been doing well at Hibs, but says it still came like a bolt from the blue. 'It was a very pleasant surprise, but a surprise nonetheless. After the success Dick had enjoyed, I thought Rangers would've appointed another foreign coach. Perhaps they were downsizing a bit, I'm not sure, but I was delighted to accept and my agent agreed terms very quickly.

'I was fortunate to inherit a team that Dick had spent a lot of money on. He won the treble in his first season as Rangers manager, but he said to me when I joined, "Alex, I can't do any more with these guys, I've done enough. It needs someone else and I leave it to you."

'At the time, Celtic were on the resurgence under Martin O'Neill, and we had been on the receiving end of that. When I took over in mid-December, Celtic had a big lead in the league, and even though we lost just one game from 20 before the end of the season, we still finished second.

'Dick had stepped upstairs by this time and he was always available if I needed a chat. We would have a cup of tea most days and talk about the team, but it was completely my strategy and I brought in my coaches. We wanted to play a wee bit faster. I made a couple of small changes, shifting Ronald de Boer to striker; Michael Mols made a comeback as he had been struggling with injuries, and Lorenzo Amoruso was out the team at that time as he'd been injured. One of the first things I did was call Lorenzo, and I said, "Big man, I want you back in my team." His reaction was first class. He said, "Hey boss, congratulations on getting the job, I look forward to working with you." He was over in Italy at the time but the big fella came back into the team and was phenomenal for me.

'We injected a bit of urgency, and stopped trying to walk the ball into the net. We started winning games again and you could see the confidence growing as a result.

'I also had a good chat with Ronald de Boer. I knew a lot about the history of Dutch football, and a lot of their players. I was pretty much a student of foreign football at that time. And I recall one of my coaches telling me he had been in the treatment room while Ronald was receiving attention for a knock, and he was busy telling the physio how impressed he had been that I knew all about his career, so that worked in my favour. But my interest in my players was real.

'From the moment I joined Rangers the league was lost, but it didn't stop us giving it our best shot. We lost just three games in 38, but Celtic's consistency was unbelievable.'

Being appointed Rangers manager was far more than just another football gig for McLeish as he came from solid Rangers stock. His dad was a big supporter, and his son had followed suit. So when he walked into Ibrox to sign his contract in December 2001, it was the best Christmas present imaginable.

He said, 'Walking up the marble staircase to sign my contract was, quite simply, the thing dreams are made of. It's an incredible part of Ibrox and just screams history and tradition. As a young guy growing up in Glasgow, and my dad being a big Rangers fan, there was only one way I was heading. Sadly I didn't get to as many games as I would've liked, as I was playing most Saturdays, but I will never forget the first time Dad took me to Ibrox. We got to the turnstiles and he said, "right, here we go," and he lifted me over. That was the way of it in those days. There would be all these kids milling around outside the ground looking for a lift over.

'When I got inside what really captivated me was the splash of colour and this huge pitch. Rangers were wearing a new blue strip with red-and-white socks, and Morton had on a yellow top with blue shorts. I was completely mesmerised by the whole spectacle. I was only a kid at the time, about nine or ten, and you have to remember that most things were black and white in those days.

'When I got to the beginning of my teenage years I was playing football all the time, either with the school, Boys' Brigade or the boys' club. But the game against Morton was my introduction to the wonderful world of live football, and it was magical.'

McLeish spent his entire playing career with Aberdeen – bar a couple of appearances for Motherwell as player-manager – yet another talented west of Scotland lad snatched from the jaws of the big two Glasgow clubs.

He said, 'I was at Glasgow United Boys' Club, and we often played against Rangers and Celtic, and a lot of other well-known boys' clubs at the time. Some of my mates were getting S [schoolboy registration] forms at 13 and 14, and even 15, but even though I was getting recognition, and told that the likes of Luton Town were coming to watch me, nothing ever came of it.

'But during the ages of 15 and 17, I took quite a stretch, and grew about four or five inches. I had trained with St Mirren a few times while Alex Ferguson was there, and I was at Hamilton Accies for a while. Getting to Hamilton from Barrhead on the bus was difficult in those days but I was dedicated to my football. I was desperate to get started with a club, and for a while I thought it might be at Hamilton, but I left when there was no sign of an S form, and went back to the boys' club.

'I was offered a trial at Chelsea, and was just about to pack my bags and head south when my mum showed me a small cutting from the *Evening Times* which read, "Aberdeen are watching Glasgow United's young centre-half Alex McLeish." I had that wee bit of paper for years, but I didn't hear anything for the biggest part of that season, and with my 17th birthday looming you start to think you've missed the boat. Then, all of a sudden we play in this cup final at the Racecourse in Paisley.

'Aberdeen's chief scout Bobby Calder had apparently been sending representatives from the club to watch me most weeks, and he invited the manager Ally McLeod to that final in Paisley. Someone told Bobby they were looking at the centre-half with red hair, but unfortunately the centre-half in the other team also had red hair! When told this, Ally said, "I actually like the centre-half in the other team," which was me, thank god!

'After the game, our coach took me aside and told me that Aberdeen wanted to come and see my parents on the Monday. So, Bobby Calder came to our house in Auchenback, in Barrhead, as promised and he really did look the part, dapper dressed with the trilby, etc. He came into the house and handed my mum a box of chocolates, which was nice. He told my parents he wanted me to become an apprentice professional with Aberdeen. This was the moment I'd been waiting for. It was my only offer, but if you're only going to get one, then it's best coming from one of the top sides in the country.

'Bobby Calder asked if I'd had any interest from either Rangers or Celtic. I hadn't, but he said he'd heard that both Old Firm clubs were circling, and that was why he'd brought Ally McLeod to the game. Bobby was based in the west of Scotland, and had his finger on the pulse. In those days Aberdeen had taken a lot of boys from the central belt. When I headed up to Aberdeen for my first day at my new club, there were ten boys from the west of Scotland on the same train. The only other one who made the grade was Jim Leighton. Jim was from Johnstone and a big Rangers fan.'

As Rangers manager, McLeish won a treble in his first full season; a great achievement given how strong the Celtic team of that era was. He said, 'It's only when I look back I realise just how amazing it was. To have achieved that in my first full season, I think, "God, how did that happen?" Truth is, both Rangers and Celtic had marvellous teams at that time. Martin O'Neill went on record as saying that was Celtic's best team since the Lisbon Lions. That season, Rangers and Celtic could've been in the English Premier League top four – and naturally we would've been third!

'I suppose it makes our achievement all the better as Celtic were so strong, but it went right down to the wire, as we always knew it would. We spoke to the players at the start of the season and said that every single point would be crucial, and that we had to remain on the pace from start to finish. Of course we dropped points here and there, like Celtic did, but thankfully we won it in the end.

'Working with those players was a joy. We had great faith in them and set them loose. One of the tactics we employed against Celtic was to play three up top against their three defenders.

'It meant an overload for our defence but we had a good strategy and managed it well, and we enjoyed some good success against Celtic that particular season. I think Martin actually switched to four at the back the following season and we found it harder to play against them. It was a bold tactic and we knew their wing-backs could cause us problems, but we had schooled Fernando Ricksen and Arthur Numan so well that they could cope with it.'

McLeish insists there was a healthy rivalry between him and his opposite number at Parkhead. 'Total respect,' is how he put it, but he added, 'We are both winners and winners love to win, but I would pop in to his office after the game for a chat, and vice versa.

He played at the top level and was used to winning things; a man after my own heart in that respect, but it's not as if either of us would ever say, "Let's go out to Satty Singh's for a meal with the girls some time." We were at clubs who expected to win but we had a good relationship and I still speak to Martin to this day.

'It was the same when Gordon Strachan got the Celtic job a couple of years later. We had been team-mates at Aberdeen for six years, and shared lots of good times. One of the first things he said to me on arriving at Celtic was, "Let's go out with the women some night," and I just kind of nodded to him, but in my head I was saying, "Gordon, that'll never happen," and it didn't. A while later he said, "I soon realised you were right and that it would never happen." Managing Rangers or Celtic is a full-on job, 24/7. That was all.

'Gordon and I always got on well but this situation was unique and there was no room for sympathy. I was absolutely bursting to win the Old Firm games, and it was also an opportunity to put one over on an old mate. Gordon came in and did a great job at Celtic, but the bottom line is you're only interested in your own team.'

The 2004/05 season was the big one. On the final day, Celtic just had to turn up at Fir Park, collect the points and the league trophy, and head home to Parkhead for the party. But what started out as a routine shift for the helicopter pilot turned into one of the most iconic days in Rangers' history. McLeish recalled, 'Sometimes when you have upsets and disappointments, like the Scotland job, you think to yourself, "I'm a dumpling," but then you look back and start to think, "Hang on, maybe I wasn't too bad!"

'Apart from the birth of my kids, Helicopter Sunday is simply the biggest thrill of my life. The roar at Easter Road when Motherwell had equalised against Celtic was the biggest spine-tingler imaginable. We were winning 1-0, and that was enough; we were in the driving seat, and we weren't exactly hanging on in the second half because Hibs were sitting in, desperate not to lose a second, as goal difference was crucial to ensuring they qualified for Europe.

'We had been drilling into our players all week the need to win at Easter Road. We had to put the events at Fir Park out of our minds and come away from Edinburgh with a victory. We all expected Celtic to win, but if something unusual happened, and there is always a case for one team beating another in football, then we had to be in a position to take advantage of that. Imagine Celtic lose and we fail to win. The players would've regretted it for the rest of their lives, and I think I would've given up the game forever!

'I'll never forget the sight of big Marvin Andrews and Sotirios Kyrgiakos impersonating ball-playing centre-halves by strolling up the park with the ball, and I'm screaming at them to get back. "Don't cross that halfway line," I'm shouting, because all it takes is a single counter-attack and that's us. But we managed the final minutes superbly and got the job done.

'It's ironic that the two teams who took centre stage that day were the two clubs I'd managed, but that's often how football works out, and both came good. It was a wee bit farcical at the end when Hibs were staying in their box, hell-bent on preventing us from scoring a second, but it worked out as they ended up beating Aberdeen to a European spot by just two goals!

'I would've been honoured to win one trophy with Rangers, but to have won two titles – and the way we won both – was just incredible. But we made great memories on Helicopter Sunday. What a day. Title number 51!'

So who would be a Rangers manager? Sign a contract, go on an emotional rollercoaster ride for a few years (if you're lucky) and resign/get sacked/leave by mutual consent before holing up at a mountain retreat to recharge the batteries. And repeat.

McLeish said, 'Managing Rangers is exactly that; an emotional rollercoaster ride. We are one of a unique bunch of clubs who must win every week. There are perhaps 12 clubs in the world like that and if they don't win every game there are inquiries and hell to pay.

'After the treble we lost a lot of players, including Amoruso, Ferguson, McCann, Mols, Numan, etc.: about eight or nine from our core group. That decimated us. David Murray knew a lot of agents and there were players with great pedigrees coming in on free transfers but who were maybe just at the stage of their careers where you weren't sure about their legs. So we didn't get a chance to prepare properly for the following season due to the high turnover of players.

'On Helicopter Sunday I had Dado Pršo and Jean-Alain Boumsong lined up to come in. I had signed them in the January, and that's good preparation, but we didn't prepare properly for the season after the treble.

'Many of the new players didn't arrive at Ibrox until a fortnight before pre-season training, so while Pršo and Boumsong already had it in their heads that they were coming, the others didn't.

'Managers at the bigger clubs definitely have a shelf life, but when I watched Stevie Gerrard celebrate the title win, I wished it had been me. But it's the expectation levels. Take the season we lost all the players; you know you still have to produce a winning team but you've just lost virtually a full first team and with it all the associated continuity. And you wonder why there is so much criticism. I'm not saying that's the fans, because you're reading all this stuff in the press, and I know if you're not winning it comes with the territory of being the manager of Rangers.'

McLeish admits he was delighted when Rangers appointed Steven Gerrard because he admired the former Liverpool player's insatiable appetite for the game. 'He was already coaching the Liverpool youngsters, and you wouldn't say that's the type of preparation required to be the next Rangers manager, but they knew Stevie's ambition for management and they knew what they were getting in terms of an individual's appetite for victory. You could see that written all over his face every time he played or scored a goal. It was an astute move by the Ibrox powers-that-be. I'm sure Dave King was instrumental in it as he has good contacts at Liverpool and is friendly with Kenny Dalglish. I can't think who could have done any better.'

McLeish had been willing Rangers on to title number 55 for some time, but knew it was coming. 'We'd had a good shout last season and the season before, but those winter breaks did us no favours. Stevie has done it differently from me. I came in and had to win right away because I'd inherited a team that was expected to win; De Boer, Mikey Mols, Amoruso, all these guys had been brought to the club to win trophies, but Stevie did it by building a team bit by bit, which was difficult for him because he was doing it at a time when there wasn't a level playing field in Scottish football as Celtic had such a big advantage. Rangers were playing catch-up but the supporters were patient with Stevie. They had been through so much in previous seasons but could see the bigger picture and what the manager was trying to achieve. And for the loyalty the supporters showed to the club when they were down the divisions they fully deserved this title.

'Stevie has done it almost in a Jürgen Klopp type of way, because when Klopp arrived at Anfield he had centre-half and goalie problems, and he didn't quite have the centre-forward formula he wanted. It took him a couple of seasons to get Virgil van Dijk, because he was playing guys like Lucas (a midfielder) in the centre of defence, and you could see he didn't have the legs when teams like Hull City were punting the ball over his head and running beyond him.

'For me, recruitment was massive and not only have guys like James Tavernier excelled, not so long after he was getting a lot of criticism, but all of a sudden guys like him and Kamara have put it all together and were playing to a really good standard.

'One area of the pitch in which we had struggled for a couple of years was at centre-forward. Alfredo Morelos had a lot of suspensions, which was upsetting the continuity, and we only really had Jermain Defoe to fall back on. And when he wasn't playing the manager would have to move players like Scott Arfield up front, and that was where it fell down a little. So when Kemar Roofe came in he caused a bit of a stir, while Cedric Itten was also contributing, albeit mostly from the bench.

Defoe would accept where he is in the game at the moment, delighted just to be a part of that, and when he comes on you can see he still has it, but when the two new strikers came in, it definitely took the pressure of both Morelos and Defoe, and the form Morelos hit in the latter stages of the season was terrific. That would be down to him having competition for his jersey.'

McLeish insisted that Rangers could look forward to the 2021/22 Champions League with optimism, testing themselves at the higher level without the need to feel inferior. 'Look at the games against Porto last season; they showed themselves to be a top team in this season's Champions League by knocking out Juventus. Rangers beat and drew with them last season and I don't think the Portuguese side have made too many changes since then.

'There are two ways to build a successful team. The first, the way Rangers have done it, is to build gradually, and pick the right players for the right positions. The second isn't an option. They can't go out and buy Kylian Mbappé to help them win the Champions League, so they have to take each step as it comes. Finance is the most important aspect of football these days, but Rangers, in the past couple of seasons, have earned the right to buy the players they have because of the way they have performed domestically and in Europe. I would expect them to do a wee bit of damage in the group stages next season; it's not outside their capabilities. That, in turn, would bring in more revenue, while giving players experience of playing at another level. The future is definitely bright.

'Personally, I'm proud of what I achieved at Rangers. You tend to look back on your failures, which is probably the negative Scottish way, but if I look at my four and a half years at Ibrox, I'll say to myself, "Wait a minute, you've done not too bad big man!"

'You learn quickly as a football coach that the most important part of the job is to make the fans happy, and it's not by telling them jokes. I got a big thrill leading Birmingham City to victory over Arsenal in the League Cup Final at Wembley in 2011, but to win trophies with my boyhood heroes was extra special. I'd always thought I would be happy if I managed Rangers for a season, which a lot of people would give their right arm to do, but to go there and win seven trophies with the help of a fantastic staff and set of players, was a dream come true. But, as has been the case for the last ten years, it would have meant very little without the wonderful Rangers supporters – they are the real stars of this show.'

Sir Brian Donohoe

Irvine, Ayrshire

Celtic 1 Rangers 1
Scorer: Morelos 38
21 March 2021

Peace was about to break out in the decorative corridors of the House of Commons. A delegation from the Westminster Rangers Supporters' Club had been invited to attend a video showing of the 1967 European Cup Final between Celtic and Inter Milan, organised by the Westminster Celtic Supporters' Club as part of the evening's entertainment to follow their AGM. Pre-show drinks were being served as the Rangers contingent entered the room. They were warmly welcomed by their hosts, and along with an aperitif or two, and some genial banter, it was all very amicable. Like the bubbly and beer, the extended hand of friendship was going down a treat.

That was until the star attraction went missing, and try as they might to find the elusive video tape, concealed within its no-thrills Blockbuster plastic casing, the Westminster CSC had no luck. The show was just a few minutes from starting. The lights had been dimmed and guests were beginning to take their seats. But the blasted VHS tape was nowhere to be seen.

Hang on, the tape wasn't the only thing missing. The Rangers supporters' club delegation had also disappeared. Perhaps they had remembered a prior engagement!

It was the latest scandal to rock the near 200-year-old Pugin-designed House of Commons, and while the plot may not have rivalled that of Guy Fawkes's audacious attempt to blow up Parliament, it set tongues wagging for the next few days.

'The tape was returned the next morning,' said Sir Brian Donohoe, the former MP for Central Ayrshire, and secretary of the Westminster RSC. 'Thankfully, they saw the funny side of us pinching their video, although we didn't hang around to find out how disappointed they were the evening before.

'I helped run the club for a while although we were in the minority amongst Scottish MPs. Mind you, it wasn't just Members of Parliament who were in the Westminster RSC, we also had a couple of members from the House of Lords, including Jim Wallace, the Liberal Democrat politician, while a number of police officers were members. So we had quite a large membership, and it was a fairly useful set of people, because we did a lot of lobbying on behalf of the club.

'It wasn't all work, though, as one evening we invited Walter Smith to dinner in the House of Commons, but I can tell you it was an expensive night given Walter's taste in good red wine. It was a highlight of my tenure as secretary, and well worth the bill.

'We were especially busy during the club's time of crisis from around 2011 onwards, and we also hosted the administrators at the House of Commons to see what we could do to help the situation. It is certainly not a time in our history we would want to see repeated.

'We didn't often get the chance to watch games together but as a group we were invited to Ibrox a couple of times, normally for midweek games, which we couldn't make as we were so far away.'

Brian is a lifelong Rangers supporter and went to his first game with his father, an away match at Kilmarnock – the town of his birth. He said, 'I don't really look upon myself as ever becoming a Rangers supporter – I was born one and to this day I still hate wearing anything green!

'My first visit to Ibrox was a fantastic experience. I can't remember our opponents – as it was so long ago – but I was completely taken with our stadium. It was a colossus and such a mind-blowing experience. I still get "that feeling" when I enter the ground, and one that now feels like walking into a "fortress". I love going up the marble stairs on the very odd occasion I'm invited.

'When I first started watching Rangers my favourite players were Eric Caldow, Jim Baxter, John Greig, and my fellow Ayrshireman Norrie Martin. Of course, the most successful period I remember was when Terry Butcher et al. were playing and we were regularly winning the league. But while I remember Rangers winning many titles, the first wasn't in 1948, the year I was born because unfortunately we didn't win it that year, although we did in 1947 and 1949. But the first title I truly recall was in 1965, as that's the year I started working!'

By that time, Brian was going to the games with his mates and they would get the train from Irvine to Glasgow Central and walk from the city centre to the stadium. 'These were great days. It took us half an hour or so to walk from the town, but there would be plenty of other people walking to the stadium, so we weren't at any risk.

'When my father took me to the games we would take the car, but there was something liberating about going to the Rangers games with my mates. And then it was time for me to take my two sons to Ibrox and we had season tickets for the Govan Rear, but we were only a couple of rows from the front, so we had great seats.'

Like all Rangers supporters, Brian enjoys nothing more than watching Rangers put one over on their old rivals, so he tuned in to the match at Celtic Park – immediately before the league split – hoping to see another victory. In the end it was a 1-1 draw, but he insisted he was happy enough with both performance and result.

He added, 'If truth be told, the game was a bit flat. It was as though we were still suffering a bit from the celebrations, and also as a consequence of Thursday night's game with Slavia Prague. And we were still without two of our main men, James Tavernier and Ryan Jack.

'It certainly wasn't our best performance of the season, but the result wasn't the worst either. I would've taken a draw before the game and I believe 1-1 was a fair reflection. I watched the game at home with my son and we both thought the Borna Barišić challenge on Édouard was a penalty. Even though Barišić was flat down, Édouard tripped over him and there was contact, and if there was VAR I'm sure it would have been given.

'The best way to gauge these decisions is to consider it happening in the other box. How would I have felt, and I would have been looking for a penalty!

'You win some, you lose some, and it used to be that Celtic won them all, although they won the 2019 League Cup because of a mistake by the match officials. We played them off the park that day and there was no way they should have left Hampden with the trophy.

'But I was delighted to see Alfredo Morelos finally break his Old Firm scoring duck. He was sharp and showed great awareness. To score when we did was important, because it would've given them a big lift going in one up at the break. It certainly wasn't one of those days when you were sitting on the edge of your seat, that's for sure. Towards the end you knew it was flattening out, and if either team had scored a second, that would have been that.

'I don't think we had a shot on target in the first half apart from the goal, but Alfredo again showed his worth to us. Not only has he been a better player this season, but he has also been a better team player, and he's clearly maturing as well.

'One of the things that struck me about the game was our inability to string any more than five passes together at any one time. Our fantastic passing has been a big feature of our play this season but it was missing at Celtic Park. We were also giving away far too many corners, and that put us under a lot of unnecessary pressure, while we didn't get into their box as often as I'd have liked.

'But we've had a fantastic season, and to have conceded just ten goals in 33 league matches is, quite frankly, astonishing. I was speaking to Ally McCoist a couple of days before the game and I suggested that Allan McGregor should be our player of the year, as he has saved us on numerous occasions. He has had an outstanding campaign. His save in the first leg of the Europa tie against Prague was simply out of this world. In all my years following Rangers I don't think I've seen better.'

'Rangers' first title in ten years!' It still rankles with Brian that we were forced to drop down three divisions in 2012, and he insists it wouldn't have happened had we been playing south of the border. 'The English football authorities would have stepped in to help one of their member clubs, unlike the ones up here. But it wasn't just the football authorities. There are only two clubs in this country playing at a similar level, and for one to want to get rid of the other, as it would make them the dominating partner, was a big mistake. I believe they did themselves a great disservice, and also their fans, by their actions, because they didn't spend the money, or concentrate on improving their team; they became complacent and that allowed Rangers to grow again, rebuild and come back strongly, and we witnessed the outcome this season.

'Had I been in their shoes I would've done the exact opposite. I would never have allowed my main opponent to go down to the bottom division. When it happened I was as sick as the proverbial parrot, particularly with the Celtic guys gloating. But listen, we are probably the better for it and now stronger as a result although it's still a hard pill to swallow.'

As a consequence of the situation the club found itself in, Brian joined Rangers First, a supporters' group set up to help the club get back on its feet, and to look at the pros and cons of fan ownership. His only interest was in seeing the group prosper. He said, 'The first I was made aware of Rangers First was when

I was approached through our Westminster Supporters' Club and asked to contribute financially, which I did.

'I thought it was a fantastic idea and so I supported it and got others to do the same, but that's when it was lean and keen, and only going to do what I thought was required, and still is required, and that was to buy the club over and have it in the hands of supporters. All I wanted to do was help. The very fact there was supposed to be transparency, good governance and independence from the club in the initial stages was all I would have supported. The problem I had was that the minute I got involved I saw nothing but self-interest, and that disappointed me greatly.

'I certainly don't regret getting involved with Rangers First, but I don't think it was wise to let one person run it. The loyalty of the fans has been there throughout, and credit to the board for putting their hands in their pocket.'

Around that time, Brian was invited to Buckingham Palace to speak to Prince Charles about how he could help with The Prince's Trust, a charity started by the Prince in the 1970s to help vulnerable young people get their lives back on track. 'I enjoyed chatting with Prince Charles and we came up with some good ideas to assist the trust. On another occasion at the palace, I found myself in the company of Her Majesty the Queen. She had recently been to Celtic Park to open the 2014 Glasgow Commonwealth Games, and I said to her, "Your Majesty, if you have been to Parkhead, then I think it's only fair you also visit Ibrox, the home of Rangers." We chatted about it and she promised to do her best to get there. I spoke to her "people" and we tried to get some dates sorted out, but sadly we couldn't make it work.'

Five years later, Brian was back at Buckingham Palace, this time the grateful recipient of a knighthood. He said, 'It was in part, payback for my absence from my family over many years and I was immensely proud to have them around me at the palace. After the investiture we visited the House of Commons before I really pushed the boat out by taking everyone to dinner at the Ritz. Well, you only get the chance once.'

It was all so far removed from Brian's early days working as an apprentice fitter and turner in the Ailsa shipyard in Troon. It was a struggle to make ends meet on his wage of £3 9d. a week, which meant something had to give, and that was often a trip to Ibrox. He explained, 'We didn't get any overtime so that meant going to see Rangers was often outside my spending capacity, which was unfortunate.'

It was while working at Ailsa that Brian first became involved in politics, and he was inspired by the famous work-in. Five major shipbuilders had joined forces to create the Upper Clyde Shipbuilders (UCS), but three years after the amalgamation, the shipbuilding consortium hit financial trouble. Rather than strike, the unions decided to conduct a work-in, to complete orders that were already in place.

Brian said, 'Working in the shipyards was the main reason I got involved in politics, and seeing the way Jimmy Airlie (a Rangers supporter) and Jimmy Reid (a Celtic supporter), leaders of the work-in, handled it, inspired me. I became a shop steward, and I suppose the rest is history.'

Brian was elected to the House of Commons at the 1992 General Election for the Cunninghame South constituency, and held the seat with a majority of more than 10,000. He said, 'It was easier than the jobs I'd previously had, and although it was several jobs rolled into one, I loved the challenge. I would spend at least 100 hours a week both in London and in the constituency. I loved the buzz of speaking in the chamber and the real tension of most of the debate was electrifying. Over my 23 years in the place, every single day was different.

'Of course, working in London would often affect my ability to get to Ibrox. Whips, who were mainly Celtic supporters, would try and make it difficult for midweek games, but to be honest they were fairly relaxed if the games were in Europe and it was a great excuse to get "up the road".'

But getting 'up the road' isn't an issue these days, and Brian admits it was wonderful to be able to watch Rangers win the league from the comfort of his living room – even though, like everyone else, he would much rather have been at Ibrox. He said, 'It has been fantastic. We won the league in style – and with a bit to spare. I didn't think for a minute we would be so far ahead of Celtic, but even had they been at the "top of their game" we would still have won it.

'When we appointed Steven Gerrard I thought it a brave decision at the time, but he has proved to be a winner, and long may it continue. But just as I am guilty of being away from my family for most of my boys' youngest years, I worry for him losing that precious time with his own family. I don't suppose many people give that aspect any real consideration.

'To celebrate our title win, I broke the habits of a lifetime by purchasing £50 of fireworks. We waited until it was mathematically impossible to be caught before letting them off – and what a show. A few folk weren't entirely happy, but I timed the "show", and it lasted just one minute 40 seconds, and they were all gone! They were stunning, though. The most explosive fireworks you can get without crossing the line into the realms of professional fireworks. Those companies must've been rejoicing when Rangers won the league. It was a bit of an extravagance, but we haven't been able to spend a lot of money this past year, so it was well worth it.

'I don't have too many doubts about next season because the club is in a good place. Not only do we have 11 good players, we now have a squad full of good players. And more will come in the close season. Kemar Roofe will be like a new player once he gets back to full fitness. He was a big part of our success until he picked up an injury, while I also like Aribo and Hagi, and when both find some consistency, our opponents should watch out!

'My hopes for the future of my club are simple. To continue to prosper and eventually get ten in a row. It's not too much to ask, is it?'

So, What Did 55 Mean to You?

They tried to kill us, sink us!
They tried to keep us down!
We stood strong, fought back!
We are champions!
We are Glasgow Rangers!

BBC Scotland Slayer @Naefearrfc

Started taking my wee girl to Ibrox in the admin season so she hasn't seen us win anything. She was nervous and excited the day we clinched the title. When we got to Ibrox, with all the singing, smoke and flags, her face was priceless!

Paul Kennedy @killiebear

My life has changed so much over the last ten years. I left Scotland, worked abroad, met my wife, moved to Wales, bought a house and had a child. My support of Rangers never wavered and I never missed a game on TV.

90minsofmadness @90minsofmadness

Total devastation when we were exiled down the divisions. We took it and filled stadiums home and away, so this title closes the door on one hell of a journey, and is for everyone who helped us back to the top.

Audrey Mills @footymadxxx

Winning #55 means EVERYTHING. The end of ten years of pain, hurt and injustice. We welcomed the chase, they were terrified of it. We climbed a mountain and now stand upon its summit as champions!

Alan McNamara @AlaaMcNamara

Being an Australian-born Rangers fan, I never give up on anything, including the club I love. Winning 55 gave me the magic and hope I needed in my grief. Thank you Rangers. More than just a team – you are my family! So proud to be a Rangers supporter.

Ann Beveridge; Sydney, Australia

55 got me through the pandemic. The isolation and restrictions of COVID-19 were harsh and dragging me down. The ray of sunshine from the team I've supported since I was a boy winning this 55th title helped save my sanity.

Allan Aikman @Thistledubhme

Everything. For those who remember the good times of bygone eras, for those who followed through the journey and for those we sadly lost along the way. This one is for all of us.

Karlarl @Karlarl184

This is our lives, every day. No other club has been through more. Only a Rangers fan knows how much this means, and that's everything. My son Teddy born 21/8/2020 – champions 07/03/2021.

John Galbraith @nashergalbraith

The completion of the journey and an epic triumph over adversity. Scotland's premier club finally reclaiming their throne.

Andrew Martin @AFM3181

'A title like no other.' Dougie Deans

Inexile @Ps95v7

It means the promise I made to my boy when he was six in 2012, 'The good times will come back,' has been fulfilled. We are the people!

HWG10IAR @ian_barrie

For me this is the best title we've ever won. I will never take a title for granted again; nine years of hurt, heartbreak and humiliation, mixed with huge relief; a year of losing people close to our hearts. Massive pride in our loyal supporters. Simply WATP.

John Gemmell @John_gemmell54

It's about our DNA. We were knocked down and had a long climb back. We played a patient game and now we're back and holding on tightly with both hands.

Stephen @stephenb1962

The absolute world. All the bumps in the road make this so special. Onwards and upwards. 55

FollowFollow @WHutch81

They tried to kill us but we wouldn't die. Took us ten years but 55 is here and we are back where we belong. WATP

Andrew Clelland @AndrewClelland5

Everything! My daughter's first time seeing us as champions. It's been one hell of a journey, but Gerrard got us to where we deserve to be. Natural order has been restored. Back where we belong.

Shell @MLArmstrong85

It will make me appreciate the good times even more. Will never take Rangers for granted again. 55 is therapy.

MacGerrard @MacGerrard_

Up there with attending Easter Road with my dad as a 12-year-old when Colin Stein scored to win the league and stop their ten in a row. I wish my dad was here today.

IMcDPHOTO @IMcDPhoto

After drying my eyes, first thoughts were for my grandpa, my great uncle Tommy and uncle John; Sandy [Jardine] and Fernando [Ricksen]. They would be proud of our generation supporting our team through the last ten years to bring back 55.

Fraser McArthur @fraser_mcarthur

After admin, demotion, cowboys running our club, Mike Ashley trying to ruin us, to getting Dave King & co., Stevie Ge55ard and his team lifting the title with six games left. In all my 63 years this is simply the best.

Ellen Wallace @KTBlady1

Tears of unbridled joy. My heart is whole once more. I need to say sorry to my fantastic wife and kids, but none of you will bring me the peace and happiness today has.

Neil Young @Neil_Young80

Nine years of hurt wiped in one weekend. Natural order restored.

Douglas Connor @Douglas_Connor

Striving for success is healthy. Strong people believe failure is part of the process, and we are the people who have been strong together on this journey. Once again, our club is the best.

Davie Bear @daviebear64

A long, hard ten years, but what a journey! And to do it the way we have this year – amazing! Simply the best!! #55

Jamie Beattie @Jamie_Beattie7

I'm so happy. Living in England now and my wife and children will finally understand why I've been throwing money at a sleeping giant for ten years. All for this. The happiest a Rangers Da can be!

El Tel @ElTeltheBell

We have retaken our city. Glasgow belongs to Rangers. Glasgow belongs to us!

Chris Mayhead @chrismayhead

Having both grandparents still with us to be part of my nine-year-old son Zayn's first title means the world. This team is what family is all about and I'm so grateful to be a Ranger.

Alex Strachan @alex40w

Amazing accomplishment after everything that's happened, and in the year of my 55th birthday.

Karen @karenspb1

From the low of admin on Valentine's Day 2012, being dumped in the bottom tier, losing Fernando, to the dearly departed who loved our club, we are back where we belong #55

TorqSkye @iammrrodriguez

To loosely quote Souness: 'Since the birth of my two children, this is by far the best day of my life.' I'm a 50-year-old man, been an emotional wreck all weekend. My love for my club is real.

Wullie @wullblake

My Rangers-mad daughter turned 16 on 21 March. So happy for her to finally see her team back on top. WATP #champions #55

Ally Fairgrieve @u111658

55 is our reward for believing: trains to Montrose and Arbroath knowing you can't make kick-off; balls stuck in puddles and last-minute winners at Brechin; standing on planks of wood at East Fife, but never giving up on our wonderful club.

D Gilchrist @gilky75

It's been one unbelievable journey from folk trying to make a fast buck to our 'rookie' manager – probably the greatest story in football.

Mike Graham @MikeGra11679676

You are born a Ranger. It's in your DNA. Through thick and thin there is nobody else that can give you the highs and lows from the day you're born to the day you die. Then you start all over again in Rangers heaven.

Marly @tycoch7

Back where we belong. They tried to destroy us but only galvanised us. What does it mean to me? Everything.

Wylie Coyote @Wylie72coyote

The defining moment in a long, hard road from oblivion, to the summit of Scottish football, backed all the way by the most loyal fans in the world.

Gordy A @Gordygfl

Watched Rangers since I was nine or ten. Now 71. After the past nine years I worried I wouldn't see times like this again, so it's extra special. God bless the Rangers

jimkpl @jimkpl1

The feeling of joy and release from this win surpasses anything I've known while following Rangers and I've been going since 1978.

William Findlay @wulbear

Watched in horror the events of 2012. Bled dry by snake-oil salesman. Got our club back; a bumpy ride, but this is a moment I thought may never happen. Elated.

TomForsyth55BigToe @nrpsimpson

Winning 55 means the end of the hardest ten years. Was delighted when we beat them [Celtic] on penalties in 2016, but this is just pure unadulterated joy!

RFCLoyal2020 @cameron19900407

It's incredible. From total despair in 2012, then through the lower leagues, to our rightful place as champions of Scotland. Incredible, fantastic feeling, the best.

Idb1969 @idb1969

From being where we were to coming back up to win 55. It means everything. Thanks to the board, management and players. We will all enjoy this moment!

Katie McGowan @katiemcgowan200

All those jelly and ice cream jibes; the times when I didn't think we would survive; scraping results against lower-league teams; attacks from the SFA and SPFL, and showing them we are still the people!

Alan Ryder @legendofgid

Great to be back at the top.

Stewarty0907 @Stewarty0907

It means everything, but most importantly restores order.

BigMurdy @TheRealBigMurdy

A feeling of unbelievable joy. I had forgotten just how good it feels.

Billy McGunnigle @yogiblair2

The last 12 months have been horrendous but in the midst of it all Rangers have given us a level of joy I feared we may never see again. Our greatest title victory for so many reasons. Thank you Stevie G.

WATP @Durrant54

This one is for my grandkids; the future of this wonderful club. They will go on to witness many more successes, contribute to its development and earn their own place in its history. Very proud Bluebelle Granny.

Cher @chermag

I said way back in 2013 it would take us four years to get back to the Premiership, and another four to be competitive, and hopefully no more than two years to become champions again.

Bobthecane @bobthecane

FOR ABSENT FRIENDS
MAY HEAVEN KEEP
THE MEN THAT SLEEP

Gary Mccord @Mccordgary

We have had our days of anxiety
Our trials to be overcome
We have emerged stronger
Let the others come after us.
The whole Struth and nothing but the Struth

Colin @AbsntFriends

A great sense of joy and happiness beyond what you would normally feel in any other happy moment.

Cheerioterrymunro @davie2_me

Everything.

MB55 @MotherwellBear

Life.

Peter @peterhay3

More than everything. To see my son celebrate his first Rangers title after years of misery.

Dean @Urban1Dean

#55 Our support has stuck by the team despite the lows. We still believed we would return to the top. There are many who never saw us complete the journey but we will remember them in our hearts and this title should be dedicated to the fans!

Graham #55 @cantbearsed_

It's karma. in 2012 they tried to end us as a club, we've been kicked and belittled ever since. Today we wiped the smirk from their faces. Back where we belong, at the summit of Scottish football. This is only the beginning.

Stirling Bear @stirlingbear55

Coming from the lowest point in our history, overcoming the entrenched enemy within, the lifting of title #55 fills me with immense pride over the efforts of so many legends of our great club.

Donald Collins @DonaldGVL

For me, winning this title mutes all the pain and hurt of the last ten years. It won't take it away, and we can never forget that other clubs wanted us dead and buried.

Andrew Muir @drusincmur

Seeing people so happy will stay with me. I grew up watching us win things that often you just took it for granted. To go without makes you appreciate it so much more. A title no one will ever forget

Louch @StephenLouch

After what we've endured over the last ten years, I didn't think I'd ever witness the utter joy of winning the title again. It was so special. Thanks to all at RFC.

Jimmy @Jimmy20449586

55 is for the men and woman who sadly aren't here to see us win it.

DM @DazMo1970

Congratulations to all Rangers folk around the world. Maybe a wee pre-season friendly at Windsor Park to celebrate?

Advocatus Diabili @Dissoi_Logoi_

It's like the end of a journey with so many bumps, but which we can look back on with such pride and be very happy where we are – back in our rightful position!

Gary King @gprking

#55 is the moment our darkest days ended. They kicked and mocked us, but no more. A generation of fans, including my nine-year-old son Rhys, hadn't experienced the joy of being on top, but they better get used to it. We are the people.

stuart.mcwhinnie @stuartyboy78

I reckoned this was the end of the journey. Maybe it isn't. Maybe the journey never ends. The last ten years have shaped us as a club and a support. It's created a connection that perhaps wasn't there before. Maybe this is the end of the beginning. #55

Jens @Jens1872

My son. Eight years old now and seeing his first title.

CCC @Obanlad1970

Started following in 1963; witnessed the highs and lows. Passion has never waned, but today, 7 March 2021, I'm an emotional mess. I've cheered, I've cried, my heart is bursting and I couldn't be happier.

@HGSM18

We had to wait ten years, but we're back where we belong. I was in tears; that's how much it means to me. Congratulations to the manager, his backroom team, the players and employees of Rangers FC. Most loyal supporters in the world. WATP

Walker Robert @WalkerRobert73

To celebrate with my three boys, the first without my dad. My youngest Josh showed how much it meant as the minute the title was confirmed, he went straight up stairs and brought down the Rangers watch my dad gave him.

Bobthe dob @boabfaenewton

We always had pride, passion and belief. The journey has been long and hard but we are back. 55 times the kings of Scotland #55

Big Red @bigredhood79

Being able to celebrate with my family and my wee grandson. #true blue memories made to last a lifetime.

James Craig @jamesc1912

Socrates talked about questioning everything. You get some hard answers but if you keep going and believe, you might just be okay.

Marty @MartyMmcflywhy

The immense pride I feel being a Ranger; never doubting we'd be back. This is only the beginning.

Wurly @BrianBtinternet

55 means everything to me! After all we've been through these last ten years, we deserve it more than anyone.

Stevie @Stevinho83

We made it.

Andy Countach @CountachAndy

It means everything, absolutely everything!

George MacDonald @GingerRanger86

Justice and redemption. From being in tears at Ibrox at our first game in the Third Division, after thinking we'd lost our club, to this. Haven't stopped smiling watching all the fans' videos!

Bear from the North @Northernger

#55 million times more than I ever thought it would mean. The devastation of everything that has happened since 2012 can now be put to bed. We are the people. Rangers have always been special and 55 is simply the best.

El naranja 55 1872 @ElPedro1872

After all the ups, downs and disasters of the last ten years, it has been emotional to say the least, but nothing will beat this feeling!

Paul @BigPawBear

I did it for love! Others hated on us, but my focus, thoughts, financial backing and support was all for Rangers. I pride myself in my love for my club!

Robert Dalziel @BletheringBob

Winning 55 was massive as my young sons, Ryan David and Mason Caleb, have witnessed the worst period in our history, and been there in SE5 for the journey back to the top. Thank you Rangers family. #Champion55

David AG Welsh @DavidWelsh1984

I believed sitting in the home end at Tannadice watching Brian Laudrup secure nine in a row was the best title I would see, but watching Rangers win #55 a day before my 40th was just incredible. Unbelievable ten-year journey.

John Bain @bainy81

Seeing my nine-year-old celebrate like it's the best thing that's ever happened made my day even better that I thought it could be.

Jamie Graham @jamiegr76012989

It's like how you expect true love to be; almost the same as having a child!

Duncan McKay @DumcanMckay

Everything – it means everything!

Kellya55 @kellyk19781

Really important and critical for the new generation of Rangers supporters.

Terry Ferguson @tferguson1970

Like waking up from a never-ending nightmare

A Gunn @Agunn777

If you'd told me ten years ago, while in the depths of despair, that we would prevail in this season of all seasons – 55 for us, ten for them, I might just have taken it.

Bruce Ross @rbr4166

#55 means an end to a decade-long torrent of ridicule and abuse, and a reminder there are always better times ahead. It's for those we lost along the way; for Alex, wee Jackie and KB, celebrating in the Rangers Supporters' Club in the sky!

55hepster @johnsheppard76

The day we clinched the title was so emotional; so happy for my daughter Olivia as she's been everywhere to watch the Rangers!

BORN A BEAR @ccbarl1873

When we were confirmed as champions, I almost broke down. My wife asked what was wrong, and when she found out it was 'football-related' she was 'relieved' as she thought someone had died!

Samuel Cameron

Winning title 55 was one of the best feelings in the world and we have our legend of a manager to thank. Steven Gerrard, I salute you.

Gillian Fiona Reilly, loyal Rangers fan

Some submissions have been edited for clarity.